BIKING
puget sound

50 Rides from Olympia to the San Juans

BILL THORNESS

Biking Puget Sound *has something for everyone.*
—*Seattle Magazine*

It's a decent wager that many bike riders—beginners to veterans—will find some sort of revelation in where to ride within the pages of Thorness' book.
—*North Kitsap Herald*

Bill's creation is all someone would need in order to select an enjoyable route for a two-wheeled adventure anywhere between Thurston County and the San Juans.
—*Washington State Grange News*

This guide is a great resource.
—University Book Store Staff Favorites

Thorness will steer you off the well-pedaled path with his new guidebook, which features clear, easy-to-follow maps and—equally important—elevation charts and time estimates for each ride.
—*Seattle Weekly*

BIKING
puget sound

*50 Rides from
Olympia to the
San Juans*

BILL THORNESS

THE MOUNTAINEERS BOOKS

THE MOUNTAINEERS BOOKS
*is the nonprofit publishing arm of The Mountaineers Club, an organization
founded in 1906 and dedicated to the exploration, preservation, and
enjoyment of outdoor and wilderness areas.*

1001 SW Klickitat Way, Suite 201, Seattle, WA 98134

© 2007 by Bill Thorness
All rights reserved
First edition: first printing 2007, second printing 2008, third printing 2009

No part of this book may be reproduced in any form, or by any
electronic, mechanical, or other means, without permission in
writing from the publisher.

Manufactured in the United States of America

Copy Editor: Kris Fulsaas
Cover and Book Design: The Mountaineers Books
Layout: Mayumi Thompson
Cartographer: Moore Creative Design
All photos by the author unless otherwise noted.

Cover photograph: *Burke-Gilman Trail* © L.J. McAllister
Frontispiece: *A view of Mount Si*

Library of Congress Cataloging-in-Publication Data
Thorness, Bill, 1960-
  Biking Puget Sound : 50 rides from Olympia to the San Juans /
Bill Thorness. — 1st ed.
    p. cm.
  ISBN-13: 978-0-89886-943-9
  ISBN-10: 0-89886-943-9
  1. Bicycle touring—Washington (State)—Guidebooks. 2. Bicycle
trails—Washington (State)—Guidebooks. 3. Washington (State)—
Guidebooks. I. Title.
GV1045.5.W2T56 2007
796.6409797'7—dc22
                                        2006039226

♻ Printed on recycled paper

*To my companion on and off the trails—my wife, Susie Thorness—
without whose support and camaraderie this project would have
been work instead of play.*

———————————

CONTENTS

THE ISLANDS

SKAGIT COUNTY

SNOHOMISH COUNTY

PIERCE COUNTY

THURSTON COUNTY

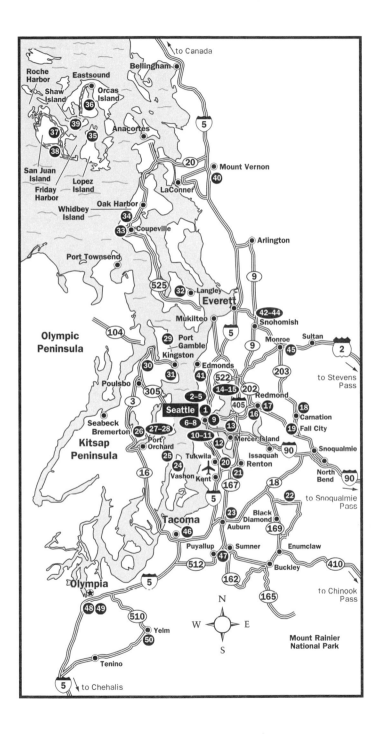

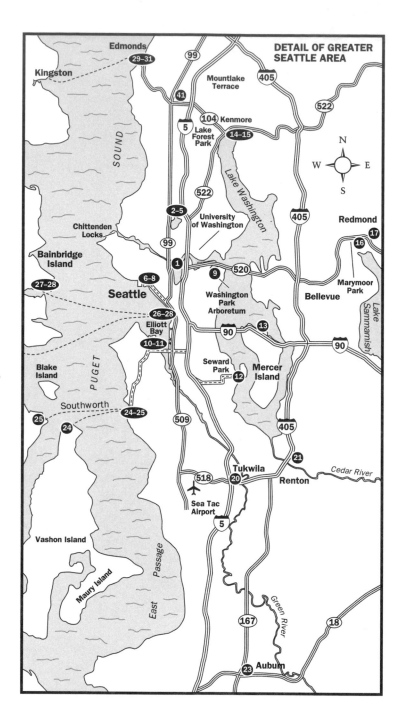

MAP KEY

‑‑‑‑‑‑‑‑‑‑‑‑‑	two-lane road
═══════════	four-lane road
▬▬▬▬▬▬▬	trail
	lake, ocean
	river
(5)	US interstate highway
(101)	US highway
(1)	state highway
◉	city or town
⌁	lighthouse
✈	airport
→	direction of tour
🛉🛈	restroom
Ⓢ	start of bike tour
] [	bridge

maps not intended for navigation and are not to scale

BIKING PUGET SOUND RIDES AT-A-GLANCE

No.	Title	Difficulty	Length (in miles)	Elevation Gain (in ft)	Time allowed (in hrs)	Points of Interest
1	Burke–Gilman Trail	Easy	24.6	250	2.5	University of Washington, Magnuson Park
2	Green Lake and Northwest Seattle	Moderate	14.2	520	1.5	Golden Gardens Park, Ballard locks, shopping districts
3	Carkeek and Golden Gardens Parks	Moderate	20.0	1110	2.5	city parks, Ballard locks
4	Magnuson and Ravenna Parks	Easy	16.0	320	1.5	city parks
5	Green Lake to Edmonds	Moderate	25.2	1330	3	Edmonds city center, underwater park, ferry dock (to Kingston/Kitsap Peninsula)
6	Magnolia and Discovery Park	Moderate	10.5	590	1.5	Olympics views, park, Ballard locks
7	Queen Anne and Seattle Center	Moderate	10.8	535	1.5	shopping district, Space Needle, SAM Olympic Sculpture Park
8	Downtown Seattle	Moderate	10.1	100	1.5	SAM Olympic Sculpture Park, ferry dock (to Bainbridge Island, Bremerton/Kitsap Peninsula), International District, Seattle Public Library, Pike Place Market
9	The Arboretum, Capitol Hill, and East Lake Union	Moderate	12.7	485	1.5	Washington Park Arboretum, Volunteer Park, REI flagship store, Lake Union waterfront
10	West Seattle	Easy	16.0	720	2	Alki Beach, ferry dock (to Vashon Island, Southworth/Kitsap Peninsula), Seattle Chinese Garden
11	Duwamish Trail	Easy	26.0	20	2	Fort Dent Park, Duwamish River access points
12	South Seattle and Seward Park	Easy	16.3	400	2	park, Lake Washington waterfront, Mount Rainier views
13	Mercer Island Loop	Easy	15.8	485	1.5	Luther Burbank Park, winding lanes
14	Lake Washington Loop	Strenuous	53.6	1835	6	multiple waterfront stops, parks
15	Sammamish River Trail	Easy	28.4	30	2.5	Marymoor Park, Velodrome, Red Hook Brewery
16	Redmond to Issaquah and Preston	Strenuous	51.7	1625	6	Issaquah shopping district, secluded Preston trail
17	Redmond to Carnation	Moderate	43.4	1410	5	farms, Cascade mountain views
18	Carnation to Snoqualmie Falls	Moderate	23.6	460	2.5	farms, Snoqualmie Falls overlook
19	Fall City to North Bend	Moderate	21.8	620	3	Mount Si views, Snoqualmie Falls overlook

No.	Title	Difficulty	Length (in miles)	Elevation Gain (in ft)	Time allowed (in hrs)	Points of Interest
20	Green River and Interurban Trails	Moderate	40.8	80	4	suburban parks
21	Cedar River Trail and May Valley	Moderate	29.7	520	2.5	rural roads, Lake Washington waterfront
22	Green River Gorge and Black Diamond	Moderate	28.7	960	3	rural roads, Green River Gorge view
23	Auburn to Flaming Geyser State Park	Moderate	35.2	830	3.5	park, farms, bakery, geyser
24	Vashon and Maury Islands	Strenuous	39.8	2500	6	farms, Point Robinson lighthouse
25	Port Orchard	Easy	30.9	360	3	coastline biking, Olympic Mountains views
26	Bremerton to Seabeck and Scenic Beach	Strenuous	37.0	2760	4.5	tiny towr, state park, Olympic Mountains views
27	Bainbridge Island Loop	Strenuous	35.4	2030	4	Olympic Mountains views, parks
28	Winslow to Fort Ward	Moderate	21.6	970	2	military ruins, Olympic Mountains views
29	Point No Point and Little Boston	Moderate	27.9	1270	3	lighthouse, Native American center
30	Port Gamble and Poulsbo	Moderate	33.4	1225	3.5	Chief Sealth's grave, mill town, Scandinavian town
31	Indianola and Chief Sealth's Grave	Moderate	18.8	1080	2.5	Chief Sealth's grave, old port town
32	South Whidbey Island: Freeland and Langley	Strenuous	41.5	1910	5	artistic town, rural roads
33	Central Whidbey Island: Coupeville and Fort Casey	Easy	13.6	440	2	coastal views, military ruins, farm roads
34	Central Whidbey Island: Oak Harbor and Fort Ebey	Moderate	20.5	1220	3	military ruins, farm roads
35	Lopez Island	Moderate	37.2	1330	4.5	rural roads, waterfront views
36	Orcas Island	Strenuous	22.2	1440	3	farms, artistic town
37	San Juan Island: Lime Kiln and Roche Harbor	Moderate	32.6	1860	3	coastal views, whale watching, historic park, marina, farms
38	San Juan Island: Cattle Point	Moderate	27.5	1000	3	historic park, coastal views
39	Shaw Island	Easy	14.9	840	2	secluded roads, historic school
40	Skagit Flats and Tulip Fields	Moderate	38.9	50	4	farm roads, tulips (in season), artistic town
41	Interurban Trail and Mukilteo	Strenuous	47.7	1380	5	ferry dock (to Clinton/Whidbey Island), urban exploration

No.	Title	Difficulty	Length (in miles)	Elevation Gain (in ft)	Time allowed (in hrs)	Points of Interest
42	Centennial Trail	Moderate	47.5	620	4	rural, tree-lined trail
43	Snohomish to Everett	Moderate	23.7	690	3	slough and river
44	Snohomish to Monroe	Moderate	33.5	600	3	tourist town, farm roads
45	Monroe to Sultan	Moderate	24.7	740	2.5	Cascade Mountains views
46	Downtown Tacoma, Point Defiance, and the Narrows	Moderate	27.5	1200	4	museums, waterfront, shady park, ferry dock (to Tahlequah/Vashon Island), university campus
47	Foothills Trail	Easy	29.8	380	2.5	rural scenes, Mount Rainier views
48	State Capitol and Central Olympia	Moderate	18.7	340	3	capitol campus, city center, parks
49	Chehalis Western and Woodard Bay Trails	Easy	29.8 & 14.7	200 & 120	3 & 1.5	rural scenes, sculpture park
50	Yelm–Tenino Trail	Moderate	27.2	320	3.5	small towns, rural scenes

ACKNOWLEDGMENTS

Many thanks to cyclists across the Puget Sound region for pointing me in the right direction on my two-wheeled travels. Valuable guidance was provided by the Rides Committee and staff of the Cascade Bicycle Club in Seattle. Individuals from across the region providing particular assistance include Paul Ahart, Dave Gardiner, Jan Johnson, Kristin Kinnamon, Pete Lagerwey, Darcy Patterson, Kent Peterson, Jim Shedd, Jeff Smith, Kat Sweet, Jim Taylor, and Tom Wilson.

Thanks to John Lehman at R&E Cycles' great repair shop for keeping me on the road during two years of research, and to the editorial and marketing staff at Mountaineers Books for keeping me on track during the writing. Thanks also to the inspiration of Erin and Bill Woods and their area cycling bible, *Bicycling the Backroads Around Puget Sound*, as well as *Touring Seattle by Bicycle* and *Touring the Islands*, both by Peter Powers and Renee Travis—and, unfortunately, both out of print.

Finally, my deepest appreciation to the many friends who offered encouragement, support, and companionship on the trails, particularly Bill Alkofer, Sherri Cassuto, Matt Dunnahoe, Tom Evert, Alison Evert, Ted Fry, Andreé Hurley, Sylvia Kantor, L.J. McAllister, Tim Olson, Rob Peterson, Neil Planert, Amy Reed, Pam Shea, Valerie Tims, Norm Tjaden, and Jack Tomkinson.

INTRODUCTION

What are you doing this weekend?

If you're like me, the answer probably involves escape. Get out of the office, off the telephone, away from cash registers, cubicles, customers, or bosses. Get into a different mindset, which probably means a different physical setting.

This book is for all those people who want to get away, do a little exploring, and get some fresh air into their lungs. My goal was to create a selection of cycling day tours that expose users to all our major bike trails and on-road bike routes. It's divided somewhat equally among urban, suburban, and rural settings. Because these 50 rides are sprinkled throughout the greater Seattle area, many people will find tours close to home. With a couple of exceptions, all rides are within an hour's drive of central Seattle.

We are fortunate to live in a cycling wonderland, with the beauty of nature found everywhere, from diverse city parks to agricultural valleys, from waterfront lanes to island coastlines to mountainous back

Overlooking Nestlé's Carnation Regional Training Center

roads. Climb a hill and be rewarded with a view of a sparkling cityscape, glittering blue bays, or towering snowy peaks. Pick blackberries by the side of a rural road, or take your comfort stop at a farm stand bursting with fresh produce. Our temperate climate allows for recreational biking nearly year-round, and an improving network of trails offers increased safety for beginners and families.

When you see a pack of spandex-clad cyclists in a "pace line" on sleek, high-tech bikes, you may think the sport of cycling sprouted recently to serve these athletes—but you would be wrong. Biking in Seattle has a history nearly as old as the city itself. The first bicycle was brought here in 1879, and by 1900—when the first automobile was spotted on our streets—the 55,000 residents of Seattle owned 10,000 bikes. (Seattle cyclists have been magnanimous in sharing our roads with cars ever since.) Also in 1900, an assistant city engineer, George Cotterill, created a bicycling map for residents that showed a 25-mile system of paths he had identified in his walks around the city. Those paths became some of the best cycling routes we still ride today, such as winding, tree-lined Lake Washington Boulevard.

Our enthusiasm for biking has grown along with our population, and the network of trails and street routes has greatly expanded to meet the need. A survey by Cascade Bicycle Club released in 2006 identified a "Regional Bicycle Network for Puget Sound" that encompasses 1521 miles of trails and roadways, and in 1999 a travel survey revealed that 59 percent of the region's residents own a bicycle. New trails are being created from old railroad rights-of-way, and many modern road projects include accommodations for cyclists. Each year, thousands commute to work by bike, and tens of thousands take part in organized rides and tours, such as the enormous two-day Seattle to Portland (STP) event.

You don't have to join in group tours, ride an expensive bike, or wear high-tech clothes to enjoy the many benefits of cycling—although a properly fitted bike and specialized gear can enhance the experience. Simply choose a route that fits your abilities and interests, and give it a try. This book contains many rides that are suitable for those who haven't been on their bike in a while; start with the flat, paved, off-street routes like the Foothills, Burke-Gilman, Sammamish River, Chehalis Western, and Centennial trails. Commuters can search the maps for interesting ways to get to work. More challenge can be gained by navigating city and suburban streets or taking on a hillier, lengthier route. Many of the tours are designed to be linked, so that the experienced cyclist may find new challenges or different destinations. To truly get away, load your bike with the travel essentials and try the five-day tour of the San Juan Islands included here.

This book is being augmented by a website *www.bikingpugetsound .com*, that will be updated and republished periodically. Hopefully, with the enthusiasm and involvement of this book's readers, the list of rides on the website will grow and evolve, remaining current and accurate.

Researching this book has provided me and my patient, energetic wife with a wonderful new depth of awareness about our region. You learn much more about getting around, interesting stops, and wonderful sights from the vantage point and the human-scale speed of bicycling than from any other form of transportation. One enjoyable exploration creates the desire to have another, so you can imagine what 50 such outings will do.

See you on the trail!

EQUIPPING FOR A RIDE

When you hop in your car for a trip, you probably don't think too much about safety or reliability. Most cars come with air bags and spare tires, and once you add a flashlight and an emergency kit, you can forget it.

But when you get on your bike for a ride, it helps to give a bit of thought to what you might need. Preparation can make the difference between a minor inconvenience and an unpleasant experience. Add a few amenities to increase your enjoyment.

Think about getting equipped for a ride in three basic categories: yourself, your bike, and your home bike-repair shop.

Yourself

Getting yourself ready for a ride involves health and comfort. First, choose a ride that matches your current physical abilities. Most people don't want to begin the season with a hilly, 50-mile ride.

Second, plan how to keep up your stamina. A full water bottle and some high-energy snacks will be welcome down the road. Many riders will "bonk" (suddenly find themselves sapped of energy) if they don't periodically fuel up.

Third, carry a small pack of first-aid supplies, including pain relievers and bandages. Apply sunscreen before each ride.

Fourth, the proper clothing for the conditions is important. The most common advice for outdoor enthusiasts in the Northwest is to "layer": Wear layers of clothing that work together to keep you warm and dry but allow you to strip off some of them so you won't overheat. Start with padded bike shorts, which come in the clingy, form-fitting style or as loose shorts with a padded, suspended brief. To keep from chafing, don't wear additional underwear underneath. Tee shirts or tops should be made of new quick-drying, breathable material rather than cotton, which can stay wet with sweat and cause chills.

Tights or water-resistant biking pants are good for wet or chilly conditions, and fleece vests under waterproof shell jackets add warmth up top. In the winter, turtleneck-style shirts or pullover neck warmers hold in your body warmth. To warm your extremities, check out these specialty items: an ear-warming headband, a microfiber skull cap, a nose and chin mask, glove liners, socks that are a blend of wool and microfiber, and stretchy, water-resistant shoe covers.

Fifth, a helmet and gloves are safety necessities, and good shoes and eyewear are helpful. King County and many western Washington communities require helmets by law. The primary consideration with a helmet is how it fits, and any good bike retailer will help you choose. Some helmets have sun visors, and some have more vents than others for better air movement so you can keep a cool head.

Cycling gloves obviously offer warmth, but they also provide safety by making sure you keep a good grip on handlebars and brake levers for steering and braking in wet conditions, and they have palm padding that protects the hand's tender nerves from bruising that can cause numbness on a long ride. Choose flexible biking gloves that provide good padding—fingerless for summer, full coverage for winter.

A solid pair of bike shoes will keep your feet happy. Most important is a stiff sole, so the pedal pressure is dispersed across the foot rather than localized in one spot. Equip your bike with clipless pedals and match them to shoes that allow you to clip onto your pedals. Although it takes some getting used to, clip systems provide a more efficient pedal stroke so you'll expend less energy.

Finally, wrap-around eyewear protects your eyes from sun, road grit, and rain and increases safe riding by keeping your eyes from watering or drying out. Sunglasses are especially a good precaution against the sun's rays when it's low on the horizon right before sunset, which can be quite blinding.

Your Bike

Bike design has become something of an art, and there are many styles available, offering a choice for each rider's individual needs and desires. The type of riding you intend to do—commuting, mountain biking, short tours, long tours—will dictate the type of bike that's best for you. The best approach is to find a quality bike shop with knowledgeable staff who know how to fit a bike to each customer. Test-riding a number of different manufacturers' bikes will showcase the bikes' differences. If you already have a bike but didn't have it fit to you, consider having this done at a good shop.

What extras you put on your bike will also be dictated by your type of riding, but there are a few basics that everyone needs.

At least one water bottle must be carried; most of them are mounted on the frame to be accessible while riding. For long rides, some wear a backpack "hydration pack."

Carry a lock; it provides peace of mind when you take breaks, and it is necessary if you need to leave your bike in an emergency, such as after a breakdown.

Speaking of breakdowns, distance riders should carry a tire patch kit, an air pump, a small bottle of oil, tire wrenches, and a "multitool" for repairs. These might not be necessary if you're just riding to the corner store, but you'll want to avoid being stranded on a rural road or on the way to work.

Every rider should know how to do a few basic repairs: reattach the chain if it slips off; unhook the brakes and take off a wheel for repair; patch or replace an inner tube. More advanced repairs (which many people leave to their bike-shop mechanic) include tightening or replacing the chain, replacing a broken spoke, and adjusting the brakes.

On a day tour, carry an extra inner tube as a replacement in case the blowout is bad or if you don't want to hassle with a repair. Pack a rag to clean up after repairs. Consider taking a two- to three-hour course in basic bike repair, offered by most bike shops and bike clubs.

Finally, to avoid major problems on the road, have professional service on the bike's mechanical systems done at least once every other year.

If you might be riding at night, plan ahead and carry lights. Washington state law requires a front white light and rear red reflector for bikes operated in hours of darkness. I believe every bike should have a rear red light that flashes brightly. Check the batteries on your lights regularly. Reflectors on the front and rear of the bike, on your clothing, on pedals, on the seat post, on wheels—on anything that might give you better visibility to the navigator of that moving ton of automobile steel—are well worth the investment.

To carry your lock, bike repair kit, extra clothes, food, cell phone, camera, extra batteries, or whatever else you might want on the trail, you'll need some sort of pack. Commuters often carry their basics in backpacks—especially the messenger-bag style—and keep their bikes very light. Many touring riders use a pack or saddlebags (commonly known by the French term, *panniers*) mounted to a rack above the back wheel. A waterproof pannier or a pair of them offers the most cargo space. There are seat-post bags, handlebar bags, and front panniers as well. For just a few things, try a small, removable handlebar pack or seat-post bag big enough for a map, snacks, and a lock. Choose a pack combination that suits your riding style.

Comfort over a long ride will be dictated by the soreness of your rear end, so a specialized seat may be a welcome amenity. Many seats

Riders head west on the newest section of the Burke-Gilman Trail in Ballard.

are padded with foam or gel, and higher-end models are anatomically designed for men or women.

Handlebars, too, can be upgraded for comfort. Choices include padded grips or added handlebar ends and "aero bars" that allow different hand positions.

Add a bell for safety, to be used when passing pedestrians or other cyclists. Another item that helps provide proper control and navigation is a rear-view mirror. These come in many styles, attaching to helmets, eyewear, or handlebars.

Add a bike computer, which also mounts on the handlebars, to chart your distance and the difficulty of the terrain and to keep track of miles ridden. Knowing how far you've gone helps you plan routine maintenance and replacement of components such as tires and chain.

Your Shop

Most people park their bike in their garage, but a little planning and a couple of extra service items will keep it in better shape. Hang your bike on hooks or a rack between rides, especially if it's going to sit for a while, to keep it from getting banged up. A number of rack styles are available, and a good one doesn't have to be expensive.

A quality floor pump is essential; one with a built-in, easy-to-read gauge is a welcome luxury. Tires need to be pumped up every few days, so leave the pump out and ready for use.

Carve out a little space on nearby storage shelves for a bottle of chain oil, extra inner tubes, a set of tools, and a book on bike repairs. Use the oil on your chain regularly, wiping clean the grit to keep the links limber.

If you plan to do your own maintenance and repairs, invest in a repair stand that will hold your bike off the ground.

If you want to keep in shape for biking year-round, buy a stationary trainer. By hooking up your bike's rear axle to the trainer, you can train indoors and improve your stamina for the trail.

Finally, for a quick getaway, keep a basket nearby that holds your helmet, gloves, lights, and packable items.

BASIC GEAR FOR BICYCLE TOURING

Water and snacks
First-aid kit and sunscreen
Layered clothes
Padded shorts
Helmet
Gloves
Bike shoes
Eyewear
Lock
Patch kit and pump
Lights

CYCLING SAFELY

One of the prime concerns of new cyclists regarding road touring is the need to co-exist with automotive vehicles on city streets and highways. Having had many near-misses and one direct hit, I can sympathize. But I also believe that, with proper understanding of the risks and safety precautions, riding on streets and roads doesn't have to be dangerous. Risks exist even on the off-street paved trails, but these, too, are manageable. It's mostly a matter of getting comfortable with situations that might arise.

Cyclists can greatly reduce their risk of accidents with vehicles, other cyclists, and pedestrians by using proper bike safety gear and observing safe riding practices. In many cases, following safety precautions also means following state and local laws.

Whether you're just out running a few errands or taking one of the tours in this book, cycling safely should always be your first goal. If you continually practice the basics—wear a helmet, carry and use the proper lighting, follow traffic laws—safety will become second nature, making you increasingly comfortable in all traffic conditions.

Wear a Helmet

Protect yourself by always wearing a helmet when riding. Helmets are required throughout King County, including in Seattle and many other areas covered by tours in this book—and rightly so. Nationally, bicycle crashes kill approximately 900 people a year and injure more than half a million of us. A review of bicycle helmet effectiveness studies by the Harborview Injury Prevention and Research Center concludes that helmets can cut the risk of head and brain injuries by 70 to 88 percent. The Washington State Department of Health says that 75 percent of all bicycle-related deaths involve severe head injury, and 20 percent of all head injuries in children ages five to 14 are caused by bike accidents. Look for the American National Standards Institute (ANSI), Snell Foundation, or American Society for Testing and Materials (ASTM) symbols on helmets when shopping.

A helmet is effective only if it fits properly and is fastened snugly. Most bike shops can help you find the right helmet for your head and your riding needs. If the shop doesn't offer knowledgeable help with fitting, go somewhere else. If you're in charge of children, make sure their helmet straps are fastened and the straps are snug.

Some public-service campaigns offer helmets at reduced cost or free. Cascade Bicycle Club operates regular events to distribute free or low-cost helmets to low-income individuals, school children, and nonprofit groups. Health-care organizations, including Mary Bridge Children's Hospital in Tacoma, also offer such a service.

Light Your Ride

Bicycle lights are also governed by law. Washington state law mandates a front light and rear reflector to be used when riding during the hours of darkness. The front light must be white and visible from at least 500 feet away. The rear reflector must be red and make you visible from all distances 100 to 600 feet to the rear when the low beam of a vehicle's headlights hits you. The law also allows for the use of a red rear light visible from a distance of 500 feet.

Most night cyclists install a battery-powered red light on the rear seat post or rack of their bikes. Many people also use a clip-on red light that can be attached to their clothing, backpack, or helmet. Most red lights, and many headlights, offer a flashing mode as well as a steady-light mode, and often the flashing mode seems to make a rider more visible.

If you want to "go green," use rechargeable batteries or a generator that will eliminate the dead-battery problem. The drawback to generator systems is that they are heavy.

In addition to lights and reflectors, reflective tape can be used on the bike and on clothing to make you more visible. Add it to pedals, shoes, fenders, rims, jackets—anywhere that a car's headlights might shine. Also wear light-colored clothing for night riding. Visibility in all conditions should be your goal.

Follow Traffic Laws

A bicycle is considered a vehicle and is subject to the same laws as a car when you ride it on the roadway, which includes bike lanes and parking lanes. Simply following the same laws as motorists will cut the risk of bicycling by quite a bit.

Traffic laws are primarily a set of standards to which everybody in society basically adheres. Such rules are the only way that I can reasonably be assured that another driver will act predictably. If we know the rules—and can be penalized for not following them—most of us will follow along with the crowd. For cyclists, the threat of a fine is often replaced by a much more painful penalty: the risk of getting physically injured. I believe that by following the same rules as a vehicle, I can be more predictable and thus less likely to be hit by another vehicle, which could be a car or another bike.

The most useful traffic rules are outlined in Figure 1. The graphics show the two best ways to execute a left turn, how to ride predictably between a traffic lane and a parking lane, and what hand signals to use when turning.

Cyclists should always assume that they are invisible to drivers of cars and trucks. That will cause you to be more cautious when you're in a bike lane and, due to these traffic conditions, must pass cars on their right (which should never be done otherwise). Be on the lookout for a driver turning right, directly in front of you (or left, if you are in a left bike lane on a one-way street). If you're riding on the sidewalk, slow to a pedestrian speed when crossing driveways and intersections.

Cars are not the cyclist's only road worries. Stay alert for potholes, railroad tracks, and pavement that is slippery with rain or oil. Watch for pedestrians entering a crosswalk or jaywalking in your path. Animals, such as dogs protecting their territories or deer dashing across a rural road, can be quite a surprise. Unseen hazards can cause a startle reaction, which may not be a big deal if you're alone on a road but could be a big problem if you jerk your handlebars just as a car is passing you. Practice remaining calm and steering consistently when in difficult conditions. Stand up on your pedals to reduce the jolt of an uneven road. Whenever

USE HAND SIGNALS

Hand signals tell motorists what you intend to do. For turn signals, point in the direction of your turn. Signal as a matter of courtesy and safety and as required by law.

RIDE CONSISTENTLY

Ride as close as practical to the right. Exceptions: when traveling at the normal speed of traffic, avoiding hazardous conditions, preparing to make a left turn, or using a one-way street.

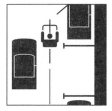

CHOOSE THE BEST WAY TO TURN LEFT

There are two ways to make a left turn: 1) Like an auto: look back, signal, move into the left lane, and turn left. 2) Like a pedestrian: ride straight to the far-side crosswalk, then walk your bike across, or queue up in the traffic lane.

USE CAUTION WHEN PASSING

Motorists may not see you on their right, so stay out of the driver's "blind spot." Be very careful when overtaking cars while in a bike lane; drivers don't always signal when turning. Some other smart things to be alert for: car doors opening and cars pulling out from sidestreets or driveways.

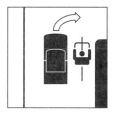

AVOID ROAD HAZARDS

Watch for sewer grates, slippery manhole covers, oily pavement, gravel, and ice. Cross railroad tracks at right angles. For better control as you move across bumps and other hazards, stand up on your pedals.

GO SLOW ON SIDEWALKS

Pedestrians have the right of way on walkways. You must give an audible warning when you pass. Cross driveways and intersections at a walker's pace and look carefully for traffic. In some communities, cycling on sidewalks is prohibited by law.

Credit: City of Portland Office of Transportation, Portland, Oregon

Figure 1

Bicycling scarecrow in a San Juan garden

possible, ride in the direction of car traffic when crossing bridges on walkways to avoid perilous collisions with oncoming bikes.

Verbal notice or hand signals will help avoid a crash with another cyclist. If you're slowing or stopping and you know there are cyclists behind you, extend your left arm downward with your open palm facing back. If you're overtaking another cyclist and going to pass, use your bell or yell "Bike on your left" as a warning. Make sure you can be seen and heard under the conditions of the road.

Other signals may help fellow cyclists ride more safely. If you're behind others in a group of bikes and a car approaches from the rear, yell "Car back!" to inform the riders in front. If you are leading other riders and come upon a hazard on the road, such as broken glass, extend your arm down and point to the hazard with a sweeping motion. When crossing railroad tracks, signal their presence by sweeping your arm at an angle behind you.

Many of these laws and rules apply equally to a paved bike trail as they do to a road. You might want to signal riders behind you when you come upon a small child on her first bike ride or see some debris on the trail. A crash with another cyclist can be very damaging to bike, body, and spirit, so do your best to ride safely.

Safely Use Buses and Ferries

In the Puget Sound region, most buses have racks for two bikes, and some new buses have racks that hold three. There is no extra charge for the bus to carry your bike.

It's a simple procedure to pull down the bike rack, set your bike's wheels into the tracks, and pull the retaining bar over the front wheel. But always get the bus driver's attention before you approach the rack, and when you're getting off, let the driver know that you'll be removing your bike from the rack. Note that buses do not allow bikes with gas motors to use the bike rack, but electric-powered bikes are OK.

The two drawbacks to this system are limitations on the number of bikes any bus can carry and the prohibition of taking your bike off the bus in the downtown Seattle "ride-free area." Unloading in the ride-free area is prohibited as a safety measure, because so many buses stack up at downtown stops. If you're heading downtown, plan ahead and exit the bus where the ride-free area begins. If you're waiting for a bus and it arrives at your stop with a full bike rack, you are stuck waiting for the next bus; bikes are not allowed inside buses. However, you might consider taking another route that drops you somewhat near your destination and simply riding the rest of the way.

Washington state ferries are commonly used by cyclists, and there are a few tricks to safely boarding and disembarking a ferry.

Enter the ferry dock along with the car traffic and pay at the vehicle toll plaza, unless instructed otherwise. There is a small surcharge for bikes, although cyclists should lobby the state to remove this as a measure to support the environment and citizen health.

First-time ferry riders should follow the lead of other riders waiting at the loading ramp. Bikes queue up in front of the cars in a signed waiting area and receive a verbal signal from dock workers when it's time to board. On some ferries, cyclists are required to walk up the ramp. Once onboard, cycle to the bow of the ferry and tie up with the provided ropes attached to eyebolts along the rails. If you leave the car deck, remember that exposed bike-shoe cleats are not allowed on the passenger deck.

When exiting the ferry, again wait for the verbal signal. Cyclists should move to the right off the ferry ramp, because motorcycles and cars will soon be coming behind. If you're uncertain about riding on and off the ramps, it is acceptable to walk your bike. Also, it's a good idea to gear down when entering the ferry, because the exit ramp at many ferry docks gets somewhat steep at low tide, and the road departing the ferry often quickly turns uphill.

COMMUTING BY BIKE

Thousands of people in the Seattle area have discovered the benefits of commuting to work by bicycle, and bike commuting numbers seem to grow with every traffic backup or spike in gas prices. In 2006 King County estimated that more than 15,000 people participated in the May "Bike to Work Day," and the City of Seattle estimates that 4000 to 8000 people commute into downtown daily. With a bit of preparation, you can reap the many advantages of bicycle commuting and suffer minimal risks.

One of the major benefits will be to your health. Bike commuting allows you to integrate a daily workout into a busy schedule. The exertion provides a natural way to arrive at work more alert, so you may experience less reliance on caffeine. By leaving your car at home, you'll contribute to the overall air quality of our area.

Keeping control of your schedule is another plus. How many times have you been stuck in traffic and arrived late to work? When you bike, you can say goodbye to transit schedules, traffic reports, freeway backups, and parking hassles. King County published some interesting statistics on its bike commuting web pages in spring 2006. It estimated that driving time from the University District to Pike Place Market would be 15 minutes in light traffic or 35 minutes in heavy traffic. By bike at a moderate pace, the trip would take 30 minutes. How often does "light traffic" describe rush hour in Seattle? Score another one for bikes.

If you're thinking about "cyclommuting," some important considerations include route planning, proper equipment, personal safety, bike security, mass transit interaction and work amenities.

Route Planning

The shortest distance between two points may be over the top of a big hill, which is probably not the kind of sweat-inducing exertion you want to go through before arriving at work. Therefore, your criteria for the best route to work may include finding one that is as flat as possible. Or it may be a combination of shortest and flattest, allowing for a little hill climbing if it means saving 15 minutes of commute time.

The City of Seattle currently has about 28 miles of shared-use paths; 22 miles of on-street, striped bike lanes; and about 90 miles of signed bike routes. Other area cities and suburban communities contribute many more miles, and some of them even link up. Many of those paths and routes have been used in this book, so chances are good that some leg of your commute can be part of a recreational tour.

Next, get yourself city and county bike maps; see the Recommended Resources at the back of this book. The maps show bike trails, striped-and-signed bike lanes on city streets, and through streets with relatively lower traffic.

Finally, test your route on a pleasure ride before using it for work. Time yourself, check road and traffic conditions, and look for possible amenities you'll need, such as a bike shop or bus stop. Many people commute partway by bike and partway by bus, or they use the bus if the weather turns bad. After you've become familiar with your route, you might enjoy adding length to it after work to increase the level of exercise.

EMPLOYER SUPPORT OF BIKE COMMUTING

Bike commuters who want to lobby their employers for parking facilities and work amenities can get help from Bicycle Alliance of Washington, a nonprofit organization that supports bike safety and commuting. These are a few of BAW's 31 ideas to support bike commuting:

Loaner Cars. Make loaner cars available to bicyclists for use in case of emergencies or personal errands that require a car while at work.

Health-Care Coverage. Reward bicyclists with better health-care coverage. This might include extended benefits, lower rates, or a lower deductible. Similar programs are offered for nonsmokers.

Employee Awards. Reward outstanding employees, customers, students, etc., with a new bicycle or with other bicycle-related items. A reflective vest, safety lights, a mirror, or a helmet with the person's name and the organization's insignia are awards that convey support for bicycling and concern for a person's safety.

Bike Lease Program. Lend or lease bikes for an established period of time—say, 30 to 90 days. This allows people to try bicycling without having to buy a bike. This program could be structured as a program to lend or lease with an option to purchase. Purchase price could be discounted.

Stranded Bicyclists. Implement a program to assist bicyclists who become stranded when their bikes break down.

Recruitment Awards. Reward employees who recruit new bike commuters.

Enhancing Your Safety

Commuters often face the issues of riding in the dark, navigating in heavy traffic, and riding in the rain. You can enhance your safety under these difficult conditions, and for general riding, by adhering to a few safety precautions.

First rule: You can never be too visible to cars. Many commuters use two rear flashing red lights, one mounted on the seat post or rack on their bike and a second on their jacket, backpack, or helmet. Use a halogen headlight to be more visible to traffic you'll meet at intersections and to more easily spot potholes or other road obstructions.

Some cyclists use lights in rainy weather during the daytime as well as after dusk. Many wear lighter-colored clothes in winter. Reflective, water-resistant orange or yellow bike jackets are the most common clothing item among bike commuters.

Second rule: Assume that drivers don't see you. Navigating in traffic is a challenge not to be taken lightly. Watch for cars changing lanes, stopping suddenly to grab a parking spot, or turning in front of you.

For instance, people who've just parked their car often don't check the bike lane before opening their car door. Give yourself 4 feet of space to avoid being "doored" by people getting out of parked cars. Stay in a traffic lane if no bike lane is available, and don't weave into the parking lane just because there's an opening between parked cars—maintain a straight, predictable course.

A note about sidewalk riding: You may think it is safer, because you're away from the traffic, but it carries its own hazards. Consider the driveways and intersections you must cross. Most drivers are not expecting bikes on the sidewalks, and if you arrive in a crosswalk at the last second, don't be surprised if a driver doesn't see you. Also, because of the width of sidewalks and the many obstructions on them, you're more likely to fall over, hit another biker, or hit a pedestrian.

Seattle does not prohibit biking on sidewalks, although it is illegal in some communities. The law says that when a bike is in the roadway, it is to be treated as a vehicle, but on the sidewalk, it is to be treated as a pedestrian. Moving at pedestrian speed on a sidewalk is wise.

Speaking of laws, it's in everyone's best interests for all bike commuters to obey traffic laws, especially stop signs and signals. Do it primarily because an oncoming car with the right-of-way will definitely not be expecting a cyclist to pop out against the light. Often, drivers speed up to catch a yellow light or beat a red one, making it even more dangerous for a biker hoping to get a jump-start when a light's turning green.

Secondarily, stay legal for the sake of your fellow bikers: For every scofflaw cyclist, there's a motorist shaking his head and assuming all cyclists act the same way. That attitude will make the streets more dangerous for all of us, because a motorist with that opinion is less likely to "share the road." Consider the bottom line: How much time is really saved by jumping a red light or illegally cutting through traffic? Relax and be safe.

One final note on traffic signals: You as a biker can make them change, and you don't have to go to the curb and push the pedestrian

Vashon's celebrated Bike in a Tree

walk button. Look for a "magnetic loop" cut into the pavement in the driving lane or bike lane. In Seattle, they're often marked with a T; in Bellevue, they're marked with an X. Positioning yourself on top of this loop engages a sensor that triggers the signal as though you were a car. Thank you, technology wizards!

Third rule: Get used to getting a little wet. If you commute year-round in the Puget Sound area, you're bound to be riding in the rain. Especially in the winter, riding in the rain is unavoidable, and lower temperatures make it easy to get chilled. But often even winter days contain dry spells, and many rainy days accumulate relatively little rainfall. The best approach to riding in the rain combines caution, preparation, and common sense.

Good raingear is your best defense. If you're a damn-the-torpedoes rider, shop for waterproof outer clothing; if you ride only when there's a light mist, perhaps water-resistant gear will suffice. The drawback to waterproof gear is that it is generally not breathable, so you can really heat up in it. However, you might be surprised how fast rain soaks through water-resistant outerwear. Err on the side of staying drier. Buy gear with zipper vents to relieve the steam within.

Shoe covers will keep your feet drier, and a helmet cover will do the same for your head. Keep a dry towel on hand to clean your eyewear. Carry a plastic bag and rubber bands to cover your bike seat if you need to leave your bike out in the rain. Take an extra pair of socks and gloves to use for the ride home in case yours haven't dried by then.

Riding safely in the rain entails making yourself more visible and knowing the limitations caused by a wet bike. Use extra lights, and make sure your raingear has reflective patches or strips. Leave more space for braking, and proceed a little slower down hills. Assume that other riders aren't being as cautious as you, and give them wider berth.

If you get caught in a really nasty squall, there's no shame in pulling over and opting out; a warm and dry bus seat awaits.

Mass Transit Interactions

Transit systems are getting savvy about bike commuting and have a number of programs to support it. In one recent year, King County Metro counted more than 300,000 people putting their bikes on the bus racks. It's a simple and quick backup to riding if you run out of energy or the weather turns nasty. For procedural and safety information about using transit systems, such as buses or ferries, see the Cycling Safely section earlier in this introduction.

If you participate in a van pool, you can also take your bike. Metro says about 40 percent of its vans currently have racks, and it will install bike racks on van-pool vans upon request.

Bike Security

More bus-system park-and-ride lots are installing bike lockers for use by commuters, so you can bike from your home to the park-and-ride, store your bike safely and out of the elements, then catch the bus into work. In 2006 Metro's lockers were free, although there was a $25 "key deposit." The ferry dock on Bainbridge Island has an expansive "bike barn" for use by commuters.

Those not using bike lockers at park-and-ride lots need to safely secure their bikes for the day at their workplace. Enlightened employers provide dry bike parking in garages or their buildings. If this is not available where you work, consider lobbying management for some facilities. Bikestation Seattle in Pioneer Square is providing a good commercial model for bike storage services. In 2006 Bikestation charged $1 per day for secured storage or $96 for an annual pass. It's a significant step up from chaining your bike to a sidewalk rack for the day, exposed to weather and possible theft.

Workplace Amenities

Arriving at work all hot and sweaty or soaking wet after your bike commute is usually not a good idea. In fact, it can be downright off-putting to co-workers and bosses.

Bike commuters have many ways to handle this situation. At the most basic level, some bring their own towels and take a quick sponge bath in the restroom. Others join a health club near work and make that their first stop.

Again, enlightened employers support the efforts of their healthy, nonpolluting cyclommuting employees by installing locker rooms with showers. Locker rooms serve not just bike commuters but also runners or others who like to exercise at lunchtime. The lockers should be large enough to hold suits or dresses at night and bicycle bags, shoes, and a helmet during the day. They absolutely need to be in a heated space and ventilated, because no cyclist wants to put on the morning's damp bike clothes before their ride home.

A good tip for making the bike commute easier is to drive or take the bus to work one day a week and leave a supply of work clothes in your locker. It makes for a quicker, lighter ride in the morning, the clothes won't get wrinkled, and it allows storage of garments such as suits or jackets that don't easily fit in a bike bag.

~~~~~~

BIKING TO SCHOOL

The idea of commuting conjures up images of adults heading to work, but it can also be applied to children going to school. The Bicycle Alliance of Washington operates a program called "Safe Routes to School" that encourages kids to ride their bikes or walk to school.

The effort, funded by the Washington State Traffic Commission, gives children more exercise and cuts down on the traffic generated by parents parading their kids to school by car. See the contact information in the Recommended Resources section at the back of this book.

~~~~~~

RIDING WITH CHILDREN

Almost every community covered in this book has a route or two that is safe for taking small children on their first public rides on their own bikes. I most often see preteens riding with their parents on the dedicated trails, such as the Burke-Gilman. These trails seem like the safest places for new riders—children or adults—to enjoy the outdoors from atop a bike.

In her excellent book *Bicycling with Children,* Trudy Bell delves expertly into all the issues parents must tackle when getting their children on the bike trail, from toting toddlers to reining in teens. She even offers a detailed system for teaching your child to ride a bike. I recommend her book to any parent wanting complete instructions, but here I also present a few of her ideas that are germane to taking children on day rides on trails in this book.

First, a child needs to know how to balance, steer, pedal, and stop before riding in public. I have seen children on bike trails who weave from side to side or who react with a wobbly turn when overtaken by a

Family riding at Green Lake

rider coming up from behind. These create dangerous situations when children are in the presence of adults who are riding fast or commuters who are locked into their daily routine. Of course, when adult riders see small children ahead, they should be on their best, most careful behavior. Bell advises that when an adult is riding with a child, the adult ride behind and slightly to the left to coach the child and warn of oncoming vehicles.

Bell suggests that beginning riders should choose locations that are relatively free of distractions (including joggers, in-line skaters, and dog walkers). That would eliminate most of the Seattle area's dedicated, paved bike trails. If you're riding with a child who's just learning trail etiquette, try using those trails at nonpeak times, such as weekday afternoons or early mornings on weekends.

Bell notes that a bicycle is not a toy—it is a child's first vehicle; hence, children should be taught the rules of the road. Some useful road rules relating to bike trails are these:

- Look before entering a trail.
- Use voice or bell when passing.
- Stop only in a safe, visible place, out of the way of other trail users.
- Obey traffic signs.
- Go with the flow of traffic, and always ride on the right side of the road or trail.
- Use hand signals to communicate turning or stopping.
- At stop signs and driveways, stop, put a foot down, look both left and right, then left again. If it's safe, then go.
- To keep from swerving, practice "no noodle arms" and look ahead on the trail.

Valuable practice can be gained by older children and teens if they are taken on lightly trafficked roads, such as a flat, rural farm road. Graduating to those outings can give a parent a chance to assess the child's skill level, too, and such outings may provide more confidence for a child when he or she is allowed to take rides without the parents.

On all outings with children, it's advisable to carry extra water, snacks, and clothes for the child. Before riding, do a helmet check and make sure shoelaces are tucked in and pant legs rolled up. Also, be sure to have repair tools to avoid having a breakdown turn into an ordeal.

Trails Suitable for Young Children
GREEN LAKE
Location: northwest Seattle. The 2.9-mile trail circling Green Lake is flat, smooth, and scenic, with separate lanes for wheels and feet. Heavy use, especially during weekends, is the only drawback. See Tour 2, Green Lake and Northwest Seattle, for details.

Crossing the I-90 floating bridge

SEWARD PARK

Location: southeast Seattle. A 2.4-mile bike and walking trail circles a center hill on the Bailey Peninsula, a thumb of land that sticks out into Lake Washington at this popular park. The trail can be very busy at times, and it contains some uneven and unpaved patches. But it is a beautiful location with kid-friendly attractions including an Environmental Learning Center and swimming beaches. See Tour 12, South Seattle and Seward Park, for details.

LAKE WASHINGTON BOULEVARD ON BIKE-ONLY WEEKENDS

Location: southeast Seattle. Let your child start practicing road riding on summer weekends when a 4-mile stretch of Lake Washington Boulevard is closed to car traffic. The street is car-free from Seward Park north to Mount Baker Beach. Check with Seattle Parks and Recreation for current bike-only weekend dates. See Tour 12, South Seattle and Seward Park, for details.

SAMMAMISH RIVER TRAIL
Location: Bothell to Redmond, east King County. This trail is one of the most widely used by Eastside families. See Tour 15 for details.

GREEN RIVER TRAIL
Location: Tukwila to Kent, south King County. You see a lot of children on this winding trail, which runs along the Green River, because there are stretches of it running right behind suburban townhomes. It is less traveled than the city trails but does not offer as many amenities. See Tour 20, Green River and Interurban Trails, for details.

CEDAR RIVER TRAIL
Location: Renton to Maple Valley, south King County. This trail is flat and long, with very few street crossings. However, it also runs right next to a very loud highway. See Tour 21, Cedar River Trail and May Valley, for details.

CENTENNIAL TRAIL
Location: Snohomish to Arlington, Snohomish County. Recently extended to stretch 25 miles into very rural farmlands, this trail is less used than ones closer to Seattle, and it has one of the smoothest surfaces of any trail. See Tour 42 for details.

FOOTHILLS TRAIL
Location: south of Puyallup, east Pierce County. One of the most rural trails, this one was recently extended. The most services will be found in Orting. See Tour 47 for details.

CHEHALIS WESTERN TRAIL
Location: Olympia, Thurston County. Combine this ride with a road trip to the state capitol. See Tour 49, Chehalis Western and Woodard Bay Trails, for details.

YELM-TENINO TRAIL
Location: southeast Thurston County. The trail runs through three small towns. See Tour 50 for details.

Trails and Routes Suitable for Older Children
BURKE-GILMAN TRAIL
Location: northeast Seattle. The granddaddy of Seattle's rail-trails, this flat trail winds 12.3 miles through the city from Gas Works Park at the north end of Lake Union to Kenmore at the north end of Lake Washington, passing other beaches and parks en route. The trail, heavily used

by commuters and college students on weekdays, is also very busy on weekends. It is necessary to cross some city streets, although the crossings are well marked. In places, tree roots have caused the asphalt to heave and crack. See Tour 1 for details.

ALKI TRAIL
Location: West Seattle. Another busy city trail, this one offers many attractions for children, such as the beach and ice cream stands. The trail truly has shared use: Part is on a sidewalk, and part is on a wide striped shoulder next to the auto traffic. See Tour 10, West Seattle, for details.

CHIEF SEALTH TRAIL
Location: southeast Seattle. This recently developed trail runs under electric powerlines across Beacon Hill. Its hills should be fun and challenging for children with more skills. See Tour 12, South Seattle and Seward Park, for details.

Rural Roads Suitable for More Experienced Riders
SNOQUALMIE VALLEY
Location: Carnation, east King County. State Route 202 is a farm road, but it does see some traffic, and if you want to ride to Fall City, you must ride a mile or so on a busy road. The rural part of it, however, provides great exposure to farmland. Access is excellent from the park in Carnation. See Tour 18, Carnation to Snoqualmie Falls, for details.

PORT ORCHARD
Location: southeast Kitsap Peninsula. Access this tour via a ferry from West Seattle, then ride the flat suburban roads that hug the shoreline to Port Orchard. There's some traffic and sections of road with no shoulder, but it's mostly flat and very scenic. See Tour 25 for details.

SKAGIT FLATS
Location: Mount Vernon or La Conner, southwest Skagit County. This route can be broken up in many ways, all of them flat but with some traffic. Start in Mount Vernon and ride through the riverine delta of Fir Island (least traffic), or start in La Conner and ride through the tulip fields (more traffic). Caution: There is some farm-truck traffic and, during tulip season, much tourist traffic. See Tour 40, Skagit Flats and Tulip Fields, for details.

HOW TO USE THIS BOOK
Each tour includes an information block (summarizing the ride's difficulty, tour time, total distance, and total elevation gain), driving direc-

tions to the starting point, a narrative describing the tour, a mileage log, a route map, and an elevation profile. Below is an explanation of each component of the information summary.

Each ride's **difficulty** rating is based on its combination of distance, elevation gain, and traffic exposure. A flat, 25-mile trail-only ride would be rated as easy, whereas the same distance on city streets or highways might be rated as moderate. Similarly, a long, flat ride might be rated as easy or moderate, but a shorter, hilly ride might be rated as strenuous. It's best to try one or two rides at the level where you'd rate your abilities, then determine whether this book's ratings are similar to your own. Use the difficulty rating in combination with the elevation profiles to get a full picture of each tour's challenges. Below is a general description of each difficulty level.

Easy: predominately flat terrain; tour distance can be ridden within two hours; a lesser amount of interaction with vehicle traffic. Try these rides if you're a new cyclist or if you're getting back in shape at the beginning of the season.

Moderate: terrain of rolling hills; some road riding in city traffic or on highways with good shoulders or bike lanes; distances can be ridden in three to four hours. Take these tours if you are comfortable on long, off-street trail rides or are an occasional bike commuter.

Strenuous: at least one challenging hill climb; may include roads with heavy traffic or no shoulders; may be longer than four hours of saddle time. These tours are for more experienced cyclists who can comfortably climb hills and switch lanes in vehicle traffic and have built up endurance for longer rides.

The **tour time** to allow for each ride assumes a moderate riding speed of 10 to 12 miles per hour and a half hour of breaks for every two to three hours of riding time. On tours where special activities are suggested, such as whale watching, museum visits, or picnicking, extra time has been added. Ferry crossings are not included in tour times. On all tours, it's advisable to start as early in the day as possible to enjoy the tour without worrying about ferry schedules or approaching darkness.

Total distance in miles and **total elevation gain** in feet for each tour were charted using the Cat Eye CC-AT100 cyclometer. **Elevation profiles** were supplemented and verified by using geographic information systems accessed at governmental websites where available.

Routes and **route maps** for each tour in this book were created through personal research and route planning. Although I have ridden each tour—in many cases, multiple times—changes in roads or trails may have occurred by publication time. Therefore, it is advisable to carry a bicycle map or road map of the area on all tours. I will endeavor to include all route changes in subsequent editions of this book.

A NOTE ABOUT SAFETY

Safety is an important concern in all outdoor activities. No guidebook can alert you to every hazard or anticipate the limitations of every reader. Therefore, the descriptions of roads, trails, routes, and natural features in this book are not representations that a particular place or excursion will be safe for your party. When you follow any of the routes described in this book, you assume responsibility for your own safety. Under normal conditions, such excursions require the usual attention to traffic, road and trail conditions, weather, terrain, the capabilities of your party, and other factors. Because many of the lands in this book are subject to development and/or change of ownership, conditions may have changed since this book was written that make your use of some of these routes unwise. Always check for current conditions, obey posted private property signs, and avoid confrontations with property owners or managers. Keeping informed on current conditions and exercising common sense are the keys to a safe, enjoyable outing.

—The Mountaineers Books

Opposite: Gas Works Park offers great views of downtown Seattle across Lake Union. (photo by L.J. McAllister)

SEATTLE

1 Burke–Gilman Trail

DIFFICULTY: easy
TOUR TIME: allow 2.5 hours
TOTAL DISTANCE: 24.6 miles; 1.4-mile side trip to Magnuson Park
TOTAL ELEVATION GAIN: 250 feet

> **Driving directions:** Take I-5 to exit 169, N. 45th/N. 50th Sts., and turn west onto N. 45th St.; proceed 1 mile. Turn left onto Stone Wy. N. and proceed south to N. 34th St. Cross 34th, and road becomes N. Northlake Wy.; proceed east. Gas Works Park is on the right in 0.3 mile; park here.

Like a number of the region's flat, broad, off-road paved trails, the "B-G" was originally created as a way to move large numbers

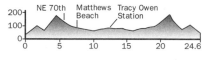

of goods. Thomas Burke, Daniel Gilman, and 10 other investors created the Seattle, Lake Shore, and Eastern Railroad in 1885 in a bid to put the city on the map by connecting their railroad to the Canadian Transcontinental Line for shipping Northwest goods to larger markets. Although the line never got past Arlington, it created a valuable link to logging communities east of Seattle in its youth. The railroad operated until 1963 and was abandoned for rail use in 1971, at which time a citizens' effort led to acquisition of the line as a recreational trail.

Some days, riding this rail-trail can seem like a mass-transit experience, and finding that open stretch for locomotion is sometimes impossible. A steady stream of bikers, walkers, runners, and skaters traverse the trail, especially from Gas Works Park through the University District. But whether you're riding a quiet, shady stretch or weaving through trail traffic on a sunny summer afternoon, the B-G provides access to and views of the best of Seattle.

Gas Works Park, at the north end of Lake Union in the Wallingford neighborhood, is a logical starting point for this tour, although the trail can be accessed at many streets crossing its 12-plus-mile route. The free parking at Gas Works Park has a time limit, so use street parking or a paid lot if you're planning a full-day excursion.

Because the trail extends in two directions from Gas Works, there are really two tours to be taken to fully see the B-G: One goes east and north to the top end of Lake Washington (the tour described here); the other goes west and north to Shilshole Bay on Puget Sound (that route

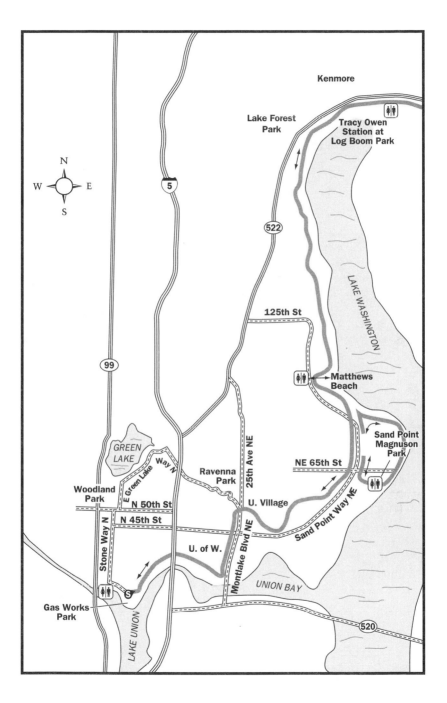

Burke-Gilman Trail in lower Wallingford (photo by L.J. McAllister)

is part of Tour 2, Green Lake and Northwest Seattle).

Most Seattle-area cyclists know the B-G, and it's a great starting route for visitors or people beginning to bike in the area. The pipe maze of the old gasworks is worth a visit, too, as well as the park's stunning views of the city across glittering Lake Union, which is often dotted with sailboats and commercial vessels and lined with houseboats and marinas.

Heading east from Gas Works Park, first climb slightly to a ridge above Lake Union's east passage to Portage Bay. Overhead looms the massive Interstate 5 bridge and more human-scale University District bridge. Under the freeway, on the south side of the trail at 0.8 mile, you'll see the *Wall of Death*, a sculpture commemorating carnival motorcycle acts.

A series of street crossings takes you onto the southern edge of the University of Washington campus. Just east of University Avenue, look up to the side of UW's recent engineering building to see a spiderlike sundial grasping the brick walls, raising the question, does time pass on a cloudy day?

Soon after you pass the high-concept clock comes the university's horticultural greenhouses, a good place for a warming walk on a chilly day. The trail then curves north at Montlake Boulevard NE at 2.1 miles, just north of the Montlake Bridge. East are Husky Stadium and the university's intramural playfields. Curve east again at University Village shopping center. Often in summer there's a fruit vendor selling fresh cherries or peaches trailside at the busy 25th Avenue NE intersection north of the shopping center. At the east edge of the shopping center is another busy crossing at NE Blakeley Street.

If you're thinking about packing a picnic, University Village is a good place to stop for supplies. Try the mega-market QFC or numerous small delis and cafés. To enter the shopping center, turn right off the trail at Blakely and proceed one-half block to a right turn.

A nice break from the trail comes at just over 5 miles. Turn right off the trail onto NE 65th Street and coast down the hill two blocks to the massive Magnuson Park (see the Mileage Log for access details). Or you can detour to a public beach at 7.5 miles as the trail bridges Sand Point Way, then skirts the edge of smaller Matthews Beach Park. Either stop makes a great turnaround point for a shorter tour.

The last 5 miles of trail winding behind large lakeside homes afford only peeks at the blue water; occasional park benches are the trail's only amenities along this stretch. Cross McAleer Creek at Lake Forest Park, and you are close to the end of the B-G. At 12.3 miles you reach Tracy Owen Station, also known as Log Boom Park; this small green space adjacent to a private marina is a great place for a picnic lunch before turning back. For picnic provisions, ride another 0.5 mile beyond the park to a shopping area with grocery stores and coffee shops.

Instead of turning around here, you can continue east to the connection with the Sammamish River Trail (see Tour 15), which takes you another 10 miles east into the suburbs, ending at Marymoor Park in Redmond—or hang a right in Kenmore and make an entire loop around Lake Washington (see Tour 14).

MILEAGE LOG

0.0 From Gas Works Park, cross N. Northlake Wy. to access the trail, turn right, and ride east with the I-5 bridge in front of you.

1.3 Cross University Ave.

2.9 Cross 25th Ave. NE.

3.1 Cross NE Blakeley St. Caution: high traffic area.

5.3 Cross NE 65th St. For a detour to Magnuson Park, turn right.

   0.2 Cross Sand Point Wy. NE onto Park Entrance Rd.

   0.7 Curve right into parking by Lake Washington.

   0.9 Forward through bollards at northeast corner of parking onto trail.

   1.6 Left at off-leash dog area onto brief unpaved section.

   1.7 Continue forward as trail forks. Right unpaved section climbs to north playfields.

   1.9 Rejoin road by parking.

   2.2 Straight at intersection with road to sports meadow; follow exit signs.

   2.4 Right at stop sign back onto Park Entrance Rd.

   2.8 Right onto 62nd Ave. NE, road through park connecting to north complex.

3.3   Arrive at north complex. Retrace route to return.
3.8   Right onto Park Entrance Rd. to exit park.
4.0   Cross Sand Point Wy. onto NE 65th St.
4.2   Right back onto Burke-Gilman Trail.
7.5   Cross Sand Point Wy. NE on an overpass; Matthews Beach Park is on the right.
12.3   Right turn into Log Boom Park, aka Tracy Owen Station. Retrace route to return.
19.1   Cross NE 70th St.
24.6   Return to Gas Works Park to end tour.

2   Green Lake and Northwest Seattle

DIFFICULTY: moderate
TOTAL TIME: allow 1.5 hours
TOTAL DISTANCE: 14.2 miles
TOTAL ELEVATION GAIN: 520 feet

Driving directions: From I-5 northbound, take exit 170, NE 65th St./Ravenna. Turn left onto NE Ravenna Blvd. toward Green Lake, continuing north onto E. Green Lake Dr. N. Community center and parking are on the left at Latona Ave. N. Additional parking on E. Green Lake Wy. N. along east side of lake.

From I-5 southbound, take exit 171, NE 74th St. Turn right onto 74th, left onto 5th Ave. NE, then right onto NE 71st St., then right onto E. Green Lake Dr. N. Community center and parking are on the left at Latona Ave. N. Additional parking on E. Green Lake Wy. N. along east side of lake.

Many bicycle tours in Seattle take the rider to landmarks, through parks, and in front of stupendous views. Here's a ride to take when you just want to poke around neigh-

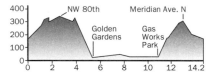

borhoods and do a little shopping. In its quick 15 miles, you ride through six unique areas where small shops abound.

Departing from the northeast side of Green Lake, ride along the lake's north shore and climb a bit to the Greenwood neighborhood, which offers a detour for some entertaining browsing. As you cross Greenwood Avenue at North 83rd Street, one block north is the Greenwood Space Travel Supply Company, the storefront effort of

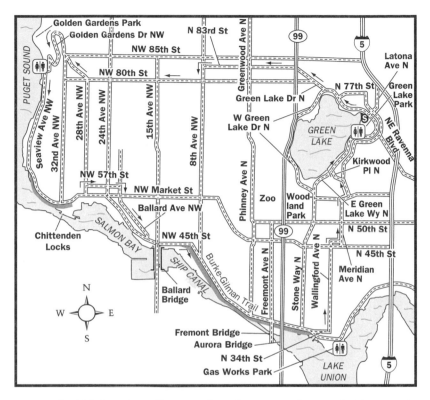

nonprofit 826 Seattle, a literacy drop-in center for youth. You won't find a better place to spend a few bucks on a book or a quirky gift for your space-traveling friends.

Back on the route, continue west on residential side streets into north Ballard. Make your way to the intersection on the bluff above Golden Gardens Park, then enjoy the quick descent on the winding, shady lane that takes you down to the waterfront park. At the bottom of the hill, ride north through the parking lots to where the trail ends at North Beach. Attractions at this popular park include sand, surf, sailboats, a waterfowl marsh, and kite flying.

Ride south along the water on Seaview Avenue NW toward Shilshole Bay and meet up with the extension of the Burke-Gilman Trail. Golden Gardens Park is the western terminus for the B-G, the granddaddy of our rail-trails, which is being finished in fits and starts through this booming neighborhood. Pass by (or dismount and visit) the Hiram M. Chittenden Locks, then turn off busy Market Street to navigate Ballard's retail core. The route takes you by the Ballard Commons Park with its skateboard bowl, then the attractive new Seattle Public Library branch with its Viking ship design and green roof, and finally down the area's old shopping street, Ballard Avenue NW, which delights with funky, small shops in two-story brick buildings.

Pick up the Burke-Gilman Trail again as you leave Ballard behind and approach Fremont. After riding through Canal Park, you can choose to either stay along the canal as the B-G takes you under the Fremont Bridge or turn onto North 34th Street and make a stop in "the center of the universe," as this neighborhood playfully calls itself. Healthy snacks can be had at the PCC Natural Market on 34th, and one block north you can watch the universe slowly expand from a perch under a huge statue of Soviet leader V. I. Lenin.

Continue east on the B-G to reach Gas Works Park. The gasworks may be rusty, but the park's big green hill offers stunning views of Lake Union and downtown Seattle. Ride north through the residential streets of Wallingford to its shopping street, North 45th. A side trip east on this street takes you to a wonderful teahouse and two old-style movie theaters, while the few blocks to the west are filled with small cafés in old houses.

A young cyclist takes a break to enjoy the sea-themed sculptures in Ballard Commons Park.

Ride north on Meridian Avenue North past Wallingford Playground to North 50th Street, where sits the artistic stone entrance to Meridian Park and the Good Shepherd Center, home to Seattle Tilth. Their organic demonstration gardens offer a quiet, welcoming respite from the retail scene. But just north on Meridian, you have one last chance to exercise your wallet as you ride through the Meridian shopping area at 55th. To celebrate the neighborhood tour, quaff a fresh brew at the Tangletown pub or pop a relatively healthy doughnut at Mighty-O.

Dropping back down to East Green Lake Way North, circle around the lake's east shore to return to parking. To work off the doughnut or ale, try a dozen or so loops on the 2.9-mile trail around the lake before racking the bike.

MILEAGE LOG

0.0 Left out of parking lot onto E. Green Lake Dr. N.

0.7 After business district, right to stay on Green Lake Dr. N.

1.1 Cross SR 99/Aurora Ave. at N. 83rd St.

1.7 Cross N. Greenwood Ave. at N. 83rd St.

2.2 Left onto 8th Ave. NW.

2.4 Right onto NW 80th St.

3.8 Right onto Loyal Ave. NW.

4.1 Forward at stop sign onto 32nd Ave. NW, which becomes Golden Gardens Dr. NW.

5.2 Arrive at Golden Gardens Park. Left to join Burke-Gilman Trail on east side of Seaview Ave. NW.

6.6 Cross Seaview Ave. at light. Caution: busy intersection.

7.2 Arrive at Hiram M. Chittenden Locks.

7.3 Left onto 28th Ave. NW.

7.4 Right onto NW 57th St.; pass Ballard Commons Park.

7.8 Right onto 22nd Ave. NW.

8.0 Left onto Ballard Ave. NW.

8.5 Right onto 17th Ave. NW for ½ block, then left onto Shilshole Ave. NW. Caution: busy intersection.

8.6 At the Y where arterial street curves left, stay right to ride under Ballard Bridge and join NW 45th St.

8.9 Cross four-way-stop intersection by Fred Meyer and rejoin Burke-Gilman Trail.

9.8 Arrive at Fremont Canal Park.

10.2 At N. 34th St. stay on trail to go under Fremont Bridge and along canal; for side trip to visit Fremont's shopping area, exit trail onto 34th.

10.4 If visiting Fremont, cross Fremont Ave. N. and continue east on the bike lane on N. 34th St.

10.8 Cross Stone Wy. N. and continue east on N. 34th St. Take trail on right for side trip to Gasworks Park.

11.1 Left onto Wallingford Ave. N. Caution: busy intersection.

12.1 Left at N. 45th St., then immediately right around QFC to stay on Wallingford Ave. N.

12.2 Right onto N. 46th St.

12.3 Left onto Meridian Ave. N.

12.8 Right onto N. 55th St.

13.0 Left onto Kirkwood Pl. N.

13.1 Left to stay on Kirkwood Pl. N. as arterial curves right.

13.3 Right onto E. Green Lake Wy. N.

14.1 Left onto East Green Lake Dr. N. Caution: busy intersection.

14.2 Left at Latona Ave. N. to end tour.

3   Carkeek and Golden Gardens Parks

DIFFICULTY: moderate
TOUR TIME: allow 2.5 hours
TOTAL DISTANCE: 20 miles
TOTAL ELEVATION GAIN: 1110 feet

Driving directions: From I-5 northbound, take exit 170, NE 65th St./Ravenna. Turn left onto NE Ravenna Blvd. toward Green Lake, continuing north onto E. Green Lake Dr. N. Community center and parking are on the left at Latona Ave. N. Additional parking on E. Green Lake Wy. N. along east side of lake.

From I-5 southbound, take exit 171, NE 74th St. Turn right onto 74th, left onto 5th Ave. NE, right onto NE 71st St., then right onto E. Green Lake Dr. N. Community center and parking are on the left at Latona Ave. N. Additional parking on E. Green Lake Wy. N. along east side of lake.

At some of our magic places where streams meet Puget Sound, city parks have kept development at bay, just as devoted volunteers now keep the wetlands and banks free of invasive species. It's being done

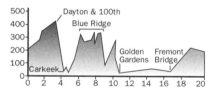

to support the return journey of oceangoing salmon. Keep the salmon in mind as you ride this tour. Each species carries its own struggle: The leisure world of humans seeking health and strong legs through biking might be a bit less essential than the salmon's upstream spawning cycle, but no less noble.

Begin your journey by cycling along Green Lake's north shore and then north through Greenwood's residential streets before turning west to Carkeek Park. This gem is somewhat of a well-kept secret, tucked away in a neighborhood far from freeways or even major arterial roads. It's really a series of ravines bisecting surrounding neighborhoods. Numerous hiking trails are open to a person walking the park. To a biker, it's a down-and-back proposition. At the parking lot, a grassy knoll looks across railroad tracks to the shore. Park and lock your bike, then use the over-tracks walkway to reach the beach.

Resume your two-wheeled effort by rising out of the saltwater air back through Carkeek and up into the winding, hilly Blue Ridge area. All the best view spots along the ridge have long ago been taken by large, glassy-eyed homes, so bikers must crest a road for an expansive view, drop into the valleys between, then emerge again. Do this a few times, and you may sense the genetic imperative of the salmon.

You'll also wend your way south, eventually coming out on the upper reaches of Golden Gardens Drive NW, just above yet another spot where you can dip your fingers into the salmon's watery world. A shady lane takes you quickly down to Shilshole Bay, bisecting Golden Gardens Park. Turn right and coast to the end of the parking lot, then go a bit farther north on the walking path to North Beach. Common sights here include windsurfers, kites, and gatherings of the posse around campfires.

Follow Shilshole Bay south along Seaview Avenue NW onto the newest addition to the Burke-Gilman Trail: a section west of the Ballard locks that makes this busy summer road a bit safer. At the Chittenden Locks, continue your meditation on the migration of species with a stop at the fish ladder, on the far side of the locks, which provides a salmon's-eye view of the journey.

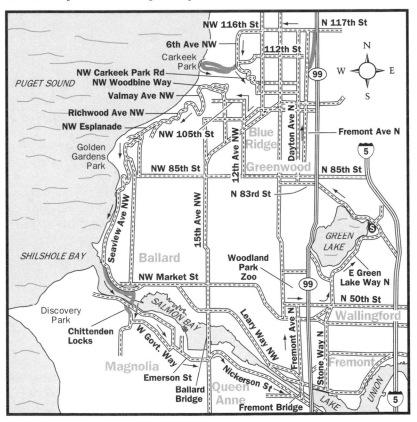

The beach at Golden Gardens Park

On the far side of the locks, climb into the Magnolia neighborhood, traversing a clattering but safe railroad trestle before coming out onto West Government Way. Take its broad bike lane down to a left that goes by Fishermen's Terminal before climbing onto the bridge over 15th Avenue West that takes you to Nickerson. Ride Nickerson, which skirts Queen Anne's north edge, to the Fremont Bridge, then cross into Fremont and take residential streets to get back to Green Lake's well-used bike lanes.

Dip your toe into the lake and consider the challenges you encountered on your course from salt water to freshwater, along major and minor tributaries, past locks and ladders, from park to park to park.

MILEAGE LOG

0.0 Left out of parking lot onto E. Green Lake Dr. N.

0.7 After business district, right to stay on Green Lake Dr. N.

1.1 Cross SR 99/Aurora Ave. N. at N. 83rd St.

1.4 Right onto Dayton Ave. N.

3.1 Left onto NW 117th St.

3.2 Cross Greenwood Ave. N. at light.

3.4 Cross 3rd Ave. NW and proceed downhill to Carkeek Park; 117th curves left and becomes 6th Ave. NW, which in 1 block becomes NW 116th St. Caution: steep grade.

4.0 Right into Carkeek Park at stop sign.

4.6 Reach pedestrian overpass to beach. Continue on one-way road to exit park.

5.2 Right to exit park, onto NW Carkeek Park Rd.

5.8 Right onto 4th Ave. NW.

6.0 Curve left as 4th dead-ends, then right onto 3rd Ave. NW.

6.3 Right onto NW 103rd St., which becomes 100th Pl. NW.

6.6 Right onto 8th Ave. NW.

6.8 Left onto NW 105th St.

7.1 Right onto 12th Ave. NW.

7.2 In 1 block, left at Y onto NW Woodbine Wy. at sign for Blue Ridge.

7.4 Left at Y with NW Norcross Wy. to stay on NW Woodbine Wy.

7.8 Right onto Valmay Ave. NW.

8.0 Right onto NW Blue Ridge Dr.

8.5 Left at Y onto Richwood Ave. NW.

8.8 Right onto NW 100th St.

8.9 Left at T at Blue Ridge Club onto Triton Dr. NW.

9.0 In ½ block, right onto NW Esplanade.

9.2 Left at Y onto 31st Ave. NW.

9.3 Right onto NW 95th St.

9.4 Straight onto View Ave. NW.

9.8 Right onto Golden Gardens Dr. Caution: fast-moving traffic on curving descent.

10.6 Arrive at Golden Gardens Park. Left to join Burke-Gilman Trail on east side of Seaview Ave. NW.

11.8 Cross Seaview Ave. at light. Caution: busy intersection.

12.5 Arrive at Hiram M. Chittenden Locks. Walk bike through locks to Magnolia exit.

13.0 Exit locks onto W. Commodore Wy., jog right 10 yards, then left onto 33rd Ave. W. Caution: steep uphill grade. Trail begins on railroad bridge at street end.

13.2 Curve left off trail onto 32nd Ave. W.

13.4 Left onto W. Fort St. briefly, then left at stop sign onto W. Government Wy.

14.1 Left onto W. Emerson Pl., which becomes W. Emerson St.

14.3 At 21st Ave. W., join roadside trail on the right.

14.5 Rejoin street at bridge approach, climb ramp, and stay right. Follow signs to Nickerson. Caution: may be heavy bridge traffic.

14.8 Coming off bridge, stay right at Y to stay on W. Nickerson St.

16.3 Left onto Fremont Bridge; merge into turning lanes or use crosswalks to enter bridge walkway/bikeway. Caution: high traffic, complex intersection.

16.6 Continue forward on Fremont Ave. N. on north side of bridge. Climb long grade out of Fremont.

17.7 Right onto N. 50th St. to SR 99 underpass.
17.9 Continue forward at stop sign to stay on N. 50th St.
18.2 Merge to left-turn bike lane between vehicle lanes to turn left onto E. Green Lake Wy. N.
19.8 Left onto Green Lake Dr. N. Caution: busy intersection.
20.0 Left at Latona Ave. NE to end tour.

4   Magnuson and Ravenna Parks

DIFFICULTY: easy
TOUR TIME: allow 1.5 hours
TOTAL DISTANCE: 16 miles
TOTAL ELEVATION GAIN: 320 feet

Driving directions: From I-5 northbound, take exit 170, NE 65th St./Ravenna. Turn left onto NE Ravenna Blvd. toward Green Lake, continuing north onto E. Green Lake Dr. N. Community center and parking are on the left at Latona Ave. N. Additional parking on E. Green Lake Wy. N. along east side of lake.

From I-5 southbound, take exit 171, NE 74th St. Turn right onto 74th, left onto 5th Ave. NE, right onto NE 71st St., then right onto E. Green Lake Dr. N. Community center and parking are on the left at Latona Ave. N. Additional parking on E. Green Lake Wy. N. along east side of lake.

Northeast Seattle provides a relaxing excursion on a summer afternoon. This short tour connects two of the city's most popular parks on a gentle route between Green Lake and Lake Washington and reveals a third park that is a hidden gem.

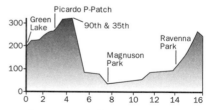

Begin and end the tour at Green Lake, one of the favorite fitness spots for Seattleites. Cross onto the most luxurious, if brief, bike lane in Seattle: NE Ravenna Boulevard. Bikes get equal space with cars here, and for a half-dozen blocks you're cycling under a broad tree canopy with room to spare.

Jogging north in the University District, the route continues on a brief gravelly trail above Ravenna Park. A stop on the pedestrian-bike bridge at 20th Avenue NE provides a sneak peek at the hidden haven below: Ravenna Park's ravine. A hard-packed dirt trail runs its length.

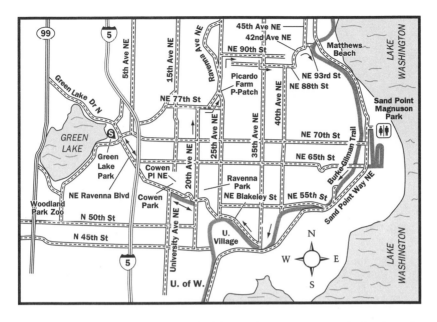

The Ravenna neighborhood holds another unique Seattle landmark: the Picardo Farm P-Patch. It is the oldest and largest of Seattle's community gardens. From a street-side view of its sunken garden north of University Prep, you can see back-to-the-land types tending vegetables and plucking weeds from the fertile soil.

From Ravenna, climb north into the Wedgwood neighborhood and then descend in a winding downhill loop east to the Burke-Gilman Trail. Heading south on the B-G, you'll soon be at your midtour break. Exit the trail at NE 65th Street and drop down to Warren G. Magnuson Park.

Previously a U.S. Navy base, this sprawling complex is now a city park and possibly the zenith of the "multiuse" concept. Ride past the short-term transitional housing for homeless families and the offices and performance spaces for nonprofit organizations. The former brig, now a community center, sits in front of a community garden and an off-leash dog park. Past the dog park are trails to the Lake Washington waterfront. You'll also find playfields, a boat ramp, an amphitheater, meadows with walking trails and large sculptures. Whew!

Cyclists might opt for reclining on the grass or lounging along the off-leash area fence to watch the canines frolicking. When your break is over, ride south again on the B-G, pass University Village shopping center, then depart the trail to cut northwest along Ravenna Park.

On a warm day, savor a noticeable drop in temperature as you visit this verdant urban canyon. A recently daylighted creek babbles

Ravenna Ravine

alongside much of the trail. Visible among the dense greenery above are the bridges of the streets you traveled earlier. Walking trails angle up the ravine on each side, and a broad main path is lined by large Douglas-firs and western red cedars.

After a visit to the ravine, ride back along its upper rim, then emerge at the edge of Cowen Park, across which begins the wide thoroughfare that brought you from Green Lake and will take you back there again.

MILEAGE LOG

0.0 Right onto E. Green Lake Dr. N.

0.3 Get in left lane and continue through intersection at NE 71st St. onto bike lane on NE Ravenna Blvd.

1.2 Left onto University Wy. NE, which becomes Cowen Pl. NE.

1.3 Left onto 15th Ave. NE, then immediate right onto a trail just south of the bridge.

1.5 Left onto 20th Ave. NE, on the bike and pedestrian bridge.

2.5 Right onto NE 77th St.

2.7 Left onto Ravenna Ave. NE.

2.9 Left onto 25th Ave. NE, which in 1 block becomes Ravenna Ave. NE. Picardo Farm P-Patch on the right.

3.0 Left to continue on Ravenna Ave. NE.

3.3 Right on 25th Ave. NE.

3.6 Right on NE 90th St.

4.1 Right onto 35th Ave. NE.

4.3 Left onto NE 88th St.

4.7 Left onto 42nd Ave. NE. Caution: Narrow road, limited visibility.

5.0 Left onto 45th Ave. NE.

5.1 Right on NE 93rd St.

5.2 As road curves left, go right on brief trail connecting with Burke-Gilman Trail, visible through trees; turn right onto B-G.

6.7 Left onto NE 65th St.

6.9 Cross Sand Point Way onto Park Entrance Rd. in Warren G. Magnuson Park.

7.4 Curve right to enter parking area.

7.5 Continue forward through bollards onto trail.

7.7 Rejoin parking and continue forward along lake.

7.9 Forward through bollards at northeast corner of parking onto trail.

8.6 Left at off-leash dog area onto brief unpaved section.

8.7 Continue forward as trail forks. Right unpaved section climbs to north playfields.

8.9 Rejoin road by parking.

9.2 Straight at intersection with road to sports meadow; follow exit signs.

9.4 Right at stop sign back onto Park Entrance Rd.

9.7 Right onto 62nd Ave. NE through park to north complex.

10.2 Arrive at north complex. Right onto NE 74th St. to community center, amphitheater, community garden and off-leash area.

10.4 Road ends at off-leash area. Retrace route.

10.6 Left onto 62nd Ave. NE to retrace route through park.

11.0 Right onto Park Entrance Rd. to exit park.

11.2 Cross Sand Point Wy. onto NE 65th St.

11.4 Left onto trail.

13.6 Cross NE Blakeley St. Caution: high traffic area.

13.8 Cross 25th Ave. NE, then immediately exit trail to the right and turn left onto Ravenna Pl. NE. Caution: busy intersection.

14.1 Right onto NE 55th. In one half block, turn left into park. Creek and ravine trail are adjacent to playfield.

14.3 Exit park back onto 55th; turn right.

14.4 In one block, curve right onto NE Ravenna Blvd.

14.5 As Ravenna curves left, stay straight into alley next to park.

14.6 Cross 20th and continue on NE 58th St., then angle right to brief, unpaved trail next to ravine.

14.8 Exit trail at 15th Ave NE. Cross 15th and angle left onto Cowen Pl. NE.

14.9 Right onto NE Ravenna Blvd., merge to left bike lane.
15.7 Proceed straight through intersection at NE 71st St. onto E. Green Lake Dr. N.
16.0 Left at Latona Ave. N into parking to end tour.

5   Green Lake to Edmonds

DIFFICULTY: moderate
TOUR TIME: allow 3 hours
TOTAL DISTANCE: 25.2 miles
TOTAL ELEVATION GAIN: 1330 feet

Driving directions: From I-5 northbound, take exit 170, NE 65th St./Ravenna. Turn left onto NE Ravenna Blvd. toward Green Lake, continuing onto E. Green Lake Dr. N. Community center and parking are on the left at Latona Ave. NE. Additional parking on E. Green Lake Wy. N. along east side of lake.

From I-5 southbound, take exit 171, NE 74th St. Turn right onto 74th, left onto 5th Ave. NE, right onto NE 71st St., then right onto E. Green Lake Dr. N. Community center and parking are on the left at Latona Ave. NE. Additional parking on E. Green Lake Wy. N. along east side of lake.

Edmonds is a well-loved Seattle suburb because of its homey downtown, wonderful views across the water, and easy access by ferry to Kitsap Peninsula. On top of that, it's a great ride from Green Lake.

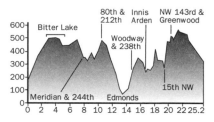

Heading north, the route barrels through the neighborhoods of Greenwood, Bitter Lake, and Shoreline. For a taste of officially sanctioned kitsch, make a stop at the Viewlands Hoffman Receiving Station, a Seattle City Light power substation at Fremont and North 107th. The northwest corner of the industrial enclosure contains a curious set of handmade wind sculptures made from kitchen items. It's a tribute to the quirky pastime of Emil Gehrke of Grand Coulee, who created and maintained the rusting art.

The way north is a combination of city streets and yet-to-be-connected sections of the Interurban Trail. At the Aurora Village Transit Center, where you cross into Snohomish County, bike lanes take you

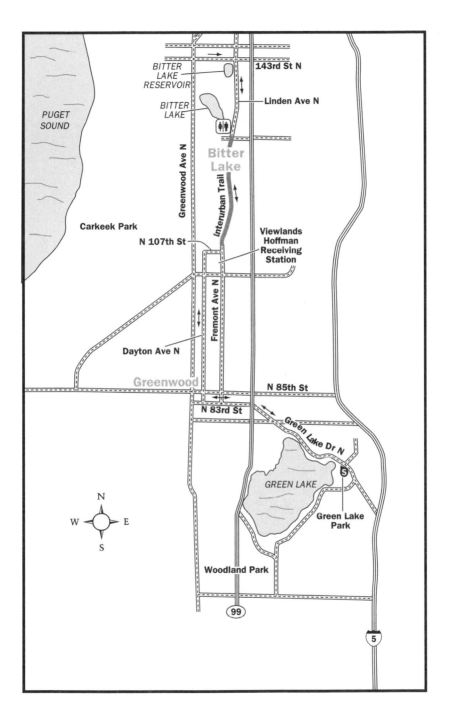

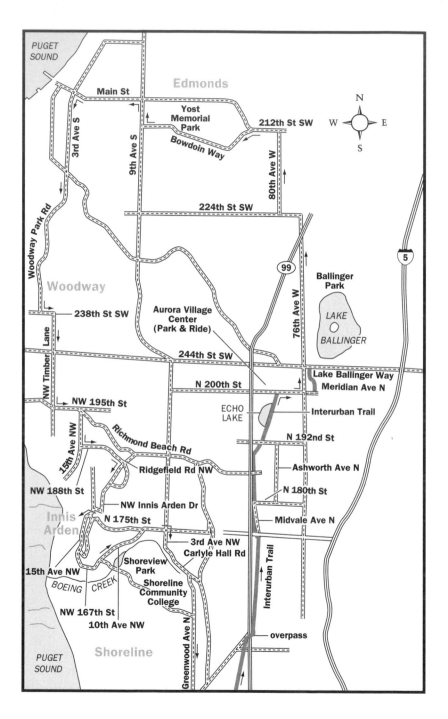

Divers in the underwater park adjacent to the Edmonds ferry dock

into Edmonds, past busy, bus-laden streets near the Lynnwood mall.

Enter downtown Edmonds by turning onto Main Street at Ninth Avenue and pedaling past a plethora of shops to a roundabout formed by a brick fountain. Just to the north are the local historical museum and, on summer Saturdays, a vibrant farmers market.

A favorite way to enjoy Edmonds is to pop into the bakery or one of the cafés and grab a bit of food and drink to go, then coast down to the water's edge. North of the ferry dock is the extensive Brackett's Landing Park with sandy beaches, rocky outcroppings . . . and underwater trails. You'd need a bit more than Lance Armstrong's lung capacity to visit *these* trails without scuba gear, though you can watch others come and go on their watery "hikes" in full wet suits and loaded down with air tanks, flippers, and lights. From the shore, you can view a map of the park, which is marked on the surface with colored buoys. Benches, restrooms and a well-kept stretch of sand make it easy to spend an hour or two waterside.

There are many choices for the route home. The easiest ride is to retrace the trip you took on the way north. But a more interesting and challenging way is to explore the hilly neighborhoods of Woodway, Shoreline, and Innis Arden. To do this, head south into Woodway, a community known for its large, tree-enclosed properties. Along its well-maintained roads you'll see the gardens and water views enjoyed by its residents.

From the aptly named Timber Lane, you enter King County once again, into the neighborhood of Richmond Beach in Shoreline. Explore it by taking a side trip to Richmond Beach Park, well signed off its main street, Richmond Beach Road, then continue on to 15th Avenue NW, a right turn at the inviting Richmond Beach Coffee.

With a left turn at 188th, you're entering one of Seattle's more exclusive neighborhoods: Innis Arden. The area's main attraction is also its challenge for cyclists: hilly terrain that results in fantastic views west to the Olympics and the Sound. This roller-coaster route continues to the east side of Shoreline Community College and Shoreview Park, which provides a challenging hillclimb. Babbling Boeing Creek accompanies the road a way. Once you've topped the hill, you're soon back in the Seattle neighborhoods where you began, for a relaxing spin south to Green Lake.

MILEAGE LOG

0.0 Left out of parking lot onto E. Green Lake Dr. N.

0.7 After business district, keep right to stay on Green Lake Dr. N.

1.1 Cross SR 99/Aurora Ave. N. at N. 83rd St.

1.4 Right onto Dayton Ave. N.

2.2 Right onto N. 107th St.

2.4 Left onto Fremont Ave. N.

2.6 At 110th St., merge right onto Interurban Trail.

3.6 Merge onto Linden Ave. N. at N. 128th St. Restrooms available on the left at Bitter Lake Playground.

4.5 Cross N. 145th St. at Seattle city limits and rejoin Interurban Trail.

5.0 Cross N. 155th St. and then SR 99/Aurora Ave. N. on two bike/pedestrian overpasses. Caution: sharp turns on overpass.

6.1 Cross 175th, trail continues on near (west) sidewalk on Midvale Ave. N.

6.7 Turn right on sidewalk at 185th at Gateway shopping center.

6.8 Left on near (west) sidewalk at Midvale to continue on trail.

7.6 Right onto N. 200th St. at Aurora Village Transit Center.

7.8 Cross Meridian Ave. N., turn left onto trail in 100 yards.

8.1 Cross 244th St. SW/Lake Ballinger Wy./SR 104 and continue north into Snohomish County, where Meridian becomes 76th Ave. W.

9.5 Merge right onto sidewalk on SR 99/Aurora Ave. N. for 1 block, then left to cross Aurora at stoplight at 244th St. SW

9.9 Right onto 80th Ave. W.

10.7 Left onto 212th St. SW.

10.9 Angle left to Bowdoin Wy.

12.0 Right onto 9th Ave. S.

12.2 Left on Main St.

12.7 Arrive at fountain at 5th Ave.; park for downtown visit. (Detour straight ahead 5 blocks to waterfront.)

12.8 At 3rd Ave. S. and Main St., turn south onto 3rd; continue south onto Woodway Park Rd.

14.5 Left onto 238th St. SW.

14.6 Right onto NW Timber Ln., which becomes 112th Ave. W. then 20th Ave. NW.

15.6 Left onto NW 195th St.; at Y, stay right on Richmond Beach Rd.

15.9 Right onto 15th Ave. NW.

16.2 Left onto NW 188th St., which becomes Ridgefield Rd. NW. at stop sign.

16.6 Right onto NW Innis Arden Dr.; keep right onto NW 177th St.

17.2 Left onto 14th Ave. NW, which becomes 15th Ave. NW in 1 block.

17.6 At Y, stay right to continue on 15th Ave. NW, which becomes NW 167th St.

18.0 Straight onto 10th Ave. NW at stop sign.

18.5 Right onto N. 175th St.

18.7 Right onto 3rd Ave. NW, which becomes Carlyle Hall Rd.

19.2 Right onto Greenwood Ave. N.

20.1 Left onto N. 143rd St. Caution: busy intersection.

20.4 Right onto Linden Ave. N.

21.4 Merge onto Interurban Trail at NW 128th St.

22.4 Right onto NW 110th St. as trail ends.

22.6 Left onto Dayton Ave. N.

23.8 Left onto N. 83rd St.

24.0 Cross SR 99/Aurora Ave. N. and make a soft right onto Green Lake Dr. N.

24.5 Left to stay on E. Green Lake Dr. N.

25.2 Right at Latona Ave. NE into parking to end tour.

6   Magnolia and Discovery Park

DIFFICULTY: moderate
TOUR TIME: allow 1.5 hours
TOTAL DISTANCE: 10.5 miles
TOTAL ELEVATION GAIN: 590 feet

Driving directions: Take I-5 to exit 169, 45th/50th Sts., and turn west onto 45th. Proceed west as 45th becomes 46th, then Market St. Turn left onto 15th Ave. W. and cross over Ballard Bridge. As 15th becomes Elliott Ave. W. just south of Magnolia Bridge, turn left onto overpass at W. Galer St. to Terminals 90/91. Proceed 1 block, turn right to go under bridge, then right again to dead-end at 16th Ave. W. Parking is trailside on 16th.

This short tour skirts the edges of hilly Magnolia and stops for a visit at the locks and an exploration of the grand open spaces of Discovery Park.

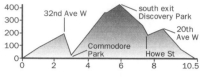

Start and end the tour at the Terminal 91 Bike Path parking, conveniently located on Elliott Bay between Magnolia and Queen Anne. The bike path is a paved trail that runs between the Interbay train tracks and a large Port of Seattle terminal. Smell the creosote and listen for the huffing of the locomotives as you ride this 1-mile stretch north. Watch for oncoming cyclists at two points where the trail narrows and at one spot where it climbs up over the tracks. Exit the path at Burlington Northern Santa Fe Railway's Balmer Yard, where you'll often see hulking train engines idling on their tracks at the road's edge as casually as a pizza delivery car while their operators visit the yard's office.

Climb a bit to Thorndyke, then continue north on a long, gradual uphill course in a wide, well-marked bike lane along Gilman Avenue West. A side tour can be taken at West Emerson Place to Fisherman's

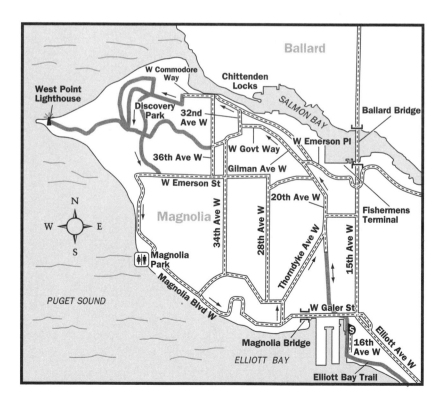

Fall is a great time to visit the Hiram Chittenden Locks and find salmon in the adjacent fish ladder.

Terminal, two blocks east. You can purchase seafood from those who caught it, right off the back of their boats.

The climb becomes a bit steeper and you will feel the length of the hill as you curve west onto West Government Way. Crest the hill, then turn right and in two blocks you're on a clacking wooden (but quite safe) pedestrian-bike trestle that spans railroad tracks. Just down the hill to the north is the Hiram Chittenden Locks, a connection between Magnolia and Ballard. Ride down to the locks, but not through them. Bikers are required to dismount and walk through the busy, touristy site.

The Magnolia side of the locks features a grassy, terraced hillside that is a great place to kickstand-back and watch the frothy water shoot forth from the spillway adjacent to the fish ladder. The fish ladder is worth a visit when the salmon are jumping. Its subterranean viewing area is marked by a series of 6-foot shiny metal waves set onto the concrete plaza.

Depart the locks by turning right onto West Commodore Way adjacent to the Magnolia entrance. This route takes you up to the northeast corner of Discovery Park, Seattle's largest park, at 534 acres. Discovery contains large open meadows, wooded trails down to Puget Sound, and stunning views of the Olympic Mountains and area waterways.

A ride through the park is a relaxing tour of closed roads dating from when this was a bustling military base. Today there's still a small cadre of military families occupying some of the old Fort Lawton housing, and a massive golfball-shaped radar installation still exists. On the edge of the grand meadow, the main road forks, with the right branch going down to the bluffs that overlook Puget Sound. Continue on the middle branch to exit by the south parking area.

Magnolia's bike route is one of the best-signed in the city, so follow the signs through the well-manicured neighborhood of stately homes with great views, and in a few minutes you arrive at Magnolia Park, which provides a panoramic view of Elliott Bay and downtown Seattle.

The bike route curves along another segment of Magnolia Park, which sports restrooms in a chalet-style building adjacent to the road. Pick up Thorndyke and coast down the long, straight arterial with views of the Interbay rail yards and Queen Anne Hill. Turn right at 20th to return to the Elliott Bay Trail—or, if you're going to loop Queen Anne too (see Route 7), continue on Thorndyke to the next stop sign.

MILEAGE LOG

0.0 From parking, ride north on Terminal 91 Bike Path. Continue into rail yards under Magnolia Bridge. Caution: trail narrows at two spots.

0.6 Leave rail yard at a Y and bear right onto city street.

1.0 Right onto Thorndyke Ave. W., which becomes 20th Ave. W., then Gilman Ave. W., then W. Government Wy.

2.4 As Government Wy. curves left, continue straight briefly on W. Fort St. Note sign for bike route to Ballard Locks.

2.5 Right onto 32nd Ave. W. As road turns left after 2 blocks, cross onto paved trail opposite.

2.6 Cross bridge over railroad tracks.

2.7 Cross W. Commodore Wy. and enter Commodore Park, on south side of ship canal locks. To depart, turn right onto W. Commodore Wy.

3.2 Left onto 40th Ave. W.

3.3 Right at sign for Discovery Park, then straight past road signed for Daybreak Star Cultural Center. Follow right edge of parking lot, proceed through bollards onto trail, and follow green "Bike Route" signs.

4.7 Cross street just to left of Hawaii Circle, then left onto a sidewalk trail.

4.9 Right to follow Bike Route and South Parking Lot signs.

5.0 Right at a T in trail.

5.3 Take middle trail as road forks.

5.5 Right onto W. Emerson St. at park's south exit.

5.7 Left onto Magnolia Blvd. W.

7.5 Veer right onto W. Howe St. for 1 block. Cross bridge.

7.8 Right onto Magnolia Blvd. W. at stop sign. Magnolia becomes W. Galer St.

7.9 Restrooms available roadside in Magnolia Park.
8.4 Left onto Thorndyke Ave. W.
8.5 Right at intersection with Condon Way W. to stay on Thorndyke.
9.5 Right onto 20th Ave. W. Proceed past BNSF Balmer Yard.
9.9 Left onto trail through rail yard.
10.5 Arrive at parking to end tour.

7 Queen Anne and Seattle Center

DIFFICULTY: moderate
TOUR TIME: allow 1.5 hours
TOTAL DISTANCE: 10.8 miles
TOTAL ELEVATION GAIN: 535 feet

Driving directions: Take I-5 to exit 169, 45th/50th Sts., and turn west onto 45th. Proceed west as 45th becomes 46th, then Market St. Turn left onto 15th Ave. W. and cross over Ballard Bridge. As 15th becomes Elliott Ave. W. just south of Magnolia Bridge, turn left onto overpass at W. Galer St. to Terminals 90/91. Proceed 1 block, turn right to go under bridge, then right again to dead-end at 16th Ave. W. Parking is trailside on 16th.

Queen Anne is another short loop like the Magnolia tour (see Tour 6), climbing up and around one of Seattle's many populated hills. On this brief ride, you'll find tree-lined neighborhoods, a vibrant shopping street, and the tourist haven of Seattle Center.

After you follow the Terminal 91 Bike Path north for a mile, get ready for some climbing as you cross 15th Avenue West. Huff your way up one block to a right turn on 14th, which connects to Gilman Drive West, a major arterial for the neighborhood. Two lefts send you northbound on 10th Avenue West, which becomes Fulton, then curves around the south side of Mount Pleasant Cemetery. Through a half dozen twists and turns, it's easiest to ignore the tree-obscured street signs and just stay on the arterial. It delivers you to West McGraw Street.

Turn south onto Second Avenue West through this comfortable neighborhood of modest-looking homes. Queen Anne is well known as one of the city's priciest close-in neighborhoods, but it's the location rather than the homes, some of which are of average size and tightly packed. Ride the sidewalk through West Queen Anne Playfield, then head south to Galer Street.

Two lefts put you at the top of "the counterbalance," which is the beginning of the hilltop shopping street. The counterbalance is so named

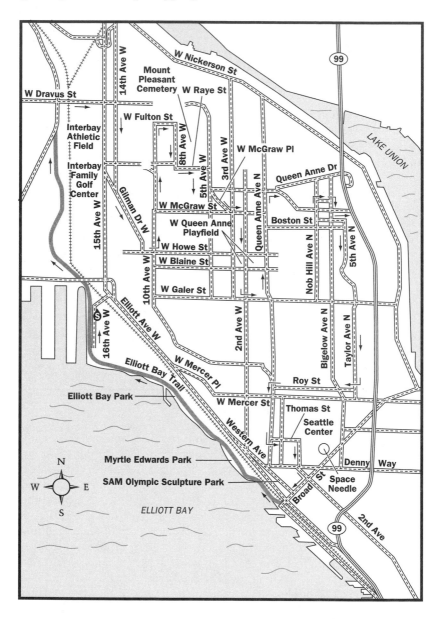

A father and son ride past the tugboat dock near Terminal 91.

because of the trolleys that once conquered the 20 percent grade of Queen Anne Avenue, using two cars linked by a cable; one was filled with concrete, the other used for passengers. As one went up, the other went down.

Riding north on Queen Anne Avenue North, you'll witness the slow evolution of a beloved business district. The mom-and-pop shops have inevitably given way to tony boutique stores and small specialty chains. The old grocery is now an upscale market and, incredibly, three gourmet coffee shops duel it out on a key corner. The locals might mourn the changes, but it's good shopping for a visiting cyclist. Stop at Pasta & Company for a deli salad, or visit Metropolitan Market for decadent chocolates. Check out the music lineup coming to the Paragon jazz club, and resolve to try it on a return visit. For excellent baked goods, stop at Macrina, just off the avenue on West McGraw.

When the businesses peter out, continue your loop around the east side of the hill, spotting views between apartment buildings across Lake Union to Capitol Hill. A ride down to the Seattle Center area of lower Queen Anne is a fast experience. Turn west onto Roy St., which has a generous bike lane that takes you past the north side of Seattle Center and into lower Queen Anne's bustling business district. Skirt the west edge of Seattle Center and approach it on Thomas St., where the Space Needle looms overhead. Tie up the bike at this entrance to the center, between the renovated plazas of the Fisher Pavilion and stylish Seattle Children's Theater, to explore the grounds.

One of the few structures in Seattle Center that has not received an external remodel—and has not needed it—is the graceful, often-imitated Space Needle. Over the years, it's only required a name change: It was originally called the Space Cage. Recline on the well-kept grass for a daydream on the city of the future evoked by the "Jetsons"-like needle before wrapping up the tour.

Continue down Second Avenue West, which will carry you to Broad Street. Turn right and ride toward the waterfront, past the new Seattle Art Museum Olympic Sculpture Park and into the bayside parks—Myrtle Edwards and Elliott Bay—whose trails lead north back to the starting point.

MILEAGE LOG

0.0 From parking, ride north on Terminal 91 Bike Path. Continue into rail yards under Magnolia Bridge. Caution: trail narrows at two spots.

0.6 Leave rail yard at a Y and bear right onto city street.

1.0 Right onto Thorndyke Ave. W., which becomes 20th Ave. W.

1.3 Right onto W. Dravus St. Proceed through stoplights and overpass at 15th Ave. W.

1.6 Right turn onto 14th Ave. W.

1.7 Take right fork at W. Barrett St. and continue on 14th.

2.3 Left at intersection of 13th onto Gilman Drive W.

2.5 Left onto W. Howe St.

2.7 Left onto 10th Ave. W.

3.4 Stay on arterial as 10th curves right into W. Fulton St., then curves again onto 8th Ave. W., then W. Raye St., then 5th Ave. W., and finally W. McGraw Pl.

4.2 Left onto W. McGraw St., then right onto 2nd Ave. W.

4.5 Cross W. Howe St. and travel on 2nd southbound to the trail bisecting West Queen Anne Playfield.

4.7 Exit the playfield at W. Blaine and 3rd Ave. W. Continue south on 3rd.

4.8 Left onto W. Galer St.

5.0 Left onto Queen Anne Ave. N.

5.7 Right onto W. Smith St.

5.8 Soft right onto W. McGraw Pl., which curves left and becomes W. McGraw St.

6.0 Soft left onto Nob Hill Ave. N., then soft right onto Wheeler St.

6.2 Right onto Bigelow Ave. N.

6.3 Left onto W. Lynn St.

6.4 Right onto 5th Ave. N.

6.7 Stay left on arterial at the Y, curving onto Taylor Ave. N.

7.4 Right onto Roy St.

7.5 Cross 5th Ave. N. and continue in bike lane on Roy St.

7.9 At 1st Ave. N., merge into left lane.

8.0 Left onto Queen Anne Ave. N.

8.3 Left onto Thomas St.

8.5 Arrive at Seattle Center entrance. Right onto 2nd Ave. N.

8.7 Right onto Broad St.

9.0 Right into park trails at waterfront.

10.8 Exit park at parking to end tour.

8 Downtown Seattle

DIFFICULTY: moderate
TOUR TIME: allow 1.5 hours
TOTAL DISTANCE: 10.1 miles
TOTAL ELEVATION GAIN: 100 feet

Driving directions: Take I-5 to exit 169, 45th/50th Sts., and turn west onto 45th. Proceed west as 45th becomes 46th, then Market St. Turn left onto 15th Ave. W. and cross over Ballard Bridge. As 15th becomes Elliott Ave. W. just south of Magnolia Bridge, turn left onto overpass at W. Galer St. to Terminals 90/91. Proceed 1 block, turn right to go under bridge, then right again to dead-end at 16th Ave. W. Parking is trailside on 16th.

Some people get great enjoyment from being a tourist in their own town, but for longtime locals who work in downtown Seattle, a bike tour through the city center may seem like the last thing they would want to do on a day away from the office. However, this tour is designed to hit many high spots a tourist might enjoy, so you can either play visitor or grit your teeth and use the tour to entertain out-of-town guests.

This modest 10-mile spin would take about an hour if you rode it straight through, and it has only one gradual incline, stretching from the International District to the downtown library, so it should be within the abilities of even the occasional rider. The difficulty comes from street traffic, which can be significant during work days or on game days in the stadium area, so this tour is best ridden on a weekend, fit in around game schedules and ridden by people comfortable riding in traffic.

Head south through Elliott Bay Park, Myrtle Edwards Park, and the

Seattle Art Museum's Olympic Sculpture Park, exiting onto Alaskan Way. Although an off-street trail currently exists on the east side of Alaskan Way, waterfront road renovations may make this leg of the route significantly different in coming years.

Pass the hill-climb to Pike Place Market, then the aquarium and the tourist-magnet piers, then ride by the ferry terminal and Pioneer Square before exiting the trail at South Royal Brougham Way. Skirt the pro football and baseball stadiums and head into Pioneer Square.

You'll technically just reach Occidental Square before a right turn toward the International District. However, art and book lovers should take a little detour here. Cross South Jackson Street into the square

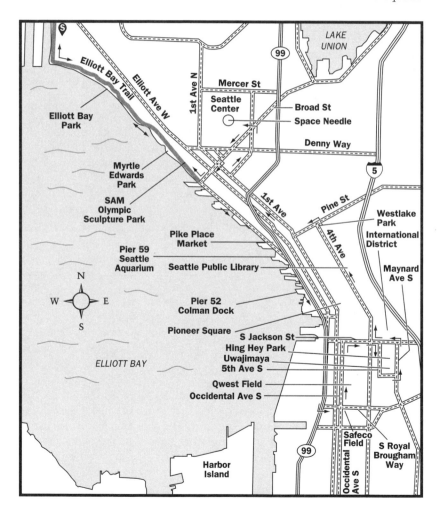

Trailside sculptures greet cyclists at the popular new Seattle Art Museum.

and chain up your bike to stroll through galleries that line the tree-covered pedestrian mall, then slip around the corner on Main Street and head to First Avenue for a visit to Elliott Bay Book Company, Seattle's premiere independent bookstore.

Cycling into the International District takes you by the evolving transit stations for Amtrak and regional rail and bus service. Both Union Station and the regional rail hub of King Street Station have been renovated, restoring architectural grandeur.

Turn right onto Fifth Avenue South and ride between the old buildings of the International District and the new, modern office towers erected recently by billionaire Paul Allen's Vulcan Corp. The Microsoft co-founder's projects border the recent Uwajimaya Village development, the tour's next stop. The expanded Asian food store created a new focal point in this busy neighborhood. Tour the store to marvel, sample, and shop for unique imported food and snack at the Asian food court.

Two blocks northeast of Uwajimaya is Hing Hay Park, which sports a colorful pagoda and a fading dragon mural on the wall of an adjacent building. All around this park, at South King Street and Maynard Avenue South, you'll find small Asian shops and cafés.

Ride north on Fourth Avenue into Seattle's business district from here, stopping for a view of the new City Hall building at James Street. The building's unusual glass awnings overhang the tan stone facade, and the paved plaza sports a series of water channels. A few blocks beyond is the Rem Koolhaas–designed Seattle Public Library at Madison Street, whose angular glass shape launched a thousand architectural reviews. Continue north on Fourth to Westlake Center, then turn left and head to Pike Place Market for another chance to stop and stroll the small shops.

Cut north through Belltown's many restaurants and apartment buildings toward Seattle Center, and approach the center grounds right under the Space Needle. It's easy to tarry at Seattle Center, grabbing a coffee or snack and watching the parade of visitors from a park bench, or strolling around the International Fountain.

Head back to the waterfront for a look at SAM's new sculpture park before finishing the tour with a ride back through the two adjoining waterfront parks.

MILEAGE LOG

0.0 From parking, ride south on Terminal 91 Bike Path, onto Elliott Bay Trail.

1.7 Exit the parks onto Alaskan Wy. at Pier 70.

1.8 At Clay St. cross to east side of Alaskan Wy. onto sidewalk.

2.2 Under Bell Street Bridge, curve left off sidewalk and cross trolley rail tracks onto beginning of waterfront trail at World Trade Center West building.

3.8 Left at S. Royal Brougham Wy. To avoid traffic, stay on the near (north side) sidewalk for next 2 blocks.

3.9 Left onto Occidental Ave. S.

4.3 Right onto S. King St., then an immediate left to get back onto Occidental Ave. S.

4.4 Right onto S. Jackson St.

4.6 Right onto 5th Ave. S.

4.7 Left into Uwajimaya Village plaza adjacent to parking.

4.8 Exit Uwajimaya where 6th Ave. meets Lane St. and proceed east on S. Lane St. for 1 block.

4.9 Left onto Maynard Ave. S.

5.1 Left onto S. Jackson St.

5.2 Right onto 4th Ave. S.

6.3 Left onto Pine St. at Westlake Center.

6.5 Right onto 1st Ave.

7.1 Right onto Cedar St.

7.3 Cedar curves left and merges into 5th at Denny. Continue through stoplight to 5th Ave. N.

7.5 Left onto John St.; arrive at Seattle Center.

7.6 Left onto Broad St.

8.2 Right into waterfront parks.

10.1 End tour at parking.

9 The Arboretum, Capitol Hill, and East Lake Union

DIFFICULTY: moderate
TOUR TIME: allow 1.5 hours
TOTAL DISTANCE: 12.7 miles
TOTAL ELEVATION GAIN: 485 feet

Driving directions: From I-5, take exit 165 to SR 520. Exit SR 520 at Montlake Blvd. Proceed east across Montlake to Lake Washington Blvd. E., then to a left turn onto E. Foster Island Rd. Parking on the left at base of Arboretum Dr.

From I-405, take exit 14 to SR 520. Exit SR 520 at Montlake Blvd. Turn left onto Lake Washington Blvd. E., then to a left turn onto E. Foster Island Rd. Parking on the left at base of Arboretum Dr.

This short tour provides close-ups of Seattle's outdoor and cultural attractions: shady wooded lanes, gardens, art, architecture, and the boating life. Toss in some views, a couple of bridges, and a bit of shopping, and you have a memorable summer afternoon.

Begin and end at the Washington Park Arboretum, a treasure trove of interesting landscapes maintained by the University of Washington. You get a good sampling from Arboretum Drive: Azaleas and rhododendrons burst with color in spring, and a small grove of giant Sequoia trees command a majestic corner.

After picking up Lake Washington Boulevard for a short ride north among the serious traffic, angle left onto the biking haven of Interlaken Boulevard. West of busy 24th Avenue East, the street becomes a trail. Wend your way up into Capitol Hill surrounded by large trees lording over steep ravines where downed logs nurse ferns and moss. Dappled sunlight filters through it all. After a steady climb, you emerge into a north Capitol Hill neighborhood of stately old homes on tree-lined streets.

Climb a bit more and enter Volunteer Park, one of the city's highest points and home to a glass-walled conservatory and the Seattle Asian Art Museum. Visit Isamu Noguchi's *Black Sun*, an inky marble sculpture that recalls a giant truck tire. This is your ideal picture stop, because through the sculpture's doughnut-hole center you can perfectly frame the Space Needle. The park's south entrance is guarded by a round brick structure that used to be a water tower; it now offers views of Seattle and its sub-

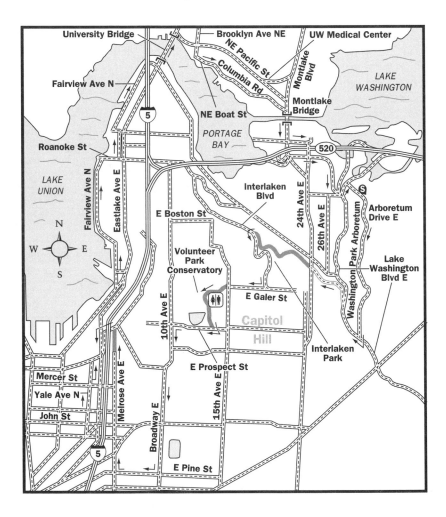

urbs from many angles through its turret windows.

Tour the vibrant Broadway shopping street, then head west toward downtown along nightclub-filled Pine Street. Ride past the flagship REI store through the booming Cascade neighborhood, then pass the biotech firm Zymogenetics, housed in the historic City Light Steam Plant, to reach Lake Union.

The ride north along Lake Union's east shore exposes you to a flotilla of homes docked at the base of the compact Eastlake neighborhood. Peek at rooftop gardens, berthed kayaks, and colorful flowerpots on the decks of these bobbing houseboats. At the heart of the neighborhood is Lynn Street Park, across the street from Pete's Supermarket. Pete the grocer led the effort to build this park, then the community rebuilt it after a driverless delivery truck caromed through its tiny space and crashed into the lake in 1995.

Continue north to pedal across the University Bridge and down

Check out great city views from the old brick water tower in Volunteer Park on Capitol Hill.

to the Burke-Gilman Trail. To finish the tour, ride east past University of Washington dorms, the Marine Studies building, and finally the massive University of Washington Medical Center complex before crossing the Montlake Bridge and State Route 520 to return to the arboretum.

MILEAGE LOG

0.0 Turn left from waterside parking onto E. Foster Island Rd., then quickly right onto Arboretum Dr. E.

1.0 Right onto Lake Washington Blvd. E.

1.2 Left onto E. Interlaken Blvd. Caution: Fast-moving traffic.

1.7 Cross 24th Ave. E. and continue on Interlaken.

1.8 As road curves left, go straight through bollards onto trail.

2.0 Rejoin Interlaken and continue straight.

2.2 Left at Y onto Interlaken Dr. E.

2.9 Right onto E. Galer St.

3.1 At intersection with 15th Ave. E., cross straight ahead into Volunteer Park.

3.3 Turn left at conservatory at the roundabout.

3.5 Arrive at Seattle Asian Art Museum, Noguchi sculpture, and reservoir.

3.7 Continue south to exit Volunteer Park at brick water tower. Turn right onto E. Prospect St.

4.0 Left onto 10th Ave. E., which becomes Broadway.

5.0 Right onto E. Pine St.

5.3 Right onto Melrose Ave. E.

6.0 Enter bike trail at end of Melrose.

6.2 Exit bike trail onto Bellevue Pl. E. Immediate left onto Belmont Ave. E.

6.3 Left onto Lakeview Blvd. E. to cross over I-5.

6.5 Soft left onto Eastlake Ave. E.

6.9 Right onto John St.; arrive at REI.

7.0 Right onto Yale Ave. N. at REI entrance.

7.3 Right onto Mercer St.

7.4 Left onto Eastlake Ave. E. Stay left to remain on Eastlake as right lane splits onto Lakeview Blvd. E.

8.0 Continue forward on Eastlake as Fairview Ave. N. merges from left.

8.1 Merge into turning lane, then left onto E. Garfield St. Caution: busy street.

8.2 Right onto Fairview Ave. E.

8.6 Pass Lynn Street Park on the left.

8.9 Curve right at Roanoke St. and climb hill 1 block.

9.0 Left at Yale Terrace E.

9.1 Right onto E. Edgar St. briefly, then left into alley before reaching Eastlake Ave. E., then left onto E. Hamlin St. for ½ block.

9.2 Right onto Fairview Ave. N.

9.8 Right onto Fuhrman Ave. E.

9.9 Left onto Eastlake. Ride over University Bridge.

10.1 Take first exit off bridge, looping under bridge and continuing to the right onto a two-way bike lane.

10.6 At NE 40th St., bike lane intersects with Burke-Gilman Trail. Left onto trail.

10.8 Right onto Brooklyn Ave., go through stoplight at NE Pacific St., and continue for 1 block.

11.0 Left onto NE Boat St.

11.3 Pass through University Hospital entry gate onto Columbia Rd.

11.7 As road ends, continue onto asphalt trail behind hospital, taking right fork to arrive at Montlake Blvd.

11.8 Right onto sidewalk to cross Montlake Bridge.

11.9 Left onto E. Hamlin St. Caution: Northbound cars U-turn here to get onto SR 520.

12.1 Right onto 24th Ave. E.; proceed through opening in barriers to bike lane.

12.2 Left onto Lake Washington Blvd.

12.7 Left onto E. Foster Island Rd. to return to parking to end tour.

10 West Seattle

DIFFICULTY: easy
TOUR TIME: allow 2 hours
TOTAL DISTANCE: 16 miles
TOTAL ELEVATION GAIN: 720 feet

Driving directions: Travel west on West Seattle Bridge, just south of downtown Seattle. Take Harbor Ave./Avalon Wy. exit. Turn right onto Harbor Ave. SW, travel 0.9 mile to a right turn into Jack Block Park, then another 0.2 mile to parking.

Visitors to Seattle are often wowed by the views, which can be spectacular, especially from the edge of the city's downtown waterfront. But how many of them know that just around the south end of Elliott

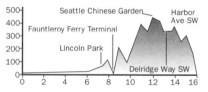

Bay lies another perspective on the city that is even more stunning? That's one of the high points of this tour, which also connects to the Fauntleroy ferry terminal.

Begin at Jack Block Park, just west of Harbor Island. This Port of Seattle facility offers free parking, restrooms, and a great look at the container shipping operations on nearby Harbor Island.

Join the trail heading north then west along Alki, and you will find numerous options for sticking your toes in the sand or stopping for snacks and drinks. Rows of white condos face Elliott Bay above Alki Avenue SW, and the street is bordered by coffee joints, small shops, and the Alki Bakery, a popular terminus for bike groups looping here from Green Lake.

Alki Beach has a history stretching back to Seattle's beginnings. On

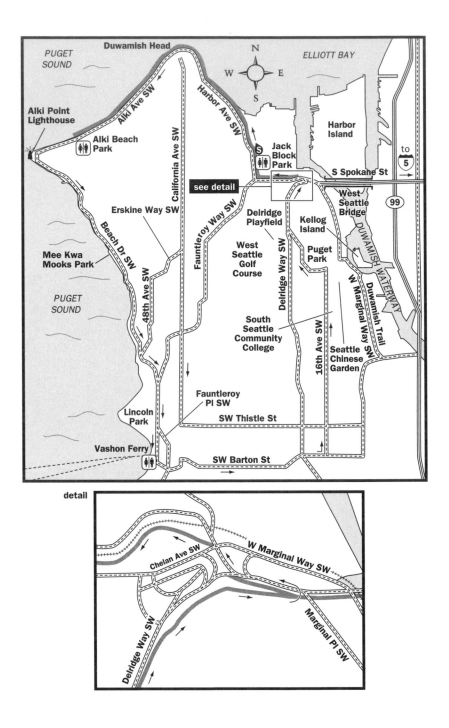

November 13, 1851, the twenty-four-member Denny Party came ashore here and, presumably not finding a Starbucks nearby, "the ladys sat down on the loggs and took A Big Cry," according to historical writings on the excellent website *www.historylink.org*. You shouldn't have that problem, but some still mourn the loss of Luna Park, a saltwater swimming pool (or natatorium) built on Alki in 1907. The park offered "warm and cold saltwater tanks, dancing, and good eats," according to a plaque that now marks the site. The park burned down in 1931, and the remains of the structure were replaced with a fish-friendly pier in 2004. If you want to keep this outing short and flat, make the Luna Park memorial or the Birthplace of Seattle monument your turnaround point.

Depart the waterfront and ride west alongside beachfront apartments and small homes holding against the tide of condominiums. Swing south around the corner of Alki Point by the historic lighthouse, which is open for visitors in the summer. It marks the southern point of Elliott Bay.

Beach Drive SW takes you past Mee Kwa Mooks Park, where Vashon Island seems close enough to touch, and south toward Lincoln Park, which offers nature trails and an outdoor saltwater swimming pool. Pass by the ferry terminal, where ferries depart for Vashon and Southworth, then climb the curving streets to West Seattle's interior.

Close the loop on this tour by riding north on 16th Avenue SW. At this point, you could stay on SW Henderson Street and drop down to

Cyclists on a tandem prepare to depart Jack Block Park.

the Duwamish Trail via Ninth Avenue SW and Highland Park Way SW, but staying on 16th provides an opportunity for one more interesting stop on the way back. At South Seattle Community College, turn into the north parking area to find the Seattle Chinese Garden. Years in the planning and fund-raising stages, the six-acre site has begun to take shape, with demonstration gardens and a wonderful pavilion. Above a wooded gorge, the garden boasts enviable city and mountain views.

Twisting streets take you down to Delridge Way SW. From there it's a quick jog across a five-way intersection on Harbor Island to the trail back to the park.

MILEAGE LOG

0.0 Depart Jack Block Park north to join the Alki Trail.

0.2 Right onto trail out of parking.

0.6 Pass Elliott Bay Water Taxi pier.

1.3 Trailside sign commemorating Luna Park.

3.0 Trailside monument commemorating birthplace of Seattle. Restrooms available on beach.

3.2 Continue west on Alki Ave. SW.

3.4 Continue on Alki Ave. SW as it curves left at Point Pl. SW.

4.0 Right onto Beach Drive SW.

6.5 At a three-way intersection, forward onto Lincoln Park Wy. SW, following sign for Lincoln Park and Scenic Tour.

6.9 Right at stop sign onto Fauntleroy Wy. SW.

8.0 Curve left onto SW Wildwood Pl.

8.2 Left onto SW Brace Point Dr., which becomes SW Barton St., then SW Barton Pl., then SW Henderson St.

10.1 Left onto 16th Ave. SW.

12.1 Arrive at north entrance of South Seattle Community College and Seattle Chinese Garden.

12.5 Stay on 16th as arterial curves left into SW Dawson St., which becomes 21st Ave. SW; then curves left again and becomes 22nd Ave. SW, then 23rd Ave. SW, then SW Oregon St.

13.3 Right onto Delridge Wy. SW.

13.8 Right onto sidewalk to join trail at intersection with SW Charleston St. where Delridge becomes on-ramp to West Seattle Bridge.

14.1 Left at trail intersection with Duwamish Trail and Marginal Pl SW.

14.2 Follow bike symbols and arrows on crosswalks to cross SW Spokane St. and W. Marginal Wy. SW at a five-way intersection, rejoining trail at plaza on intersection's northwest corner, marked by marine-style bollards across sidewalk.

15.2 Right onto Harbor Ave. SW and Alki Trail.

15.8 Right into Jack Block Park.
16.0 Arrive at parking lot to end tour.

11   Duwamish Trail

DIFFICULTY: easy
TOUR TIME: allow 2 hours
TOTAL DISTANCE: 26 miles
TOTAL ELEVATION GAIN: 20 feet

Driving directions: Travel west on West Seattle Bridge, just south of downtown Seattle. Take Harbor Ave./Avalon Wy. exit. Turn right onto Harbor Ave. SW, travel 0.9 mile to a right turn into Jack Block Park, then another 0.2 mile to parking.

This tour skirts one of Seattle's major industrial regions and stumbles upon historical connections to the living and trading patterns of Native Americans and settlers. Although this route runs past industrial areas and warehouses, it provides a vital link to riding the wonderful south King County routes. Thankfully, it's possible—amid the powerlines and bridge ramps—to find some interesting stops along the journey.

Start the tour at the Port of Seattle's Jack Block Park and head south across the challenging intersection at SW Spokane Street and West Marginal Way SW to pick up the short trail.

The route takes you through the warehouseland of South Park, where you'll see the occasional well-kept small house and interesting metal sculpture among the machine shops. If you were to crest the South Park Bridge, you would see Boeing Field, and a short side trip would take you to the airplane maker's Museum of Flight. Instead, loop under the bridge and continue south next to State Route 99.

Pass by Seattle City Light's Ham Creek Watershed, a vacant area among the warehouses where ospreys sometimes nest on the platforms atop tall utility poles.

At this point you join the Green River Trail, which heads south through Tukwila to Kent. Traverse a quiet, scenic section, cross a quaint pedestrian-bike bridge, then travel behind office parks and alongside Interstate 5 before running alongside Tukwila's busy Interurban Avenue.

Next to the river is the site of the Foster Homestead, the destination of flat-bottomed boats that brought provisions for settlers up to the

Duwamish from the Green and Black Rivers. The Black River, which was lost when the level of Lake Washington was lowered, previously joined the Green at Fort Dent.

Fort Dent Park, once a winter community for the Duwamish tribe and then a military outpost, is now a bustling recreation center. Take a break and turn around here (or continue south on the winding Green River Trail, Route 20).

On the return trip, stop at a couple more public access areas along our waterways. The unimaginatively named T107 Park is one of the

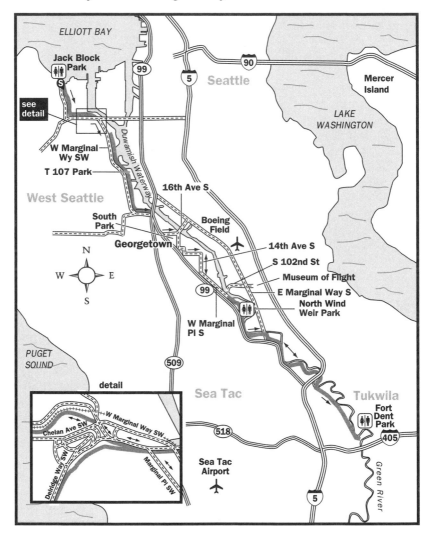

This Kellogg Island overlook enhances birdwatching from a trailside park.

"Duwamish Public Access" points, where you can watch shipping traffic and bird activity along the river. This roadside park also includes greenery and some delightful Native American plaques and sculptures that give you a hint of cultures here before shipping terminals took over. A brief stop is also warranted at T105, a smaller public access area carved out between industrial sites. The entrance to T105 is just north of SW Dakota St.

The last mile, as they say in the utility world, is the most challenging, and when this book went to press you still had to ride a brief section of busy East Marginal Way South to pick up the last leg. But it's a quick jaunt to meet up with connecting trails under the West Seattle Bridge. Head north to the flat, scenic Alki Trail (or you can climb into West Seattle via Delridge Way or turn east toward downtown Seattle).

MILEAGE LOG

0.0 Depart parking at Jack Block Park.

0.2 Turn left (south) on Alki Trail.

1.2 Turn left at Harbor Ave. SW on near-side sidewalk to stay on trail.

1.7 Follow bike symbols and arrows on crosswalks to cross West Marginal Wy. SW and SW Spokane St. at a five-way intersection, rejoining trail as it climbs under bridge's on-ramp.

1.8 Forward at intersection with Duwamish Trail onto Marginal Pl. SW.

1.9 At intersection with 17th Ave. SW, veer right onto 17th, then left onto 16th Ave. SW.

2.2 Left onto SW Dakota St. In one-half block, right onto West Marginal Wy. SW.

2.4 Cross West Marginal Wy. SW to rejoin trail on east side of street.

4.7 Cross under 1st Ave. S. Bridge on the left sidewalk as trail ends. Continue on sidewalk along West Marginal Wy.

5.4 Left onto S. Holden St.

5.8 Right onto 7th Ave. S.

6.1 Left onto S. Rose St.

6.2   Right onto 8th Ave. S.

6.4   Left onto S. Cloverdale St.

6.9   Right onto 14th Ave. S.

7.4   Left at S. Director St., then immediately right onto sidewalk trail next to 14th Ave. S.

7.5   Curve left at the Y to continue south on West Marginal Pl. S.

8.9   Cross S. 102nd St. (left over bridge for side trip to Museum of Flight) and join Green River Trail to continue southbound.

9.2   Pass restrooms in North Wind Weir Park, then cross pedestrian bridge.

9.6   Exit trail and turn right onto Tukwila International Blvd. bridge.

9.7   Turn right at end of bridge to rejoin trail.

11.5   Trail exits into parking lot, then resumes at far edge of parking.

13.4   Cross into Fort Dent Park. Restrooms, water available. Reverse route to return.

15.3   Trail exits into parking lot, then resumes at far edge of parking.

17.1   Loop under bridge at Tukwila International Blvd., cross bridge, and rejoin trail.

17.5   Cross pedestrian bridge.

17.9   At intersection with S. 102nd St., cross 102nd and continue north on West Marginal Pl. S. as Green River Trail ends.

19.3   Curve right onto 14th Ave. S.

19.8   Veer right at the South Park Bridge approach, turning left onto Thistle under bridge ramp.

20.1   Angle right onto S. Rose St.

20.2   Right onto Dallas Ave. S., then immediately right onto 10th Ave. S.

20.3   Left onto S. Kenyon St.

20.6   Right onto 5th Ave. S.

20.8   Left onto S. Holden St.

21.0   Right onto sidewalk at West Marginal Wy.

21.5   Approaching 1st Ave. S. Bridge, transfer to north sidewalk to ride under bridge ramp on West Marginal Wy. to join Duwamish Trail.

21.9   Right at West Marginal Wy. SW to stay on trail.

23.5   Arrive at T107 Park.

23.9   Continue north on West Marginal Wy. SW as trail ends.

24.1   Left onto SW Dakota St. Caution: busy street. In one-half block, right onto 16th Ave. SW.

24.4   Soft left onto Marginal Pl. SW.

24.5   Forward at intersection with Duwamish Trail to rejoin Alki Trail.

24.6   Cross five-way intersection to continue on trail.

25.6   Right onto Harbor Ave. SW and Alki Trail.

25.8   Right into Jack Block Park.

26.0   Arrive at parking to end tour.

12   South Seattle and Seward Park

DIFFICULTY: easy
TOUR TIME: allow 2 hours
TOTAL DISTANCE: 16.3 miles
TOTAL ELEVATION GAIN: 400 feet

Driving directions: From I-5, take exit 163 to Columbian Wy. Take Columbian Wy. south and turn right on Beacon Ave. S. Turn left onto S. Orcas St. and proceed east to entrance of Seward Park.

Southeast Seattle holds many charms for a nice summer day: A long stretch of Lake Washington waterfront, multiple swimming beaches, and verdant Seward Park are the highlights. But on a city

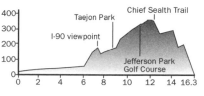

tour around this quadrant, you also will discover stunning views of Mount Rainier, a colorful pavilion donated by an Asian sister city, and Seattle's newest bike trail.

Begin this short loop tour at Seward Park, whose grand green thumb (the Bailey Peninsula) juts out into Lake Washington and faces central Mercer Island. The park itself has charms with which to while away an afternoon: a flat, paved (if a bit rough) perimeter trail; hiking trails into its hilly, wooded interior; swimming beaches; and the occasional ice cream vendor.

Head north along Lake Washington Boulevard South, which sports public waterfront almost to the Interstate 90 floating bridge. An excellent ribbon of asphalt trail runs along the Olmstead-designed avenue by the water's edge.

Whether you're on the busy street or this path, however, expect slow going on a nice weekend day, as the area fills with families and people out for a scenic drive. Conversely, on selected Saturdays and Sundays throughout each summer, this 2.5-mile section of Lake Washington Boulevard is closed to car traffic from midmorning to late afternoon. During those days, the street becomes a great place for a slow ride through the family traffic and a chance to give young children a taste of riding on city streets. Check *www.seattle.gov* for dates and details.

You leave the lakeside by jogging west under a couple of small bridges into Colman Park, which has a winding, little-used road that hauls you up to a wonderful viewpoint overlooking Interstate 90.

From here, you could continue north and drop back down to the lake, traveling through Leschi and past Madrona Park and Denny Blaine Park, continuing north to join the Burke-Gilman Trail (see Tour 1). You also could connect with the bike lane across Interstate 90 to Mercer Island (see Tour 13) or the eastern suburbs. But to stay on this tour, loop down under the view stop to ride on top of the freeway in the tunnel that takes you under the Mount Baker neighborhood and into Sam Smith Park. Note the curious art project beneath your tires: Large words set into the pavement invite a psychological game:

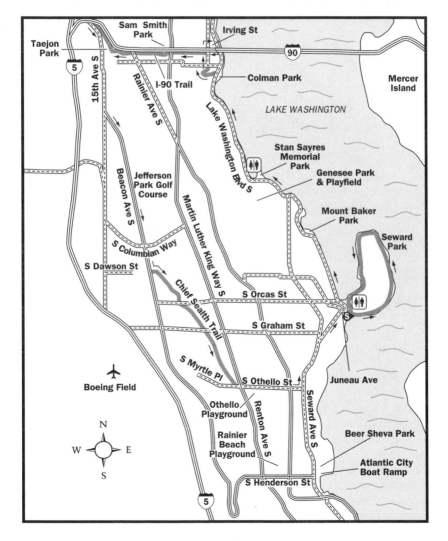

gate/cave, home/away, dawn/twilight. I would add "park/ride."

A well-appointed bike trail takes you to the north edge of Beacon Hill, where along the way a sliver of park reminds you that you're on a small planet. Taejon Park, named for Seattle's sister city in the Republic of Korea, sports a beautiful, multicolored carved wood pavilion donated by that central Korean city.

At the end of the I-90 Trail, also called the "Mountains to Sound Greenway," you are treated to great views of downtown Seattle, the stadiums, and Elliott Bay. Drink in the panorama, then head south by cresting Beacon Hill.

Continuing south, pass Jefferson Park Golf Course and join Seattle's newest dedicated bike trail, Chief Sealth Trail. Opened in 2007 as an offshoot of the light rail being installed along Martin Luther King Jr. Way, it snakes under powerlines and provides two key connections to the new rail corridor. Contractors building Sound Transit's light rail moved many tons of excavated soil into the corridor to grade the trail.

If you prefer to explore the upper neighborhoods of southwest Seattle, you could continue south on Beacon Avenue South, taking advantage of the sidewalk that runs down the wide center berm between traffic lanes. Watch for turning cars at each intersection. Beacon Avenue turns into winding, shady Carkeek Drive South, which drops down to Rainier Beach. This tour continues on the Chief Sealth trail, turning back onto city streets at Othello and picking up Seward Avenue South. For a side trip on the 1.6 mile south trail leg, turn right onto Holly Park Drive S., then right on 39th Ave. S. to rejoin the trail. It ends just north of Kubota Gardens, a wonderful city park.

MILEAGE LOG

0.0 Right onto loop trail around Seward Park to right of entrance circle.

2.6 Right onto Lake Washington Blvd. S. Ride either the street or the sidewalk.

3.2 Right into parking lot on east edge of trail.

3.4 Trail again becomes street-side walkway.

4.7 Arrive at Stan Sayres Memorial Park. Restrooms available.

5.1 Soft right into parking area; follow bike-route signs.

5.2 Left under two consecutive bridges at end of parking area.

5.3 Quick right after underpass, then left into Colman Park.

6.9 Exit Colman Park, cross S. Massachusetts St., and continue north on Lake Washington Blvd. S.

7.3 Arrive at East Portal Viewpoint above I-90.

7.4 At north end of overlook, turn right on Irving St., then right again into bike pathway. Go straight into tunnel.

7.7 Exit tunnel into Sam Smith Park.

Seattle's newest bike trail, Chief Sealth Trail, offers great views of Mount Rainier beyond the powerlines.

8.1 Left onto Martin Luther King Jr. Wy. S., then right in 100 yards to go back into park on sidewalk.

8.8 Arrive at Taejon Park.

9.1 Left onto Golf Dr. S. as trail ends at S. Charles St.

9.3 Left at a Y; stay on Golf, which becomes 15th Ave. S. after road splits.

10.1 Left onto Beacon Ave. S.

12.0 Enter path on median between traffic lanes. Caution: Watch for turning cars when crossing numerous intersections.

12.3 Left onto S. Dawson St., then immediate right onto Chief Sealth Trail.

13.1 Cross S. Orcas St. and proceed south on trail.

13.5 Cross S. Graham St., jog left 100 yards, then right to resume trail.

14.3 Left onto S. Myrtle Pl., which becomes S. Othello St. Caution: busy street. (For side trip on south trail leg, turn right onto Holly Park Dr. S., then right on 39th Ave. S. Trail ahead in 0.4 mi.)

15.3 Left onto Seward Park Ave. S.

15.9 Right at Y to stay on Seward Park Ave. S.; follow signs for bike route and Seward Park.

16.2 Right onto Juneau Ave. S. at stop sign.

16.3 Cross Lake Washington Blvd. S. into Seward Park to end tour.

Opposite: A stop at Jubilee Farm outside Carnation showcases local, small-scale agriculture, and its supportive community.

13 Mercer Island Loop

DIFFICULTY: easy
TOTAL TIME: allow 1.5 hours
TOTAL DISTANCE: 15.8 miles
TOTAL ELEVATION GAIN: 485 feet

> **Driving directions:** From I-5, take I-90 east to Mercer Island and take exit 7A, 77th Ave. SE; turn left onto 77th Ave. SE. Turn right at stop sign onto N. Mercer Wy., go through light at 80th Ave. SE, then turn left onto 81st Ave. SE. Turn right on SE 24th St. and drive to road end. Luther Burbank Park entrance on the left.
>
> From I-405, take I-90 west to Mercer Island and take exit 7, Island Crest Wy. At top of ramp, turn right onto SE 26th St. At stop sign turn left onto 84th Ave. SE and drive straight into Luther Burbank Park after another stop sign at SE 24th St.

Looking for a short, scenic ride on a sunny summer day? Consider East Seattle. That was the early name for the main community on

Mercer Island and, although it's not now officially part of the city, it certainly feels like another neighborhood—albeit one accessible only by boat or floating bridge.

Mercer Island seems to be a workout route for cyclists who live in the area, judging by the number of people engaged in a business-like trek on the quiet, wooded ring road during weekday evenings. But it also can be an enjoyable weekend ride combined with a visit to a lakeside beach, or it can easily be linked to the loop around Lake Washington (see Tour 14) or rides through Bellevue or South Seattle (see Tour 12).

Parking is easily accessible from the island exits off Interstate 90; simply head into Luther Burbank Park or find the small lots along the landscaped I-90 Lid Park.

Since this loop basically stays on one road for the entire route, it can be traveled in either direction, but I like taking it counterclockwise, which keeps the cyclist on the outside edge of the road, rather than the inside, making for better views along the ride.

Exiting the park via city streets, you pick up the I-90 Trail briefly. When entering or exiting this trail, be sure to check for commuting cyclists, who are commonly seen here, often moving fast. Head west on

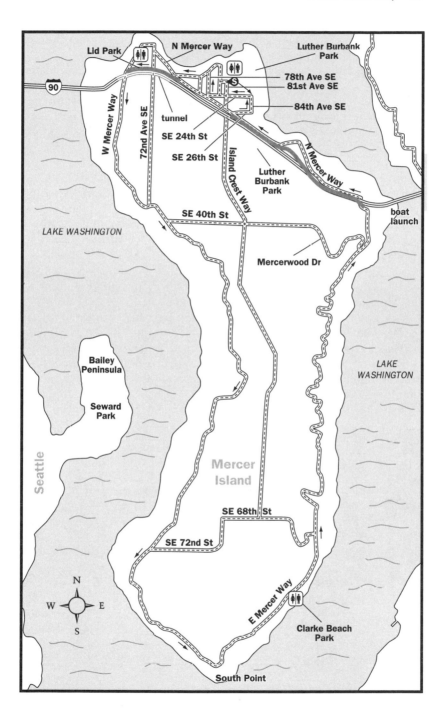

the trail, which uses sidewalks and crosses a number of streets before reaching the I-90 Lid Park.

After climbing up through the lid park and past sheltered playfields, Seattle and the Interstate 90 floating bridge come into view. Cross the park at the West Mercer Way off-ramp and head south on West Mercer Way. Gaining elevation as you ride along the island's western edge, you get peekaboo views through the trees of Seward Park across the lake and gables of the big houses fronting this side of the lake.

Development has come quite a long way since Seattle pioneer Thomas Mercer explored the island in the 1850s. Cyclists will see houses cleverly tucked into wooded hillsides and not-so-subtly looming over the waterfront. What you won't see while riding this loop is any commercial development. Services such as groceries and gas stations are confined to the island's north-central corridor. But if you brought a picnic or want a comfort stop, pull over at Clarke Beach Park at 8.7 miles. The well-kept beach and dock area has picnic tables, a grassy lawn, restrooms, and views of Mount Rainier rising behind Renton on the lake's far southern shore.

At the southern tip of the island, West Mercer Way turns into East Mercer Way, and the ride north is highlighted by a series of linked curves hugging the hillsides. Thank the road designers for grading that is well calculated to provide a fun series of turns—unless you get behind a cautious Sunday driver. There is scant room to pass a car and no shoulder on this section.

Return to the I-90 Trail at the island's northeast corner, where a brief

The I-90 Lid Park on Mercer Island

jaunt to the east would take you to Bellevue for a visit to Mercer Slough or trails running north or south (see Tour 14 Lake Washington Loop). If you want more time in the saddle, continue west and ride 1.7 miles across the floating bridge to Seattle, then head south to Seward Park for another loop and waterfront ride (see Tour 12 South Seattle and Seward Park). The addition, including the bridge and Seward Park trail, would add another 18 miles.

To finish this tour, return to Luther Burbank Park and stretch your legs with a walk to the water or around the historic school building. The park is the site of a 100-acre self-sufficient farm that was operated in the early 1900s as part of a school for boys. A waterfront plaza, beach, and sculptures are worth a look. For a post-ride beverage or some pub food, check out the Roanoke Inn, a historic spot nearby on 72nd Avenue SE. The inn was a speakeasy in the days when travel to the island was by a ferry that docked at the island's nearby northern tip, and the place retains the flavor of a welcoming neighborhood tavern.

MILEAGE LOG

0.0 Depart parking to begin tour.

0.2 Exit north parking lot by turning right onto SE 24th St. at park entrance.

0.5 Arrive at entrance to bike trail, but continue on road, which becomes 78th Ave. SE.

0.7 Left onto SE 22nd Wy., which becomes 76th Ave. SE.

1.0 Right onto trail at intersection with 76th Ave. SE, which leads through I-90 Lid Park (or continue on 76th to a right turn onto N. Mercer Wy.).

1.8 Left onto W. Mercer Wy.

2.3 Continue on arterial as it briefly becomes 65th Ave. SE but remains W. Mercer Wy. to south tip of island, then becoming E. Mercer Wy.

2.8 Views of Seward Park beyond trees and homes to the right.

5.3 Continue forward through Brook Bay neighborhood.

8.7 Right into Clarke Beach Park; descend to water.

8.8 Arrive at swimming area, water, restrooms.

8.9 Climb back to E. Mercer Wy., turning right to continue loop on winding road.

13.4 At Mercer Island boat launch just beyond community center, turn right onto bike path on sidewalk.

15.4 Right onto SE 26th St.

15.5 Left onto 84th Ave. SE to proceed to north parking.

15.6 Cross SE 24th St. to enter Luther Burbank Park.

15.8 Arrive at parking to end tour.

14 Lake Washington Loop

DIFFICULTY: strenuous
TOTAL TIME: allow 6 hours
TOTAL DISTANCE: 53.6 miles
TOTAL ELEVATION GAIN: 1835 feet

> **Driving directions:** From I-5 in Seattle, take exit 171, Lake City Wy./
> SR 522. Continue northeast on Lake City Wy. NE to Lake Forest Park,
> where road becomes Bothell Wy. NE. After entering Kenmore, turn
> right onto 61st Ave. NE, then immediately right onto NE 175th St.
> Tracy Owen Station at Log Boom Park is ahead 1 block; park here.

Water is one of the Seattle area's most plentiful natural features, making
local lakes and rivers some of our most desirable cycling destinations.
Circumnavigating the queen of our blue heaven, Lake Washington, offers cyclists a route filled with great views, enticing stops, and insight
into local history and development of our metropolitan area. A shorter
half-loop option is possible, as well as links to other Seattle tours.

Ride first through the desirable Eastside communities of Juanita
and Kirkland, leaving the lakeside almost immediately, skirting Saint
Edward, Big Finn Hill, and O. O. Denny Parks in a long, slow climb.
Dropping down into Kirkland, regain lakeside views at Juanita Bay,
where a large swimming beach at Juanita Beach Park beckons.

Just beyond the beach, a brief detour from the bike lane takes you
through Juanita Bay Park, Kirkland's largest and most historic park,
the terminus of two creeks and a calm haven for many types of birds.
Enjoy the bustling downtown Kirkland scene, then head south along
the lake, spotting numerous statues and sculptures in waterside parks,
faced by luxury apartment blocks.

Cross over State Route 520 and into Bellevue, climbing through
Clyde Hill, sliding back down to the lake, then climbing the shady,
winding lanes above the East Channel before connecting with a bike
trail again at Interstate 90.

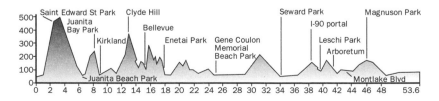

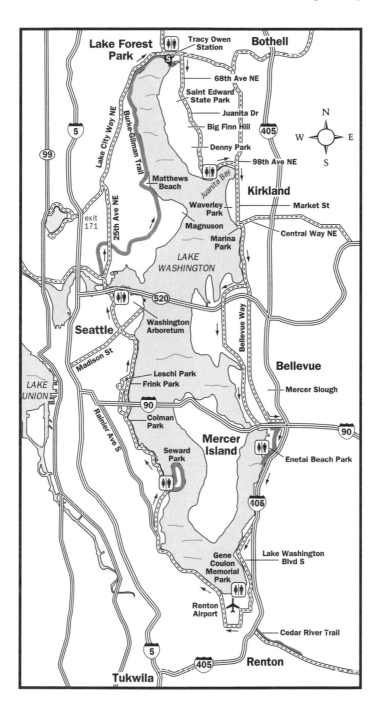

At the East Portal Viewpoint in Seattle, cyclists watch traffic on the I-90 floating bridge.

At this point, a shorter loop is an option, if you go west across Mercer Island on the I-90 bridge, then pick up the route again at the East Portal Viewpoint. It's 4.8 miles from this junction to set your wheels on Seattle soil, and the shortcut removes a 19.5-mile south-end ride, making the shortened loop 38.9 miles total.

To do the full loop, however, turn south on the trail toward Factoria. Ride through wetlands under the freeway maze, then alongside Interstate 405 on a little-used suburban road.

Next stop is Gene Coulon Memorial Beach Park in Renton at the lake's southernmost point. Sited next to the Boeing Company's Renton plant, the park is a common cycling comfort stop. Plans call for a connection to the Cedar River Trail (see Tour 21) just beyond Boeing's broad tarmacs, but until that happens, cyclists need to skirt the plant and head into downtown Renton. A turn north onto Rainier Avenue South marks the tour's halfway point.

The western route hugs the lake for most of the ride, through the neighborhoods of southeast Seattle. Return to Lake Washington Boulevard at Seward Park (see Tour 12), then leave the lakeside briefly for a view of the I-90 bridge at the East Portal Viewpoint. Continue north along the lake to the Washington Park Arboretum (see Tour 9), then cross the Montlake Bridge and join the Burke-Gilman Trail (see Tour 1), which provides a flat, pleasant end to the loop.

MILEAGE LOG

0.0 Right onto Burke-Gilman Trail and head north.

0.5 Approaching trail underpass at 68th Ave. NE, exit trail onto street-level sidewalk.

0.6 Right onto 68th. Caution: busy intersection; use sidewalk over bridge.

2.5 Pass entrance to Saint Edward State Park on the right.

1.1 Proceed straight (south) as 68th becomes Juanita Dr.

4.5 Continue on Juanita Dr. at intersection with Holmes Point Dr.; shortly, pass Big Finn Hill Park.

6.4 Arrive at Juanita Beach Park.

6.7 Right onto 98th Ave. NE.

6.8 Soft right into Juanita Bay Park onto Corduroy Rd. (off-street trail closed to motor vehicles).

7.3 Exit park onto Market St. at a Y as trail continues downhill.

8.8 Left onto Central Wy. NE in downtown Kirkland.

9.0 Right onto Lake St. S. (SR 908), which becomes Lake Washington Blvd.

11.3 Right onto NE Points Dr.

11.9 Proceed through street end at 96th Ave. NE.

12.1 Left onto 92nd Ave. NE; go over SR 520.

14.0 Left onto Lake Washington Blvd. at Clyde Beach Park (Restrooms).

14.7 Right onto 101st Ave. SE and stay on arterial, which becomes SE 5th St., then 98th Ave. SE, 99th Ave. SE, and 97th Pl. SE, before meeting up with 100th Ave. SE.

16.1 Continue straight onto 100th.

17.1 Right onto 104th Ave. SE and stay on arterial, which becomes SE 30th St.

17.5 Right onto 106th Pl. SE.

17.8 Cross 108th Ave. SE onto trail under I-90. Turn right (south) onto trail. Restrooms, water available at Enetai Beach Park.

18.4 After going under I-405 on-ramps, turn right at Y in trail.

18.8 Right to stay on trail. Follow signs to Newcastle Beach Park.

20.3 Proceed through gate in fence; turn left onto 106th Ave. SE, which becomes Ripley Ln., then Hazelwood Ln.

22.8 Right onto Lake Washington Blvd. S.

24.8 Right into Gene Coulon Memorial Beach Park, then immediate left at stop sign.

24.9 Right into parking area by pavilion. Restrooms, concessions, water available.

25.5 Right onto park road, which merges with Houser Wy. N.

25.7 Straight across to continue on Houser Wy.

26.2 Right onto N. 8th St.

26.4 Left onto Garden Ave. N.

26.8 Right onto N. 6th St.

27.1 Left onto Logan Ave. N.

27.6 Cross Cedar River, then right onto airport perimeter road. Follow bike route signs on this road around airport.

29.6 Right onto Rainier Ave. S.

31.7 Right onto Seward Park Ave. S.

33.6 Right to stay on Seward Park Ave. S.

34.1 Right onto S. Juneau St.

34.2 Left onto Lake Washington Blvd. S. at Seward Park. (Restrooms)

37.5 Right onto Lakeside Ave. S.

37.6 Left onto Lake Washington Blvd. S.; uphill through Colman Park.

38.1 Cross S. Massachusetts St. to continue on Lake Washington Blvd. S.

38.5 Arrive at East Portal Viewpoint. Continue on Lake Washington Blvd. S. through Frink Park.

38.9 Cross S. Jackson St. to stay on Lake Washington Blvd. S.

39.4 Left at Leschi Park to stay on Lake Washington Blvd. S.

40.7 Curve left at Denny Blaine Park; stay on Lake Washington Blvd. S.

40.8 Cross 39th Ave E. to stay on Lake Washington Blvd. S.

41.0 Curve left at Y; then at next intersection with 37th Ave. E. in one-half block take middle route onto E. Harrison St.

41.5 Right onto Martin Luther King Jr. Wy. Jog right at E. Madison St., forward onto 28th Ave. E., which becomes 26th Ave. E. Follow "Lake Washington Loop" signs.

42.7 Left onto E. Galer St., then right in one-half block onto 26th Ave. E. In one block, cross Boyer Ave. E. Caution: traffic.

43.2 Left onto E. Lynn St. In one block, right onto 25th Ave. E.

43.5 Left onto E. Roanoke St., then quickly right onto Glenwilde Pl. E., then left into alley. Follow Lake Washington Loop signs.

43.7 Right out of alley onto 24th Ave. E. Proceed one block to cross Lake Washington Blvd. S. Caution: heavy traffic.

43.9 Forward through bollards as street turns right, then right onto E. Hamlin St., which becomes E. Park Dr. and then E. Shelby St.

44.1 Right onto sidewalk at Montlake Blvd. NE; cross bridge.

44.3 Left at stoplight to cross Montlake at intersection with NE Pacific St. Right on sidewalk at UW entrance, circle right and follow Lake Washington Loop signs.

44.4 Right onto Burke-Gilman Trail.

45.9 Cross 25th Ave. NE to stay on trail at shopping district.

54.2 Arrive at Tracy Owen Station to end tour.

15 Sammamish River Trail

DIFFICULTY: easy
TOUR TIME: allow 2.5 hours
TOTAL DISTANCE: 28.4 miles
TOTAL ELEVATION GAIN: 30 feet

> **Driving directions:** From I-5 in Seattle, take exit 171, Lake
> City Wy./SR 522. Continue northeast on Lake City Wy. to Lake
> Forest Park, where road becomes Bothell Wy NE. After entering
> Kenmore, turn right onto 61st Ave. NE, then immediately right
> onto NE 175th St. Tracy Owen Station at Log Boom Park is ahead
> 1 block.

Suburban recreating doesn't get much smoother than a ride on the Sammamish River Trail, the flat, buffered green ribbon that hugs that river's east bank from Bothell

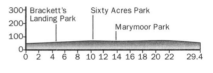

to Redmond. It's well used but mostly free of traffic noise or interruptions, and it offers comfort stops at evenly spaced intervals.

Begin at either end, at Marymoor Park in Redmond or at parks bordering the trail in Bothell or Woodinville. I suggest starting from Tracy Owen Station in Kenmore, which borders Lake Washington's north shore, because from there you get the flavor of how the Sammamish links with the granddaddy of local bike routes, the Burke-Gilman Trail (see Tour 1).

Heading northeast through Kenmore, you immediately begin to parallel the Sammamish, which connects Lake Sammamish with Lake Washington. You're also paralleling Bothell Way NE here, but the dense greenery along the trail, which is significantly below street level, makes you soon forget you're surrounded by traffic and commerce. Cycle past the Wayne Golf Course, the Park at Bothell Landing—which has services accessible via a quaint, arched wooden bridge—and Brackett's Landing Park before crossing under the massive girders of the Interstate 405 and State Route 522 interchange.

As the trail stretches out into the warehouse area of Woodinville, ride by Jerry Wilmot Gateway Park, an excellent amenity stop. Restrooms, water fountains, and attractive stone planters effusive with trees and flowers and linked with an arcing overhead trellis create a shady, comfortable place to dismount and watch the wheels go by. Just beyond the parking lot is the busy intersection of State Route 202 and NE 175th Street, which would take you into downtown Woodinville if a side trip interests you.

Continue south on the trail to view some youthful competition at the Northshore Athletic Fields (at 7.4 miles) and Sixty Acres Park (at 9.8 miles), both trailside as you head south toward Redmond. Opposite Sixty Acres, at NE 116th Street, is the northern border of Willow's Run Golf Course, just west of the trail across the river. A side trail called the Powerline Trail, accessible at 11.1 miles via an attractive red bridge, runs under the lines out to Willows Road in the midvalley.

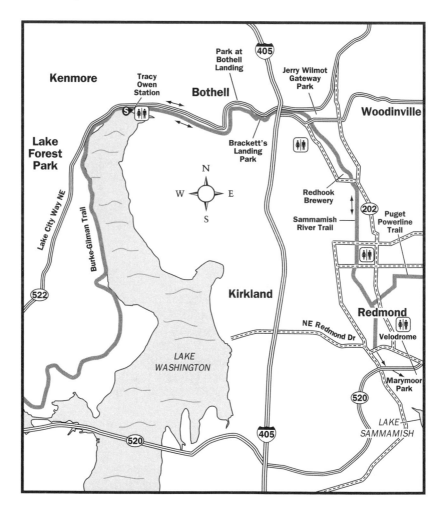

The trail parallels the Sammamish River from Woodinville to Redmond.

At 12.7 miles you reach tiny Luke McRedmond Landing, and in another two-tenths mile the trail splits, with the upper route leading to the surface streets of Redmond and the Town Center a few blocks away and the riverside branch continuing south to Marymoor Park.

Marymoor is an Eastside gem, offering open space, a constant stream of events, and numerous attractions for its many regional users. State Route 520 dead-ends at its northeast corner, giving it major access for festivals and concerts. Vast grassy fields and generous frontage along Lake Sammamish provide hours of exploration. For cyclists, the Velodrome is the logical terminus, where, if you haven't had enough riding, you can circle round and round, trying your skill at banking, passing, and group dynamics. Classes and events are often held at the Velodrome, but it is also a significant training site for racers and has a bank of bleachers from which to watch the action.

After some Marymoor-style repose, hop back on the velo and head north again to finish off the refreshing, 30-mile ride by retracing your route. As an additional treat, when you reach the Northshore Athletic Fields on the return trip, head west briefly on NE 145th Street for a stop at the Redhook Brewery's Forecaster's Public House, almost immediately on your right. Here you'll find one of the most extensive areas of bike racks outside of a public school, and with good reason: There's often scant room to fit your two-wheeler in with the crowd. If wine is more your style, pedal a bit farther on the same road to find the facing Chateau Ste. Michelle and Columbia Wineries. If you're interested in a longer ride, continue south from Tracy Owen Station on the Burke-Gilman Trail (see Tour 1) or, if you're truly energetic, continue around Lake Washington (see Tour 14).

When the Great Depression hit in the 1930s, Redmond suffered and persevered like many other American small towns. One of the legacies of that era that survives to this day is the Redmond Bike Derby. Intended as a fund-raiser for Christmas decorations and school athletic equipment in 1939, it remains the nation's oldest bike race. Signs leading into Redmond still proclaim the town as the Bicycle Capital of the Northwest.

—www.historylink.org

MILEAGE LOG

0.0 Right onto Burke-Gilman Trail and head north.

2.5 Pass the Wayne Golf Course clubhouse, then follow signs to right to cross river.

3.4 Pass the Park at Bothell Landing.

4.2 Pass Brackett's Landing Park. Trail continues on marked street for **0.2** mile.

5.7 Arrive at Jerry Wilmot Gateway Park in Woodinville. Restrooms, water available.

7.4 Pass Northshore Athletic Fields. Exit trail and turn right onto NE 145th St. here to go to wineries and brewery.

9.8 Pass playfields at Sixty Acres Park.

11.1 Pass bridge on the right that connects to Powerline Trail leading out to Willows Rd.

12.7 Trail splits, with main route continuing over Sammamish River south to Marymoor Park. Side branch leads to Redmond Town Center via Redmond Wy.

13.4 Cross back over river and pass Marymoor's ball fields.

14.2 Arrive at Velodrome. Reverse route to return.

28.4 Return to parking at Tracy Owen Station.

16   Redmond to Issaquah and Preston

DIFFICULTY: strenuous
TOTAL TIME: allow 6 hours
TOTAL DISTANCE: 51.7 miles
TOTAL ELEVATION GAIN: 1625 feet

> **Driving directions:** Take SR 520 east to West Lake Sammamish Pkwy. NE exit. Travel south 0.6 mile on West Lake Sammamish Pkwy. NE, then turn left into Marymoor Park. Inexpensive paid parking immediately on the left.

Redmond's Marymoor Park is a location from which you can go nearly any direction on a bike. Head north to Woodinville on the Sammamish River Trail (see Tour 15), into Bellevue on the State Route 520 Trail, or east to the Snoqualmie Valley over winding Union Hill or Novelty Hill roads. That leaves only one compass point left, and that's the direction for this tour: Head south toward Issaquah around Lake Sammamish.

This route south will be much enhanced for road cyclists in coming years as the recently opened East Lake Sammamish Trail is paved. Until then, I recommend looping the lake by heading south along its west side, then returning up its east side. Both roads have good bike lanes, although the west side is bikeable only southbound, and there is a brief section with no shoulder. If that is a concern, go up and back on the east side of the lake on the wide, well-paved road surface.

The lake ride is mostly a means to an end, though. Other than intermittent views and two lakefront parks (passed early in the ride), it's not an exciting destination on its own. But heading down the lake links you to more great riding, either west toward Seattle on the I-90 Trail or east toward Issaquah and beyond. The latter is the goal of this tour.

The fast-growing town of Issaquah is a place to check out. The attractions are plentiful, from the quaint shops of Front Street and homey but professional Village Theater to the in-town salmon hatchery and

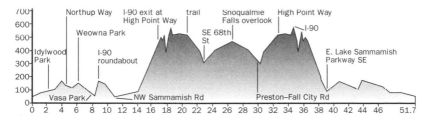

nearby hiking and mountain biking trails of Tiger, Cougar, and Squak Mountains—the Issaquah Alps. A microbrewery and candy factory offer gastronomical temptations.

Stop in Issaquah for a rest and provisions before hopping onto the freeway—that's right, Interstate 90—which takes you to the Preston-Snoqualmie Trail. Cycling on the interstate is allowed east of Front Street, but the tour picks it up at the Sunset Way on-ramp. You ride just 2 loud miles on a very wide shoulder to the High Point Way exit. High Point connects to the trail at Preston, where there also are restrooms and provisions at the Preston General Store at mile 20.1.

Beyond Preston, the trail becomes quiet and wooded. Moss envelopes the trunks of tall evergreens and bigleaf maples. Sturdy bridges cross an occasional deep ravine or riverbed. It's necessary to traverse two roads to continue up to the trail end, high in the forest, where there's a stunning overlook of Snoqualmie Falls and the Salish Lodge. This is the true heart of the ride, so plan enough time to enjoy it at a leisurely pace. Return to Issaquah by reversing the route, then ride back to Redmond on the east side of Lake Sammamish.

Note: This tour can be ridden in two sections. Simply loop Lake

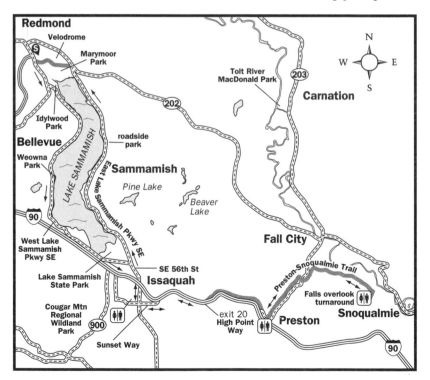

Banking turns on the Velodrome in Marymoor Park

Sammamish and drop into downtown Issaquah for a 28-mile trip, or ride the Preston-Snoqualmie Trail from a start in Issaquah for a 24-mile trip. To skip the freeway ride and take an even shorter 20-mile ride through Preston and on the trail, begin at the High Point Way exit off Interstate 90.

MILEAGE LOG

0.0 Right out of parking to West Lake Sammamish Pkwy. NE.

0.3 Left onto West Lake Sammamish Pkwy NE.

1.2 Left to stay on West Lake Sammamish Pkwy NE.

2.1 Pass Idylwood Park on the left, which offers lakefront access.

4.5 Continue straight at intersection with Northup Wy.

5.0 Pass Weowna Park.

7.9 Pass Vasa Park.

8.8 Travel three-quarters of the way around the roundabout at I-90 entrance, and turn left to continue on West Lake Sammamish Pkwy SE.

11.4 Left onto NW Sammamish Rd., which becomes SE 56th St.

12.3 Right onto East Lake Sammamish Pkwy SE. Caution: Merge left as right lane becomes I-90 on-ramp. South of freeway, road becomes Front St. N.

14.0 Left onto Sunset Wy.

14.7 Right onto I-90 via on-ramp.

16.8 Right off I-90 at exit 20, High Point Wy.

17.0 Left onto 270th Ave. SE and go under freeway.

19.2 Left onto trail at Opus I-90 business center at SE 78th St.

20.4 Cross SE 87th Pl. and continue on trail beyond trailhead parking.

22.6 Cross Preston–Fall City Rd. SE and turn right to continue on trail behind concrete barrier on east side of road. Caution: fast traffic.

22.7 Left onto SE 68th St. and cross the Raging River.

22.9 Rejoin trail at end of this short street. Trail climbs, then again runs behind roadside barriers.

23.2 Pavement ends at gravel path leading to short series of switchbacks. Walk bike up to rejoin trail.

23.3 Continue on trail at top of switchbacks.

26.3 Arrive at Snoqualmie Falls overlook at end of trail. Retrace route to return.

29.3 Arrive back at switchbacks; walk bike down to continue.

29.4 Rejoin trail at bottom of switchbacks.

29.9 At Preston–Fall City Rd. SE, turn right onto near-side sidewalk.

30.0 Cross busy road and continue on trail.

32.2 Exit trail at parking, cross SE 87th Pl., and rejoin trail eastbound.

33.2 Rejoin High Point Wy. as trail ends.

35.4 Right onto I-90 at on-ramp.

37.5 Exit I-90 at exit 18, Sunset Wy.

37.7 Merge left to turn left at E. Sunset Wy. at stoplight at end of exit ramp.

37.8 Left onto Sunset Wy.

38.4 Right onto Front St., which becomes East Lake Sammamish Pkwy. SE north of I-90. Caution: busy commercial area for **0.5** mile.

39.1 Cross Gilman Blvd., and in **0.2** travel under I-90.

40.3 Cross SE 56th St.

41.4 Pass entrance to Lake Sammamish State Park on left; restrooms, trails, beaches.

42.2 Cross 212th Wy. SE.

43.5 Cross SE 24th Wy.

46.0 Cross Thompson Hill Rd.

50.0 Left onto NE 65th St. at light and sign for Marymoor Park. Proceed through industrial park to Marymoor entrance.

50.4 Left onto Marymoor Wy. within park to return to parking.

51.7 Arrive at parking to end tour.

17 Redmond to Carnation

DIFFICULTY: moderate
TOTAL TIME: allow 5 hours
TOTAL DISTANCE: 43.4 miles
TOTAL ELEVATION GAIN: 1410 feet

Driving directions: Take SR 520 east to its end. Make first right onto Union Hill Rd., cross 178th Pl. NE, then turn right into Bear Creek Park & Ride.

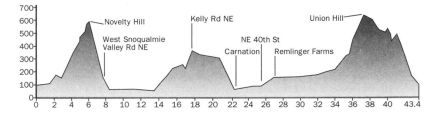

Climbing and descending the hills of Redmond to explore the farm country around Duvall and Carnation makes for a pleasant afternoon and a good bit of exercise. On a balmy summer day, you'll find plenty of two-wheeled company taking variations of this route.

Begin the tour at the end of State Route 520, where you will find the convenient Bear Creek Park & Ride, a bit northeast of Marymoor Park. Escape the shopping-area scene very quickly by heading east out of Redmond on NE Union Hill Road, then cutting through preserved marshlands and a nearby park to pick up Novelty Hill Road.

Booming development has significantly increased traffic in this area, but an adequate bike lane makes the long climb relatively safe. The traffic thins as you reach the Redmond Ridge development, and the wooded roadside opens into northern vistas. Take care as you plunge down the steep, 0.75-mile run to the Snoqualmie Valley. A winding two-lane road with scant shoulders means that cyclists should command a lane and ride with traffic on this stretch. Drivers seem to be used to it.

Pastoral views abound as you skirt the valley's west edge. The Snoqualmie River meanders through plowed fields and pastures, and picturesque farm buildings appear at intervals along the road.

The tour dips briefly into Duvall, and riders are encouraged to explore the town with a detour down Main Street and a stop riverside at the park just south of the bridge. Mountain bikers will often be seen on the unpaved Snoqualmie Valley Trail, which runs along the river as it skirts the town. Continue the route on NE Cherry Valley Road north of Duvall. After climbing its first few steep blocks, you are rewarded with views north across the river valley to Mount Baker and east to the closer Cascade peaks. Make a stop at the historic cemetery and farmstead, or pull over at the Cherry Valley Dairy's farmstand a bit farther along.

Enjoy the views while making a steady climb away from the valley, because the scenery turns green and woodsy as the road turns south. The next vista comes when again rejoining the Snoqualmie Valley after a grand slalom curve downhill to meet State Route 203, the Carnation-Duvall Road. Take care entering and riding along this stretch into

Carnation, as State Route 203 is the busiest road in the valley. Still, a wide shoulder offers safety for careful riders.

When visiting Carnation, I look forward to two things: a stop at Remlinger Farms and a visit to Tolt-MacDonald Park. Remlinger's represents perhaps the pinnacle of on-farm marketing. It holds a harvest festival, celebrates Halloween with massive pumpkin patches, and operates a farm store, café, and bakery that must be seen to be believed. It's just a mile south of Carnation, well worth the detour.

Pick up some snacks or drinks at Remlinger's and take them to Tolt-MacDonald Park. Named for a civic leader who marshaled the efforts of Boy Scouts to build the public amenities, the park holds a sweet spot on the Snoqualmie River where you can doff your shoes and cool pedal-weary feet. The park has overnight camping and plenty of day-use sites and picnic tables, as well as acres of open space. Its entrance at NE 40th Street is well signed off Tolt Avenue, the main road through town.

Depart Carnation by heading north, then cut across the valley on Carnation Farm Road. This route takes you over a scenic bridge that's next to the county's Chinook Bend Natural Area, which offers great bird-watching. A bit farther along is the historic Carnation Farm, homestead of the well-known dairy. The dairy is now part of Nestlé, and the company uses the farm as its Carnation Regional Training Facility. Care for this iconic site is seen in its well-kept, red-roofed buildings,

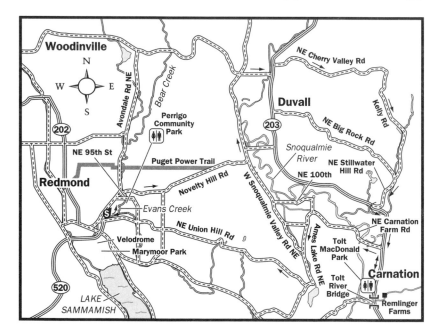

Old Carnation Road

whitewashed fences, and stately gates. Overlooking the valley is a statue of the "World Champion Milk Cow."

Leaving the valley behind, the last leg of the tour takes cyclists up a thigh-burning climb of NE Union Hill Road, which flattens out in the last few miles and then drops you back to civilization.

MILEAGE LOG

0.0 Right out of parking lot onto NE Union Hill Rd.

1.0 Left onto Evans Creek Trail through Perrigo Community Park. Turn right at **1.7** miles to access restrooms and water.

2.0 Left off trail onto NE 95th St.

2.5 Right onto Avondale Wy.

2.6 Right onto Novelty Hill Rd. after 1 short block.

5.4 Pass Redmond Ridge shopping area; restrooms, gas station.

7.2 Left onto West Snoqualmie Valley Rd. NE at bottom of hill.

10.2 Right onto NE Woodinville-Duvall Rd.

11.3 Left onto SR 203 in Duvall. (Go right to visit town of Duvall.)

11.5 Right onto NE Cherry Valley Rd. (first right, sharply uphill, after turning onto SR 203), which becomes Kelly Rd NE, then NE Stillwater Hill Rd.

21.9 Left at end of NE Stillwater Hill Rd. onto SR 203, which becomes Tolt Ave. through Carnation.

25.2 Pass entrance to Tolt-MacDonald Park at NE 40th St. in downtown Carnation.

25.7 Cross the bridge over the Tolt River.
25.8 Left onto NE 32nd St. for visit to Remlinger Farms.
26.6 Arrive at Remlinger Farms. Retrace route to SR 203.
27.5 Right onto SR 203 and recross bridge, retracing route through Carnation.
29.3 Left onto NE Carnation Farm Rd.
31.7 Pass Carnation Regional Training Center.
33.7 Continue forward onto Ames Lake Carnation Rd. NE at intersection with West Snoqualmie Valley Rd NE.
35.2 Right onto NE Union Hill Rd.
38.6 Right at T with 238th Ave. NE to stay on NE Union Hill Rd.
38.9 Bear left at stop sign at three-way intersection to stay on NE Union Hill Rd.
43.4 Left into Park & Ride to end tour.

18 Carnation to Snoqualmie Falls

DIFFICULTY: moderate
TOUR TIME: allow 2.5 hours
TOTAL DISTANCE: 23.6 miles
TOTAL ELEVATION GAIN: 460 feet

Driving directions: From SR 520, take Redmond Wy. exit and turn right onto SR 202 east (Redmond–Fall City Rd.). Turn left on NE Tolt Hill Rd., then left onto SR 203 (Fall City–Carnation Rd.). Cross bridge into Carnation and drive 0.5 mile to a left at NE 40th St. Park is at road's end.

From I-90, take exit 22, Preston/Fall City, and follow Preston–Fall City Rd. SE, which becomes SR 203 (Fall City–Carnation Rd.) at intersection with SR 202 (Redmond–Fall City Rd.). Continue straight on SR 203 across bridge into Carnation and drive 0.5 mile to a left at NE 40th St. Park is at road's end.

Spend a lazy afternoon in the lush farm country of the Snoqualmie River valley with this flat tour between two of the area's main towns. If you feel like a challenge after making the short trip from

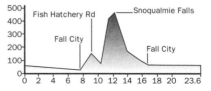

Carnation to Snoqualmie, take the 3-mile climb to view the famous Snoqualmie Falls. You can also connect this trip with the extra miles to

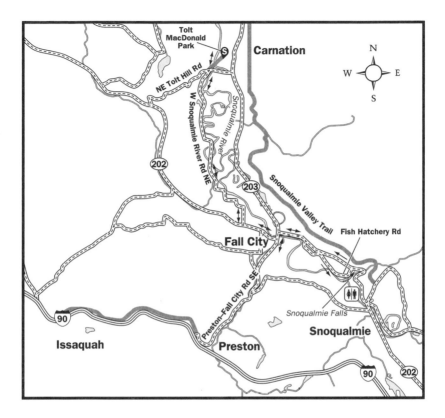

North Bend (Tour 19) or use it as a continuation of the Duvall-Carnation loop from Redmond (Tour 17).

Begin at Tolt MacDonald Park in Carnation. A row of big poplars shields your car from the afternoon sun in its free parking lot. Ride toward the river into the park and cross the attractive arched pedestrian bridge over the wide, shallow confluence of the Tolt and Snoqualmie Rivers. A short packed-earth trail takes you to the paved roads, but even the skinniest road-bike tire can handle this brief interval on the earth.

Cross busy NE Tolt Hill Road just west of the car bridge and head south on West Snoqualmie River Road NE. The curvy, shady lane is lightly used, due to the straighter and wider Fall City–Carnation Road (State Route 203) on the east side of the valley. It's not unusual to see cars stopped by the roadside, buying cut flowers or vegetables from a farm stand or admiring the bucolic scenery.

Pass by the Carnation Marsh, stewarded by the National Audubon Society, with its osprey nests and leafless dead tree "snags" in the boggy landscape, then pedal by an alternative use of the land: the trimmed and flower-bedecked Carnation Golf Course.

Productive farmland is nestled along the road, and in August you'll be treated to rows of riotous color in fields where cutting flowers are grown. Next you arrive at Jubilee Farm, with its big white barn hunched by the side of the road, gaping door open when the farmers are working, which is almost every summer day. The well-loved farm also offers processed foods and hosts regular events, such as farm tours and festivals.

This main road through the western side of the valley has been given many names, as reflected in the mileage log, but it's all one route, taking you south to the tiny town of Fall City. A bit farther along, you come to another golf course, Tall Chief, marked by a long allée of poplars leading to the clubhouse. You also may come upon lush fields of corn lining the road, as well as cattle and horse ranches along the way.

Fall City sports a tiny main street with a well-stocked market, a couple of taverns, and a take-out burger joint, as well as a riverside park that offers a good place to picnic. A curious sight is the native totem pole welcoming you to town, which seems to have a bear clutching a blue space-alien child.

If this flat, 9-mile ride from Carnation hasn't taxed your energies, continue on to Snoqualmie Falls. Cross over the river and make a

Riders find corn fields and flat, open roads in the Snoqualmie Valley.

right onto busy State Route 202 to head for the falls, cutting off onto Hatchery Road to avoid some of the traffic. It's 3 miles of riding up into the Cascade foothills, as the overhead line of mountain peaks that were visible from the valley floor give way to a thick march of evergreens growing up to the ditches on both sides and receding into the hills beyond the road ahead. The climb is steady but not overly difficult, and a wide shoulder makes the traffic bearable.

Stop at the parking area for the falls, take the short walk 100 yards to the overlook near the luxurious Salish Lodge, or make a hike out of it and take the steep 0.5-mile trip down to the river emerging from the base of the falls. Restrooms and refreshments are available here.

The ride back toward Fall City is a quick downhill. Continue retracing your route back to Carnation. End the tour by sticking your feet in the cool water of the Snoqualmie at the park in Carnation, or ride up the town's main street to the upscale tavern for a snack and a cold drink before heading home.

MILEAGE LOG

0.0 Right out of parking into camping area of park.

0.2 Cross footbridge over Snoqualmie River.

0.4 Left onto trail on other side, paralleling river.

0.8 Exit trail onto NE Tolt Hill Rd. Make immediate left onto West Snoqualmie River Rd. NE.

5.1 Left onto SE 24th St., which becomes 316th Ave. SE, then SE 28th St., then 321st Ave. SE, then SE 31st St., and finally 324th Ave. SE.

7.0 Left onto Redmond–Fall City Rd., SR 202.

7.7 Arrive at Fall City.

8.1 Left onto Preston–Fall City Rd. SE and over Snoqualmie River bridge.

8.3 Right onto Fall City–Snoqualmie Rd., continuation of SR 202.

9.1 Right onto Fish Hatchery Rd.

11.0 Left onto 372nd Ave. SE.

11.2 Right onto Fall City–Snoqualmie Rd.

12.4 Arrive at Snoqualmie Falls: parking, gift shop, overlook. Return on Fall City–Snoqualmie Rd.

15.0 Left onto Preston–Fall City Rd.

15.2 Right onto Redmond–Fall City Rd.

16.3 Right onto 324th Ave. SE, which eventually becomes West Snoqualmie River Rd NE.

23.0 Cross NE Tolt Hill Rd. and make immediate left onto trail before crossing bridge.

23.4 Right onto footbridge over Snoqualmie River.

23.6 Return through park to parking to end tour.

19   Fall City to North Bend

DIFFICULTY: moderate
TOTAL TIME: allow 3 hours
TOTAL DISTANCE: 21.8 miles
TOTAL ELEVATION GAIN: 620 feet

> **Driving directions:** Take I-90 east to exit 22, Preston/Fall City. Turn left off exit and go over I-90 on SE 82nd St. Turn right onto Fall City–Preston Rd. SE at stop sign. Go north 4.7 miles. At intersection with SR 202, turn right to follow signs that say "202 East, North Bend/Snoqualmie Falls." At Fall City, cross bridge and turn immediately left onto SR 203, Fall City–Carnation Rd. SE. Parking in unpaved lot at Fall City Community Park immediately on the left.

Take this short tour to visit Snoqualmie Falls, enjoy some rolling hills, get a great view of rocky Mount Si, and take a spin through the foothill towns of Snoqualmie and North Bend.

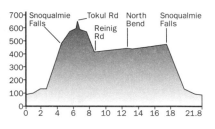

Depart from the eastern edge of Fall City and avoid most of the climb up busy State Route 202 by turning south onto Fish Hatchery Road. This quiet lane parallels the loud highway but also runs along peaceful Snoqualmie River for a time. A short climb takes you back onto State Route 202 for the last mile of climbing before reaching the impressive Snoqualmie Falls, which is always worth a stop and a look.

Cross the busy highway at the slow corridor around the luxurious Salish Lodge and continue toward North Bend on back roads, skirting the town of Snoqualmie on the outbound. The route takes you into the "Reinig Road Sycamore Corridor," where a bit of history from when the area was run by a logging mill can still be seen. A large stand of sycamores was planted by immigrants who lived in the Snoqualmie Falls company town and worked in the mill. The trees, with their mottled gray bark and heavy canopies, are now quite large and shade the edge of the valley.

Break out into a farming area and aim straight at Mount Si, which provides an impressive backdrop to the rural valley you traverse to get to North Bend. A leisurely cycling speed is perfect for examining its craggy walls. In the foreground, enjoy a King County natural area at 9.8

miles that offers trails down to a bend in the river. A neighboring ranch with its nicely maintained barns, paddocks, and pastures completes the postcard-perfect scene.

The small town of North Bend offers a number of attractions as well. Although the route calls for turning right onto North Bend Way, the town's main street, detour left one block to visit Scott's Dairy Freeze for an ice cream treat. To the right along your downtown route, pass Georgia's Bakery and Tvede's Café, which was made famous as the Mar-T Diner in the quirky 1980s television series *Twin Peaks*. You can still get Agent Cooper's favorite cherry pie at the diner, which plays up its screen notoriety. Turn right at the diner's corner to exit North Bend and continue the tour, or make another detour and head left down Bendigo Boulevard to the factory discount stores, grouped in a shopping center 1 mile south next to Interstate 90.

Plentiful local traffic is to be found on the road between Snoqualmie and North Bend, although a generous shoulder makes for a safe ride. The only exceptions are the old bridges, which have no shoulder or

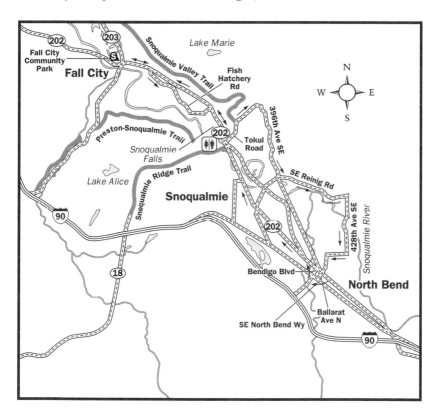

Mount Si

pedestrian-bikeway and must be traversed with caution. A rear-view mirror to gauge the traffic behind you comes in handy at such unavoidable spots.

The route takes you straight through Snoqualmie's main street, along an old rail station and train display, and past one of the most massive cross sections of a tree trunk you'll ever see. Across the street is a candy factory and a small grouping of cafés. Exiting Snoqualmie, you approach another narrow bridge, but this one has a separated pedestrian-bikeway on the right. Take care at the narrow ramp to the protected lane.

For the final leg of this short ride, pass by the lodge and the falls, then enjoy a thrilling, curving downhill ride back to the edge of the Snoqualmie Valley.

MILEAGE LOG

0.0 Right out of parking onto SR 203, Fall City–Carnation Rd. SE.

0.1 Left at stop sign onto SR 202, Fall City–Snoqualmie Rd. SE.

0.9 Right onto Fish Hatchery Rd.

2.8 Left onto 372nd St.

3.0 Right onto Fall City–Snoqualmie Rd. SE.

4.6 Arrive at Snoqualmie Falls Park. Restrooms, water, overlook to falls.

4.8 Left on Tokul Rd. just beyond Salish Lodge.

6.6 Bear right to stay on unmarked main road as Tokul curves sharply uphill. Main road becomes 396th Ave. SE.

8.4 Left onto SE Reinig Rd.

10.3 Right onto 428th Ave. SE, which becomes 12th, then 420th.

12.6 Continue forward as 420th becomes Ballarat Ave. N. in downtown North Bend.

13.0 Right onto SE North Bend Wy.

13.2 Right onto Bendigo Blvd., SR 202, which curves left (west).

16.4 Arrive at downtown Snoqualmie. Historical rail station, tree cross-section in park on the right.

17.7 Arrive back at Snoqualmie Falls; retrace route.

21.7 Right onto SR 203.

21.8 Left into parking area to end tour.

20 Green River and Interurban Trails

~~~~~~

DIFFICULTY: moderate
TOUR TIME: allow 4 hours
TOTAL DISTANCE: 40.8 miles
TOTAL ELEVATION GAIN: 80 feet

Driving directions: From I-5 southbound, take exit 156, turn right onto Interurban Ave., travel 0.5 mile, then turn right on 42nd Ave. S., cross Green River, and turn right into Tukwila Community Center parking lot.

From I-5 northbound, take exit 156, turn left onto Interurban, travel 0.3 mile, then turn right on 42nd Ave. S., cross Green River, and turn right into Tukwila Community Center parking lot.

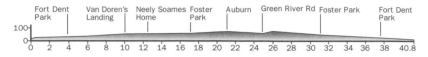

The Green River has a bad reputation, through no fault of its own. It has faced the common challenges of many American rivers that flow through urban areas: pollution, industrial uses, neglect. In true American style, let's ignore all that abuse and instead recognize this river as a historic waterway, important in Native American and early settler development, now being reclaimed as a scenic amenity and wildlife habitat. A ride down the winding Green River Trail presents a bit of that history as well as a view of suburban development that is happening south of Seattle. It's worth a leisurely spin, if only for the excellent barbecue to be found along the way. It also provides a great link to other south-end rides.

Begin the ride at the Tukwila Community Center and ride south to Fort Dent Park. The area, a former Duwamish tribe settlement, was once the confluence of the Green River with the long-gone Black River, an outflow from Lake Washington and nearby White Lake. The Washington National Guard built a small fort there after the 1855 Battle of Seattle against the tribes and named it after the battalion's leader, Frederick Dent, who was also the brother-in-law of President Ulysses S. Grant.

Skirting the edges of Fort Dent Park and heading south under the many lanes of Interstate 405 and into Tukwila's light industrial warehouse area, it's hard to imagine the open land that the Green River once wound through in its path from Mount Rainier to Puget Sound. But you do still feel the flow of nature as you bike along the flat, winding path that mostly tracks the river's route. The trail leads behind warehouses that skirt Southcenter Mall. What was once fertile farmland has been replaced largely by suburban sprawl, although there are occasional runs along plowed fields and rows of produce.

The snaking trail veers slightly westward but continues to roughly parallel Interstate 5 as it skirts the eastern edge of Des Moines and enters Kent. At South 212th Street, you leave the trail briefly and ride along Russell Road, past Van Doren's Landing Park and the Green River Natural Resources Area across the road. This former sewage lagoon now houses a wildlife refuge and wetland. On the south edge of the GRNRA, the Puget Power Trail intersects with the Green River Trail, heading east-west. Continue south, however, and soon reenter the off-road trail at Russell Woods Park.

Apartment complexes and townhomes are plentiful along this stretch, making the trail more populated with children and families. Another trailside attraction soon appears, the Neely Soames Homestead, the

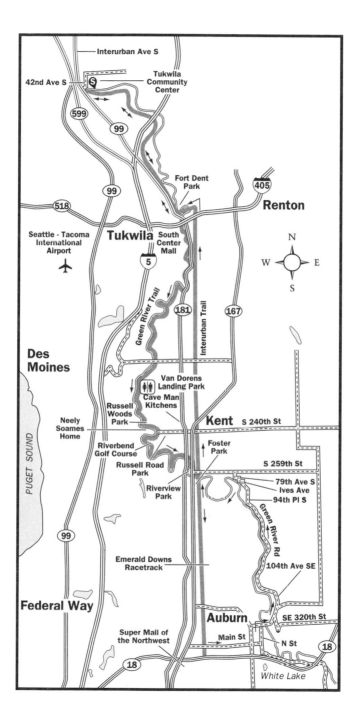

oldest standing residence in the Kent area. Due to its location at an easy river landing for steamboats headed for Seattle, it served as the area's first post office and general store.

From the frontier homestead, travel back even further in time for some prehistoric barbecue at Cave Man Kitchens, an area fixture since 1970. The original owners kept chickens on the site, and if you could catch one you'd get a free chicken dinner. Today you catch your chicken, beef, or pork sandwich smothered in sweet, tangy sauce at the counter across from the smokehouse and enjoy it at one of their brick-red picnic tables beneath a dinosaur mural on the smokehouse. To get there, head south on the trail from Neely Soames Home to where the trail again joins Russell Road. Make a left off the trail onto South 240th Street, also known as West James Street, and travel a half dozen blocks on a street bike lane to the West Valley Highway (also known as Washington Street). Make a left, staying on the near sidewalk to avoid riding on this busy street, and the Cave Man is on your left in a scant two blocks.

The Green River Trail ends at Foster Park in south Kent, linking up with the rail-straight Interurban Trail. If you wish to turn around at this point, turn left onto the Interurban back to Fort Dent. The Interurban is as linear as the Green River is curvaceous, and you're slowed only by other trail users and frequent road crossings. Heed the roads: Much of the Interurban runs between highways and warehouses, so truck traffic is plentiful. The route continues by turning south on the Interurban

Cyclists on a homemade tandem ride past the "Slip Stream" sculpture in Van Doren's Landing Park.

and checking out the homegrown style of Auburn. The return takes you winding east along the river back to Foster Park before beelining north on the Interurban.

MILEAGE LOG

0.0 Left onto near-side sidewalk out of Tukwila Community Center parking. Cross bridge.

0.1 Left off bridge down short embankment, then right onto trail. Exit trail immediately into office park parking lot and continue along river's edge.

0.4 Re-enter trail as parking ends.

1.1 Trail travels under I-5, then next to onramp.

1.4 Curve left to stay on trail at intersection with I-5 and Interurban Ave.

2.1 Cross 141st St., then left and follow bike trail signs.

2.6 Cross bridge into Fort Dent Park.

3.3 Pass under vehicle bridge, then curve left to follow "River Trail" signs and cross over the river on bridge's pedestrian/bike lane. Exiting bridge, take immediate left to stay on trail.

3.9 Right at intersection with Interurban Trail, continuing to follow "River Trail" signs. Cross under Interurban Ave. and I-405.

4.6 Exit trail on sidewalk to cross river. Left onto trail in 0.1.

6.8 Left onto arched pedestrian bridge to cross river. Right off the bridge to continue.

7.9 Pass Riverview Park.

9.0 Pass Three Friends Fishing Hole.

10.0 Pass under S. 212th St., then soft right onto Russell Road. Pass Green River Natural Resources Area.

10.3 Right onto trail through Van Doren's Landing Park. Restrooms.

10.6 Exit trail back onto Russell Road.

11.2 Right onto trail at bridge into Russell Woods Park.

12.6 Pass Neely Soames Home. (Just south, at S. 240th St., exit trail for 1.5-mile side trip to Cave Man Kitchens.)

12.8 Rejoin Russell Road briefly, then right onto trail through Riverbend Golf Complex.

13.8 Trail passes under W. Meeker St. and continues through golf course.

15.6 Exit trail onto cul-de-sac, continue forward to pick up trail again in 0.1.

15.8 Exit trail right onto Hawley Rd.

16.0 Rejoin trail at street end.

16.2 Enter Foster Park.

16.5 Right onto Interurban Trail. (Note: To shorten route, left on

Interurban Trail and return to parking in 9.9 miles.)

20.0 Pass Emerald Downs racetrack.

21.5 Left onto W. Main St. in Auburn.

22.9 Left onto N St. NE.

23.4 Left onto R St. NE.

23.5 Right onto 8th St. NE over bridge to cross Green River.

23.8 Left onto 104th Ave. SE. Caution: busy intersection.

24.6 Left onto SE 307th Pl., also known as Green River Rd.

27.5 Bear left at Y with 94th Pl. S. to stay on Green River Rd.

28.2 Left at stop sign where 94th Pl. S. comes in from south.

28.3 Left at large boulders and bollards to rejoin trail.

29.8 Trail ends under a railroad bridge. Right onto Ives Ave., then left onto S. 266th St., which becomes 79th Ave. S., then S. 261st St., then 80th Ave. S.

30.5 Left onto S. 259th St.

30.6 Cross 3rd Ave. S. and continue west on 259th.

30.9 Right onto Interurban Trail.

32.1 Continue on trail under SR 167, the Valley Freeway.

35.9 Trail crosses parking adjacent to Nelson Pl.

36.1 Continue on trail under I-405, then under Grady Wy.

36.7 Right at intersection with Green River Trail.

37.5 Right onto bike lane on bridge into Fort Dent. When exiting bridge, curve right and follow "River Trail" signs.

38.8 Right on trail parallel to Interurban Ave. at S. 141st St.

39.5 Trail curves right at I-5 onramp.

40.4 Exit trail into parking behind office park. Continue along river.

40.7 Exit parking onto trail briefly, then exit to ramp and right onto bridge to community center.

40.8 Arrive at Tukwila Community Center parking to end tour.

21 Cedar River Trail and May Valley

DIFFICULTY: moderate
TOUR TIME: allow 2.5 hours
TOTAL DISTANCE: 29.7 miles
TOTAL ELEVATION GAIN: 520 feet

Driving directions: From I-5, take exit 154 to I-405 northbound. From I-405, take exit 4A and turn right onto Maple Valley Highway/ SR 169. Take first right into Renton Community Center, proceed left, and pass aquatic center to parking by community center.

Do you ever, on a flat and open stretch of trail, just tune out your surroundings and listen to your body working with your bike? Legs operate like pistons, heart churns like an engine. Try this on

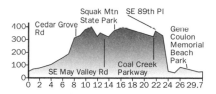

the Cedar River Trail's flat, open route, and you might get a feel for the trail's first use: as a railroad. The trail, paved from Renton to Maple Valley then continuing to Landsburg as gravel, began life as a part of the Milwaukee Railroad. Reappropriated by the government through the "railbanking" mechanism, it's a great jumping-off point for exploring the cusp of rural lands in south King County. The three-hour ride is at times loud and busy, but the exploration of the charms still existing in May Valley make it a worthy ramble through the civilization happening southeast of Seattle.

Begin the tour by crossing the bridge behind the Renton Community Center. Before heading southeast toward Maple Valley, you could take

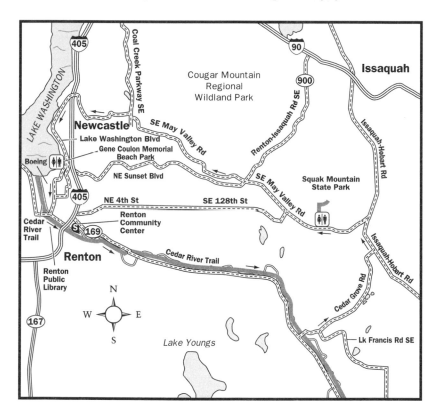

A broad, paved boardwalk runs along the Cedar River from downtown Renton toward Lake Washington.

a 5-mile round-trip detour north and trace the river's course through Renton to Lake Washington. Ride along the shallow river for a time, then rise onto the city streets and a small park near the lake. Boeing's large plant is here next to Renton's airport, evidenced by the regular roar of jet engines being tested. Return to the community center, crossing back under I-405, to begin this tour.

Head south along the river, enjoying a couple miles of peaceful, green landscape. Emerge like a locomotive out onto the fringes of State Route 169, the Maple Valley Highway, past a golf course and multiple housing developments.

The ride to Maple Valley is just over 20 miles round-trip, and the paved trail stops just short of the actual town, ending at a bridge over the river where the gravel portion begins. Exit the trail here at the Testy Chef, a small diner that locals say lives up to its name. Across the busy highway sit the Cedar Grange and the Maple Valley Grocery, but you'd need to ride about 2 miles farther south on that fast-moving street to find any other conveniences. A great suggestion, made by Erin and Bill

Woods in *Bicycling the Backroads of Puget Sound*, is to plan this trip on a Sunday when the Cedar Grange is offering its pancake breakfast.

If it's not the right day, however, there is a better way to enjoy this area. Instead of riding into Maple Valley, continue south on the loud trail only until it meets Cedar Grove Road. Follow the road up the hill, past the Cedar Grove Composting facility, with its steady stream of trucks, and on to a left at the Issaquah-Hobart Road, then onto SE May Valley Road for a long and winding route, mostly rural and enjoyable, back to Renton.

May Valley still reveals its farming heritage at spots, but those are outnumbered by signs of suburbanization. For instance, a development called Sunset Valley Farms shows a number of homes with suburban-size yards filling a small side valley that one could picture having been a pastoral family farm.

At Squak Mountain State Park, you'll find restrooms and picnic tables off the parking area. The park, replete with hiking and riding trails, stretches some distance north.

Cross State Route 900, the Renton-Issaquah Road, and then the landscape becomes more pastoral for a time. May Valley Road has minimal to nonexistent shoulders, but it is signed for 30 miles per hour, with regular reminders that it is a "recreation trail" for pedestrians and cyclists.

A brief stint onto wide and busy Coal Creek Parkway is followed by a series of narrow suburban streets with moderate hills and many twists and turns: 89th Place begats 88th Place begats Lincoln begats 44th Street, and you're in Newcastle, then back in Renton. As the streets narrow, so do the side yards, until townhomes and shopping centers give way again to Interstate 405.

Cross over I-405 and head south on Lake Washington Boulevard to Gene Coulon Park on the lake's south edge. Soon you're in downtown Renton, jogging down once again to the river, then emerging at the library and Liberty Park to return to the tour's start.

MILEAGE LOG

0.0 Begin trail behind Renton Community Center parking. Left onto trail under I-405 on a bridge crossing Cedar River.

0.1 Left on trail on west side of river.

8.4 Left onto Cedar Grove Rd.

12.3 Left onto Issaquah-Hobart Rd.

13.4 Left onto SE May Valley Rd. Caution: traffic when merging to left-turn lane.

15.0 Arrive at Squak Mountain State Park. Restrooms available.

19.3 At stop sign at 164th Ave. SE, stay on May Valley Rd.

21.5 Right onto Coal Creek Pkwy. SE.

22.0 Left onto SE 89th Pl. Caution: road curves; fast-moving traffic.

Road becomes SE 88th Pl., then SE 88th St., then 114th Ave. SE, then Lincoln Ave. NE, then NE 44th St.

24.5 At ramps for I-405, go straight over I-405.

24.6 Left onto Lake Washington Blvd.

26.9 Right into Gene Coulon Memorial Beach Park, then immediate left at stop sign.

27.0 Right into parking area by pavilion; restrooms, concessions, water available.

27.6 Right onto park road, which ends at the intersection of Houser Wy. N. and Lake Washington Blvd.

27.8 Straight across Lake Washington Blvd. and railroad tracks to continue on Houser Wy. N.

28.3 Right onto N. 8th St.

28.5 Left onto Garden Ave.

28.7 Right onto N. 6th St.

28.9 Left onto Williams Ave. N.

29.1 At Riverside Dr. S., take ramp on the right down to Cedar River Trail. Turn left onto trail.

29.5 As trail ends, take ramp up to the library, turn left onto sidewalk, then right to loop around library's east side, into Liberty Park, and ride south past skateboard park.

29.7 At light, cross Houser Wy. into short tunnel under I-405 that delivers you to trail entrance and parking area.

22 Green River Gorge and Black Diamond

~~~~~~

DIFFICULTY: moderate
TOUR TIME: allow 3 hours
TOTAL DISTANCE: 28.7 miles
TOTAL ELEVATION GAIN: 960 feet

Driving directions: Take I-5 to I-90 eastbound. At Issaquah, take Front St. exit. Turn right on Front St., which becomes Issaquah-Hobart Rd., which becomes 276th Ave. SE. Travel approximately 11 miles. Trailhead parking is on north bank of Cedar River, just south of SE 247th St.

Southeast King County, somewhat less encumbered by the rumble of development or the bustle of farm activity, is home to some of the best back roads riding still available in the area. A ride through the Green River Gorge east of Black Diamond offers quieter roads, mostly gentle terrain, and beautiful wooded scenes. This tour provides merely an introduction to

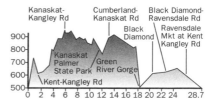

the multiple routes cyclists can create around the Green River, and it may be combined easily with other adjacent tours for many enjoyable outings of varied length and difficulty.

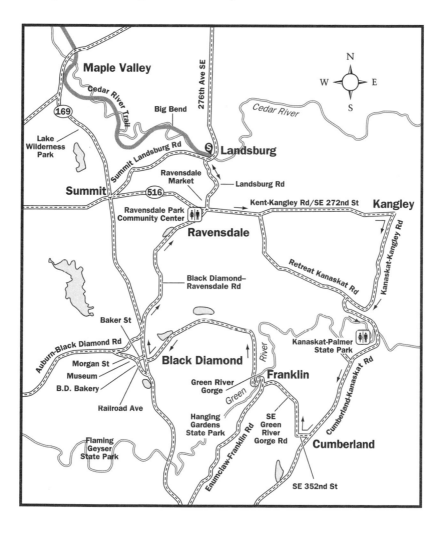

Green River Gorge

Begin this loop at Landsburg, a wide spot in the road adjacent to the Cedar River Watershed, one of the sources of Seattle's water supply. From here, water is screened, chlorinated, and fluoridated to slake the thirst of more than a million people. However, fill up your water bottle at home, because you'll find no facilities at the parking site.

What you will see is a white-water kayak training course under the bridge that spans the Cedar River. "Gates" elevated above the river are raised and lowered depending on the flow to provide a course for river rats to hone their skills. A foot trail from the parking area leads to the Big Bend open space along the river.

Ride south and east on 276th Avenue SE, which becomes Landsburg Road SE, a somewhat strenuous hill with which to begin. At the intersection of Landsburg Road SE and Kent-Kangley Road, the ride's first turn, sits the Ravensdale Market, a good stop for snacks if you plan to picnic on this ride. Restrooms are just south in Ravensdale Park. Turn left onto Kent-Kangley, the busiest road on the tour but one that sports a wide shoulder for easy riding. Cycle east past wooded hillsides and the occasional open valley sporting small ranches to a comfort stop at Kanaskat-Palmer State Park.

The 320-acre park has campgrounds and day-use areas, with restrooms, water, and picnic sites. Its main attraction is the Green River access, also a favorite of paddlers. The curving riverfront through the park goes from class II to IV, providing challenges for kayakers and rafters of many skill levels. A recreation area begins at the park and follows the river downstream almost continuously to Flaming Geyser State Park; a coalition of enthusiastic users is seeking to preserve the area and develop the recreational opportunities of this verdant ribbon that supporters call "the best of the last wild places in King County."

South of the park, turn right toward the SE Green River Gorge Road just before the tiny burg of Cumberland. This segment provides the visual high point in the ride: a winding, secluded road that leads to a sturdy one-lane bridge spanning the gorge. A stoplight warns approaching motorists of oncoming traffic, but cyclists can use the wide sidewalks to traverse the bridge. Stop midspan to enjoy its breathtaking views down into the gorge. A former inn sits boarded-up at the bridge's eastern approach, implying the grandness of this attraction to previous generations. Perhaps conservation of the area will make it a destination yet again.

The road climbs and winds, alternating past woods and clear-cuts, into Black Diamond, where a visit to the Black Diamond Bakery is virtually required for anyone pedaling into town. Depart Black Diamond heading north, then shortly angle northeast toward Ravensdale, beyond which lies the Landsburg parking site.

MILEAGE LOG

0.0 Depart parking area north of Landsburg bridge by turning south and crossing bridge.

0.2 Bear left at Y at Summit-Landsburg Rd, staying on Landsburg Rd.

1.5 Turn left onto Kent-Kangley Rd./SR 516.

2.8 Stay left at intersection with Retreat Kanaskat Rd. to stay on Kent-Kangley (also signed here as SE 272nd St.).

6.1 Turn right onto Kanaskat-Kangley Rd.

9.1 Turn left onto Cumberland-Kanaskat Rd.

11.1 Turn right into Kanasket-Palmer State Park.

12.1 Arrive at day-use area, restrooms, water, picnic tables. Retrace route to exit park.

13.2 Turn right onto Cumberland-Kanaskat Rd. when exiting park.

15.7 Turn right onto SE 352nd St., also named SE Green River Gorge Rd.

17.9 Turn right at intersection with Enumclaw-Franklin Rd. to continue on SE Green River Gorge Rd.

18.3 Cross one-lane Green River Gorge Bridge.

21.7 Road becomes Lawson St. as it enters Black Diamond.

22.6 Turn right onto 3rd St., also known as SR 169/Enumclaw–Black Diamond Rd. (For side trip to Black Diamond Bakery, turn left onto Baker St., then left onto Railroad Ave.)

23.3 Turn right onto Black Diamond–Ravensdale Rd., which becomes SE Ravensdale Wy.

27.1 Cross Kent-Kangley Rd. at Ravensdale Market. Proceed north on Landsburg Rd.

28.4 Turn right onto Summit-Landsburg Rd.

28.7 Arrive back at Landsburg bridge and parking to end tour.

23 Auburn to Flaming Geyser State Park

DIFFICULTY: moderate
TOTAL TIME: allow 3.5 hours
TOTAL DISTANCE: 35.2 miles
TOTAL ELEVATION GAIN: 830 feet

Driving directions: Take I-5 or SR 167 to SR 18 eastbound. Take first exit in Auburn, C St. SW. Left off ramp, in 0.2 mile left onto W. Main St., then left into parking by Interurban Trail in another 0.4 mile.

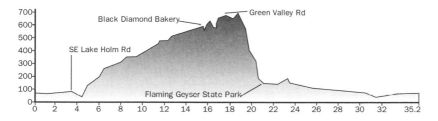

South King County is home to some excellent road biking, along rural roads and through lush farming communities. This route, heading east from Auburn, skirts new development, visits the small town of Black Diamond with a great bakery, and returns through lush, green farmland. This road tour also offers connections to rides using the area's major paved bike trails (see Tour 20, Green River and Interurban Trails), so it can be used as an extension of or connection to other rides.

Start the tour by parking next to the Interurban Trail adjacent to Auburn's quiet Main Street. Access is easy and quick from Interstate 5 or State Route 167. Ride east through town and briefly alongside busy State Route 18 as you head northeast on the shady, winding SE Auburn–Black Diamond Road. An alternate route along SE Lake Holm Road can be taken if the group wants a more strenuous activity and a quieter road, but the curvy, steep section to start, which offers no shoulder for biking, might be unpleasant for less experienced riders.

By either route, your first destination is Black Diamond and its two main tourist attractions: the railway museum and the Black Diamond Bakery. They are situated just a matter of yards from one another, in a small shopping area that also houses a bookstore and general store.

The railroad station has a well-preserved engine sitting on a short stretch of track and displays of goods shipped from the area, such as coal and logs. Other relics of the town's past are lined up, too, such as a one-room jail dating from 1910. The museum, open on summer afternoons, is worth a quick tour. The bakery is a favorite of the region's cyclists, and not just for the comfort-stop essentials of water and clean restrooms. A café offers a full menu, but there is a generous seating area for those just having an espresso drink or bakery item.

Ride back to Auburn along the country jewel that is SE Green Valley Road. Here in designated farming areas, housing developments are still nonexistent, although massive new homes of hobby farmers are sprinkled along the road. It is mostly an area of working farms, and there are picturesque barns and horse pastures on view.

Before reaching the main valley, drop down into Flaming Geyser State Park, adjacent to the road. Part of a patchwork of preserved green spaces that begins on the Green River at Kanaskat-Palmer State Park

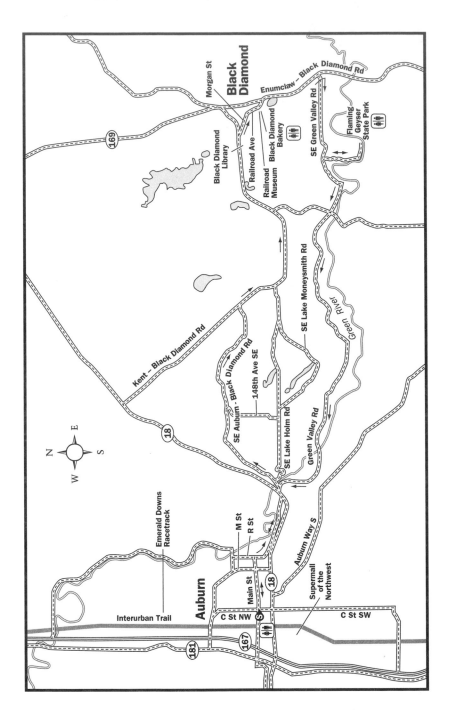

Black Diamond

Morgan St

Black Diamond Library

Railroad Ave

Black Diamond Bakery

Railroad Museum

Enumclaw - Black Diamond Rd

SE Green Valley Rd

Flaming Geyser State Park

169

Kent - Black Diamond Rd

SE Lake Moneysmith Rd

SE Auburn - Black Diamond Rd

148th Ave SE

SE Lake Holm Rd

Green Valley Rd

Green River

18

N E S W

Emerald Downs Racetrack

M St

R St

Auburn Way S

Supermall of the Northwest

Interurban Trail

Auburn

Main St

18

C St NW

C St SW

167

181

Take a break in Black Diamond to visit the historic railroad museum, just down the street from the famous Black Diamond Bakery.

and continues through the stunning Green River Gorge, this park is home to a unique sight: a flame that continually burns in a bubbling stream due to release of natural gases. It's only a short walk from the parking area to view the "flaming geyser."

The park also features mossy, woodland trails and Christy Creek, home to chinook, chum, and coho salmon. At the entrance to the park is an open area used by model-airplane aficionados, often seen buzzing their remote-control planes over the flat, grassy field.

While the road out to Black Diamond is shady with rolling hills, this route back is light, airy, and flat. There are even a couple of opportunities to pick up country farm products.

End the loop by turning back onto the Auburn–Black Diamond Road west into Auburn under State Route 18. At the turn, the venerable Neely Mansion sits on the left, a homestead of one of the first families of the area. Its grounds are open to visitors during summer weekends.

MILEAGE LOG

0.0 Right onto Main St. from parking adjacent to Interurban Trail.

1.5 Right onto R St. Caution: railroad tracks—cross at an angle; intersection with truck traffic.

3.4 Continue straight at Green Valley Rd. intersection.

3.5 Cross bridge and continue straight on SE Auburn–Black Diamond Rd. at intersection with SE Lake Holm Rd.

8.3 Merge right at intersection with Kent–Black Diamond Rd.

12.8 Arrive at Black Diamond; road becomes Roberts Rd.

15.0 Right onto Morgan St. (not signed, but first right after library).

15.6 Right onto Railroad Ave.; pass railroad museum and bakery.

16.5 Right onto 3rd Ave., which becomes Enumclaw–Black Diamond Rd.

17.5 Right onto SE Green Valley Rd.

20.4 Left into Flaming Geyser State Park.

20.8 Right into park off access road.

21.8 Arrive at parking, restrooms, picnic area. Retrace route to continue.

23.2 Left onto Green Valley Rd. when exiting park to continue tour.

31.7 Left onto SE Auburn–Black Diamond Rd.

33.7 Left onto Main St.

35.2 Arrive at Interurban Trail parking to end tour.

24　Vashon and Maury Islands

DIFFICULTY: strenuous
TOTAL TIME: allow 5 hours
TOTAL DISTANCE: 39.8 miles
TOTAL ELEVATION GAIN: 2500 feet

Driving directions: From I-5, take exit 163, West Seattle Bridge, and follow it west. Continue into West Seattle on Fauntleroy Way SW as bridge ends. Follow Fauntleroy as it curves left, then right, past Lincoln Park to reach ferry parking. Use north lot farthest from ferry, except on Sunday, when closer lot may be used. After parking, cycle 0.2 mile south on Fauntleroy to ferry dock.

Ferry across to Vashon Island for a rural 40-mile workout that is one of the most scenic to be found in our region. Off the well-traveled main road, cyclists enjoy tree-lined back roads low on traffic and high on pastoral and water views.

The inevitable hill climb to start the ride is one of the most challenging of any from a ferry dock. It's a steady, 2-mile grade, after which

you veer onto the island's west side for a long spin that takes you south down most of the island. Views across Colvos Passage to the Kitsap Peninsula and the Olympics are interspersed with valleys where deer or grazing livestock can be seen. Mostly, though, the view is a predictable tunnel of Northwest evergreens that line the roads. The way south takes you past the Wax Orchards berry operation and picturesque Misty Isle Farms and its naturally raised beef. Vashon is an agricultural island, and many small farms, a few with roadside stands offering fresh veggies, can be found along its roads.

As the route turns back onto the Vashon Highway, you're just 2 miles from the Tahlequah Ferry to Tacoma. A wonderful side trip to Point Defiance Park is only a few minutes beyond that ferry dock. However, this tour turns north and loops around the tiny Burton peninsula before continuing onto Maury Island.

A note on picnicking: On this route, retail establishments are scarce, so it's best to plan ahead and bring your provisions. However, a small store sits roadside at the entrance to the Burton area. A great midpoint to stop, rest your legs, enjoy the views, and fuel up is Burton Acres Park. The park includes beach access, restrooms, and picnic tables.

From Burton, curve northeast around quiet Quartermaster Harbor. You could skip Maury Island and shorten the tour by 8 miles by turning left at Dockton Road, but continue to Maury and you'll be delighted by the quaint lighthouse and pebbly beach at Point Robinson Park. This is a great place for an extended rest.

The small Point Robinson lighthouse, with well-informed guides that will take you up the spiral stairs to view the working Fresnel lens, is a gem for visitors. From the catwalk you can view Seattle across the narrow channel and perhaps see "hardhat" divers going into the 300-foot-deep water right off the point to harvest geoduck clams. Looming next to the lighthouse is the Coast Guard's electronic beacon, making this a rare facility where both old and new warning systems for sailors are in effect.

Walk the curved, sandy beach and view a case of excellent mariners' antiques in the gift shop before climbing back out of the park and onto the road leading back to Vashon. The ride hugs the islands' eastern coasts until climbing toward the commercial center of Vashon, offering many views of the city to the northeast.

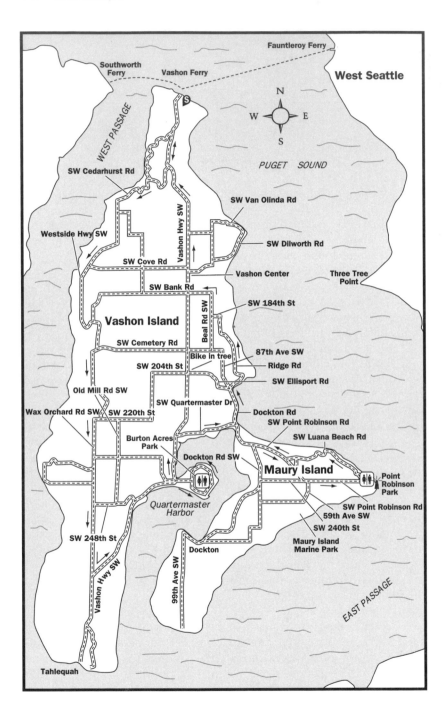

Riding past the self-serve produce stand at Plum Forest Farm

If visiting Vashon on a Sunday, be forewarned that many of its shops are closed. However, downtown Vashon docs host a number of great cafés, gift shops, and a bustling farmers market. A cycling curiosity can be found on a side trip 2 miles south of town; just off the northeast corner of SW 204th Street and Vashon Highway SW, discover a short trail into the woods that leads to a bike encased in the trunk of a large tree. From town, it's a quick and easy 5 miles to return to the ferry for the 15-minute crossing back to Fauntleroy.

MILEAGE LOG

0.0 Depart ferry uphill.
2.0 Right onto SW Cedarhurst Rd.
4.2 Road curves left and becomes Westside Hwy. SW.
8.5 Road curves right and becomes Cemetery Rd. briefly.
8.8 Continue forward as road again becomes Westside Hwy. SW.
10.3 Right onto SW 220th St.
10.5 Left onto Wax Orchard Rd. SW.

14.1 Left onto Vashon Hwy. SW.

17.2 Right onto SW Burton Dr. for a short peninsula loop.

17.7 Right onto 97th Ave. W., which becomes SW Bay View Dr.

19.5 Right back onto SW Burton Dr. to return to main road.

19.9 Right onto Vashon Hwy SW.

20.9 Right onto SW Quartermaster Dr.

22.4 Right onto Dockton Rd SW to ride Maury Island (left to short cut omitting Maury Island).

23.0 Left at Y onto SW Point Robinson Rd. as main road goes right.

24.5 Stay left at intersection with 59th Ave. SW to continue on SW Point Robinson Rd.

25.8 Right to stay on SW Point Robinson Rd. into park.

26.2 Arrive at Point Robinson Park. Retrace route to depart park.

26.7 At intersection with SW Point Robinson Rd, stay right to turn onto SW Luana Beach Rd.

29.2 Right to return to SW Point Robinson Rd.

30.0 At intersection with Dockton Rd SW, stay right to continue back to Vashon. Road becomes Dockton.

30.6 At intersection with Quartermaster, stay right to stay on Dockton, which becomes Chataqua Beach Rd SW at mile **31.7**.

31.9 Left onto SW 204th St., which becomes Ridge Rd. at mile **32.1**.

33.5 Road curves left and becomes SW 184th St.

33.7 At a T where 184th ends, turn right on Beal Rd. SW.

34.2 Left onto SW Bank Rd.

34.7 Right onto Vashon Hwy. SW.

39.8 Arrive at ferry dock to end tour.

Opposite: S'Kallam totem pole and longhouse in Little Boston

25 Port Orchard

DIFFICULTY: easy
TOTAL TIME: allow 3 hours
TOTAL DISTANCE: 30.9 miles
TOTAL ELEVATION GAIN: 360 feet

Driving directions: From I-5, take exit 163, West Seattle Bridge, and follow it west. Continue into West Seattle on Fauntleroy Wy. SW as bridge ends. Follow Fauntleroy as it curves left, then right, past Lincoln Park to reach ferry parking. Use north lot farthest from ferry, except on Sunday, when closer lot may be used. After parking, cycle 0.2 mile south on Fauntleroy to ferry dock.

The creaking of ferry pilings as the big boat snuggles up to the dock is a familiar sound to cyclists who head across Puget Sound for

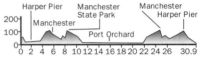

relaxing rides on the Kitsap Peninsula. Bicyclists are first on and first off the ferry—unless you arrive at the last minute—and get a front-row view of docking procedures. Disembarking at Southworth, on the far side of the Vashon Island run from West Seattle, riders are treated to one of the few ferry landings that does not require a steep uphill charge right off the dock. It's a mellow beginning for a ride that is equally relaxing throughout. Hills are few and small on this 30-mile spin along the shore toward Bremerton.

Accessibility and a moderate climate make this waterfront property desirable, so the ride passes a great variety of homes, from a surprising number of modest bungalows to the occasional luxury vacation home. At 2 miles, slip through a hidden passage to continue along the water at Harper Pier. An enjoyable early stop can be had here for an espresso at the quirky, tiny coffee shop while you watch people fishing or scuba-diving off the pier. On the café's water side, find a foot trail around overgrown bushes that leads to a one-lane road serving the homes along the beach. The road dead-ends at the bushes behind the café but connects on the other end to allow for continuous riding.

Another quaint side road exists on the outbound leg of this tour. After riding Colchester Drive SE for about a mile, veer right onto Miracle Mile Drive East for a brief jaunt (0.3 mile—perhaps that's the miracle) along a scenic side road.

Manchester provides the next diversion, where you can turn off the route toward the water and find a grocery store, pleasure-boat docks, a small park, and great views of downtown Seattle and the shipping traffic heading to Bremerton.

Just beyond the town and the fenced U.S. Navy fuel supply depot is Manchester State Park, worth a short trip down its side road. The park, alongside Clam Bay's small cove, housed a defensive military installation, the remnants of which still exist. At the picnic area you'll see a mining casement and former torpedo warehouse (now a picnic shelter), and if you continue down the old road east, you'll find a cement battery nestled among the trees. From that point, looking north across Rich Passage to Bainbridge Island, you'll realize the strategic placement of these defenses when you see the location of matching batteries among the trees at Fort Ward State Park.

Manchester State Park is also part of the Cascadia Marine Trail, so you may spot kayakers traveling and camping along this route. Offshore is Blake Island, also part of the Cascadia Marine Trail.

Next stop: Port Orchard, after a lovely 5-mile ride along the water, with views north and west over small bays and inlets. The town of Port Orchard has a relaxing marina at which to have a picnic or just kick back and watch the boat traffic in and out of Bremerton harbor. The Puget Sound Naval Shipyard is visible just across the bay.

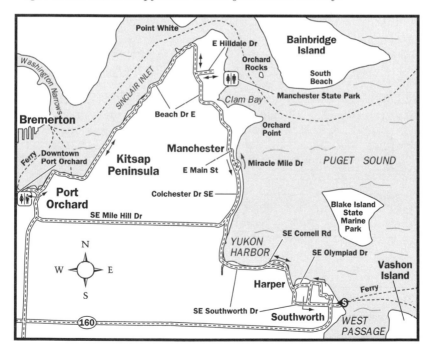

A cyclist's inspiration along flat, scenic Sinclair Inlet

A passenger ferry connects this port to Bremerton, so you can extend the tour if desired: For a longer return to your car, you could ride this ferry to Bremerton, then get on the one-hour Bremerton-Seattle run and cycle back to West Seattle from downtown Seattle's Coleman Dock (an additional 13 miles). On this tour, simply enjoy the laid-back feel of Port Orchard, try the bakery or check out the antique shops, then head back along the water to retrace your steps to Southworth. This ride gets a nomination as the one most likely to put the tang of rotting seaweed into your nose as it delivers some of the best coastal riding around Puget Sound.

MILEAGE LOG

0.0 Exit ferry onto SE Southworth Dr.

0.3 Just beyond grocery store and post office, right onto SE Cherry St.

0.7 Right onto SE Olympiad Dr.

1.1 After road curves, right to stay on Olympiad.

1.5 As Olympiad ends, right onto SE Southworth Dr.

2.0 Exit road at Harper Pier. Use foot trail to right of small café, walk bike around street-end barrier, continue on SE Cornell Rd.

2.6 Right onto SE Southworth Dr.

3.5 Right onto Yukon Harbor Dr. SE.

4.4 Right onto Colchester Dr. SE.

5.3 Right onto Miracle Mile Dr. E.

5.6 Right onto Colchester Dr. E.

5.8 Left onto E. Main St. in Manchester. (On the right at intersection are grocery and town park.)

5.9 Right onto Beach Dr. E.

7.9 Right onto E. Hilldale Rd. toward Manchester State Park.

8.2 Enter park.

8.8 Arrive at park picnic area, restrooms. Ride an additional **0.2** mile to park battery. Retrace route to Beach Dr. E.

10.1 Right onto Beach Dr. E.

15.7 Arrive at Westbay Center in Port Orchard. Turn right onto Bay St. at stoplight.

16.3 Arrive at Port Orchard marina and bay. Retrace route onto Bay St. to return.

16.9 Left onto Beach Dr. E.

24.6 Left onto E. Main St. in Manchester.

24.8 Right onto Colchester Dr. E.

26.5 Left on Yukon Harbor Dr. SE.

27.4 Left onto SE Southworth Dr.

28.4 Left onto SE Cornell Rd.

29.0 Exit Cornell by walking bike around street-end barrier at Harper Pier. Continue forward on SE Southworth Dr.

29.5 Left onto SE Olympiad Dr.

29.9 Right onto Nokomis Rd SE.

30.3 Left onto SE Southworth Dr.

30.9 Arrive at ferry to end tour.

26 Bremerton to Seabeck and Scenic Beach

~~~~~~

DIFFICULTY: strenuous
TOTAL TIME: allow 4.5 hours
TOTAL DISTANCE: 37 miles
TOTAL ELEVATION GAIN: 2760 feet

Driving directions: From I-5 southbound, take exit 164 (northbound, exit 164B) and proceed down off-ramp to 4th Ave. S. Turn right on 4th Ave. S., then right on S. Royal Brougham Wy. in 1

block. Turn right onto Alaskan Wy. S.; Washington State Ferries'
Coleman Dock at Pier 52 is 1.2 miles ahead. No parking at terminal; park in paid lots or at on-street meters.

Kitsap County is a great place to get away, and this tour takes riders
along a road less traveled than some of the northern county routes.
Explore the naval town of Bremerton, loop around Dyes Inlet, and ride
out to the western side of the county to the tiny village of Seabeck and
a secluded beach park. There are a few good hills on this tour and some
roads with no shoulders, but the traffic is relatively low and the scenic
value is high.

Bremerton, as home of the Puget Sound Naval Shipyard, seems to
be awash in navy-gray paint. On the ferry ride into port, view the USS
Turner Joy, a destroyer berthed at a waterfront pier and open for touring. Downtown Bremerton is experiencing a bit of a rejuvenation, and
it merits a visit too. A naval museum, historical museum, and downtown boardwalk are worth a look, and more small shops are opening
near the ferry.

Depart Kitsap County's largest city by skirting the south edge of
Dyes Inlet and the north edge of Kitsap Lake as you head inland along
the Seabeck Highway. The rolling hills and seemingly endless forest
give way to the tiny town of Seabeck, on the east shore of Hood Canal.
A cluster of shops alongside the quiet bay, including a café, pizza place,
well-stocked general store, and espresso stand, provide ample provisions for a lunch at the nearby town park, or have lunch in the village
and enjoy the comings and goings of locals.

The town began as an early logging settlement, known as Kah-mogk
("Quiet Waters") by Native Americans. A sawmill was begun in 1866
and operated until 1882, at which time mill operations were moved to
Port Hadlock farther north on the canal.

Just 2 miles farther is Scenic Beach State Park, which was the homestead of Joe Emel Sr., before becoming a state park. Now Emel House,
home of the Seabeck Community Club, sits between a grassy lawn and
a bluff overlooking a pebbly beach. Colorful gardens and lush forest
surround it. Across the canal, close enough to chart a climbing path,

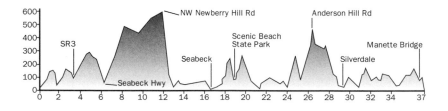

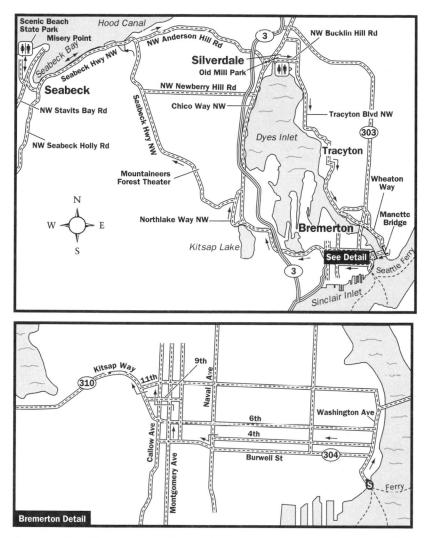

the stunning Olympic peaks loom. It's a quiet place for viewing wildlife and sealife or simply contemplating two of Washington's finest natural wonders: salt water and craggy mountains.

Reluctantly depart Scenic Beach by returning through Seabeck. The route takes riders back through Silverdale and along a nice waterfront drive on the east side of Dyes Inlet. However, the first section involves some impressive hills that must be climbed; to avoid such exertion, you could retrace the outbound route. The main route tackles Anderson Hill Road, so get ready for repeated climbs in the first few miles beyond

Scenic Beach

Seabeck, which moderate as you get closer to Silverdale, then mostly disappear as you ride along Puget Sound.

At Silverdale, a comfort stop can be taken at Old Mill Park, a roadside county park marking the north edge of the inlet. The tour's last leg takes you south through the Tracyton community, along a road signed as a Blue Star Memorial Highway route. These highways, designated throughout the country since World War II, are dedicated to men and women who served in our armed forces. The blue star refers to the star on the flag of the armed services. Often the roads have been chosen for their scenic nature, and this one lives up to the designation.

End the tour by joining the cars crossing the Manette Bridge into downtown Bremerton. This old bridge has no shoulder or walkway, so command a lane and ride with the cars on the short crossing. It is necessary to ride the sidewalk against traffic on one-way Washington Avenue for the last two blocks, or follow the "ferry traffic" signs a few additional blocks to return to the big boat.

MILEAGE LOG

0.0 Exit ferry dock onto Washington Ave.

0.3 Left onto 4th St.

1.4 Left onto Naval Ave., then right in 2 blocks onto Burwell St.

1.7 Right onto Montgomery Ave.

2.0 Left onto 9th St., then in 1 block right onto Callow Ave.

2.2 Left onto 11th St.

2.3 Right onto Kitsap Wy./SR 310.

3.6 Cross under SR 3; continue forward.

5.3 Left onto Northlake Wy. NW. Caution: busy intersection; use left turn lane.

6.5 Left at Y onto Seabeck Hwy. NW. Caution: railroad tracks with bad angle just ahead.

7.5 Pass Mountaineers Forest Theater on the right.

11.7 Cross intersection with NW Newberry Hill Rd.; service station on the right.

12.5 Pass intersection with NW Anderson Hill Rd.

16.6 Arrive at Seabeck.

17.2 Right onto Miami Beach Rd. NW.

17.5 Stay right at Y with Seaview Dr.

18.1 Left onto Scenic Beach Rd. NW.

18.2 Stay right at Y with NW Stavits Bay Rd.

18.6 Arrive at Scenic Beach State Park. Take first left to Emel House.

18.8 Arrive at Emel House parking. Retrace route to return.

20.5 Left to rejoin Seabeck Hwy. NW.

24.0 Left onto NW Anderson Hill Rd.

28.3 At roundabout just beyond SR 3 underpass, continue on NW Anderson Hill Rd. toward Silverdale.

28.6 Left onto NW Bucklin Hill Rd.

29.1 Arrive at Kitsap County's Old Mill Park.

29.8 Right onto Tracyton Blvd. NW.

33.7 Right to stay on Tracyton Blvd., which becomes Tracyton Beach Rd. NW, then Lebo Blvd., then Campbell Wy.

35.6 Right onto Wheaton Wy.

36.6 Right onto Manette Bridge to downtown Bremerton. Caution: busy bridge; no shoulder.

36.8 Left onto Washington Ave.

36.9 Where Washington turns into a one-way, switch to sidewalk for riding last 2 blocks to ferry.

37.0 Arrive at ferry dock to end tour.

27 Bainbridge Island Loop

DIFFICULTY: strenuous
TOTAL TIME: allow 4 hours
TOTAL DISTANCE: 35.4 miles
TOTAL ELEVATION GAIN: 2030 feet

Driving directions: From I-5 southbound, take exit 164 (northbound, exit 164B) and proceed down off-ramp to 4th Ave. S. Turn right on 4th Ave. S., then right on S. Royal Brougham Wy. in 1 block. Turn right onto Alaskan Wy. S.; Washington State Ferries' Coleman Dock at Pier 52 is 1.2 miles ahead. No parking at ferry terminal; park in paid lots or at on-street meters.

You know Bainbridge is bike-friendly as you pedal from the ferry to begin the tour. Kitsap Transit's Bainbridge Island Bike Barn, adjacent to the ferry terminal, offers a number of covered, secure storage units for commuter bicycles as well as some personal-size lockers. You'll also see green bike-route signs regularly along the island roads. Along the tree-covered lanes and beach drives of Bainbridge Island, you'll see a purely Northwest amalgam: a family-centered lifestyle embracing the natural world, in a setting that doesn't get much more ideal.

The tour traces the eastern curves of the island and heads north, but you'll get only occasional glimpses of the water as you head toward Fay Bainbridge State Park, a great place for the first break. The park lies at the northeasternmost point of the island. Welcoming you is the Port Madison Bell, brought from San Francisco in 1883 to be used as a "town crier" for the area, which was then a booming sawmill and shipbuilding area. There are restrooms, picnic tables, and many bleached-white logs on which to contemplate the waves and the view of Seattle. You'll see the green swaths of Discovery Park, Golden Gardens Park, and Carkeek Park, with a low point in between where lie the Ballard locks and Shilshole Bay.

Cut across the top of the island, past Madison Bay toward Agate Passage. As you turn west, the corner of Phelps Road NE and Madison Avenue NE offers a locally famous landmark. Nestled at the base of the trees is "Frog Rock," which looks like two stacked boulders with a crease across the middle. Locals keep the rock covered in frog-green paint, sporting big eyes and a bright red mouth formed by the crease. Cyclists use it as a regrouping point.

Carefully cross busy State Route 305, which connects Winslow with the Agate Passage Bridge and the Kitsap Peninsula, then turn south and you're riding roughly along the island's western edge. Skirt Manzanita Bay and conquer the roller-coaster hills leading to Battle Point Park, another welcome rest stop.

From here, the tour turns inland, along busy Miller and Fletcher Bay roads and past Island Center, which provides a quick return to Winslow if you want to cut the ride shorter. Return by turning left onto NE New Brooklyn Road, then making a right on Madison Avenue NE, which leads to Winslow Way. But continuing to the south part of the island offers a few alluring sights and one more hilly challenge.

Lynwood Center Road NE leads to NE Baker Hill Road, which is one

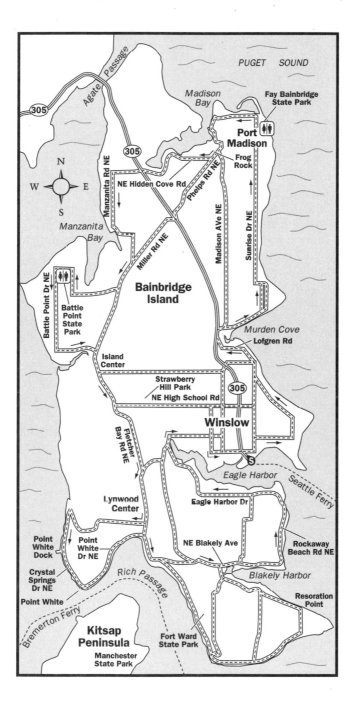

Frog Rock is a common meeting point for cyclists riding Bainbridge Island.

of the most difficult big climbs of Bainbridge, worth the effort because of the wonderful western waterfront riding along Point White beyond. If you've had enough of big hills, skip the climb and still get the beach ride by continuing south to the Lynwood Center shopping area and, just before the business strip, make a right onto Point White Drive NE, ride out to the Point White Dock, and return.

In any case, cross back east across the island at Lynwood Center, skipping the very southernmost points of the island (which can be ridden on Tour 28, Winslow to Fort Ward). Skirt the south edge of IslandWood, an incredible nonprofit environmental learning center, then ride through a hilly neighborhood on the island's east edge before reentering Winslow via Eagle Harbor.

MILEAGE LOG

0.0 Exit ferry ramp; move to right lane.
0.2 Right onto Winslow Wy. E.
0.4 Left onto Ferncliff Ave. NE.
0.6 Right onto Wing Point Wy NE.
1.3 Left onto Park Ave. NE, which becomes Grand Ave.
2.6 Right onto Ferncliff Ave. NE, which becomes Lofgren Rd.
3.5 Curve right to join Moran Rd. NE.
3.8 Right onto Manitou Beach Dr. NE.
3.9 Take right fork in road to stay on Manitou Beach Dr. NE.
4.7 Left onto Falk Rd. NE.
5.2 Left onto NE Valley Rd.
5.4 Right onto Sunrise Dr. NE.
8.2 Right into Fay Bainbridge State Park.
8.5 Arrive at parking area, beach, water, and restrooms. Retrace route to road.
9.0 Exit park by turning right onto Sunrise Dr. NE, which curves left to become Lafayette Ave.
9.7 Left onto Euclid Ave.
10.1 Left onto Phelps Rd. NE.

10.4 Pass by "Frog Rock," at intersection of Phelps and Madison Ave. NE.
10.7 Right onto NE Hidden Cove Rd.
12.4 Cross SR 305. Caution: traffic at highway speeds.
12.9 Left onto Manzanita Rd. NE, which becomes Doris Ave. NE, then NE Bergman Rd.
14.3 Right onto Peterson Hill Rd. NE.
14.8 Right onto Miller Rd. NE.
15.3 Right onto NE Arrow Point Dr., which curves north.
16.3 Arrive at Battle Point State Park. Restrooms, water available.
16.4 Exit park by turning left onto NE Arrow Point Dr.
16.6 Left onto NE Frey Ave.
16.9 Left onto Battle Point Dr. NE., which curves east.
19.0 Right onto Miller Rd., which becomes Fletcher Bay Rd. NE.
21.5 Right onto Lynwood Center Rd. NE.
22.4 Right onto NE Baker Hill Rd.
24.0 Left onto Crystal Springs Dr. NE. Caution: stop sign at end of descent.
24.8 Arrive at Point White dock. Past southern tip of Point White, road becomes Point White Dr. NE.
27.2 Right onto Pleasant Beach Dr. NE.
27.9 Left onto NE Oddfellows Rd.
28.4 Merge right onto NE Blakely Ave.
29.2 At five-way intersection, go straight across and uphill onto NE Halls Hill Rd., which becomes Rockaway Beach Rd. NE, then NE Eagle Harbor Dr./Eagledale Rd.
33.7 Road curves right and becomes Wyatt Wy. NW. Hill climb.
34.4 Right onto Grow Ave. NW.
34.7 Left onto Winslow Wy. W.
35.2 Right onto Olympic Dr. SE toward ferry dock.
35.4 Arrive at ferry to end tour.

28 Winslow to Fort Ward

DIFFICULTY: moderate
TOTAL TIME: allow 2 hours
TOTAL DISTANCE: 21.6 miles
TOTAL ELEVATION GAIN: 970 feet

Driving directions: From I-5 southbound, take exit 164 (northbound, exit 164B) and proceed down off-ramp to 4th Ave. S. Turn right on 4th Ave. S., then right on S. Royal Brougham Wy. in 1 block. Turn right onto Alaskan Wy. S.; Washington State Ferries' Coleman Dock at Pier 52 is 1.2 miles ahead. No parking at ferry terminal; park in paid lots or at on-street meters.

Tackling the entire breadth of Bainbridge Island is a full-day affair suitable for strong legs and lungs, but a jaunt around the island's south end can be handled 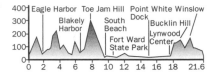 with much less time and effort. However, its challenges are still best met by a cyclist with at least moderate experience and ability. This tour explores the island's southern waterfront areas and offers views of Rich Passage, Bremerton, and the verdant hills of the Kitsap Peninsula beyond. It's a great summer morning's ride to be followed by an alfresco lunch in Winslow, or it could be planned as a picnic ride to Fort Ward.

Cycle in and out of Winslow via Wyatt Way. The outbound route

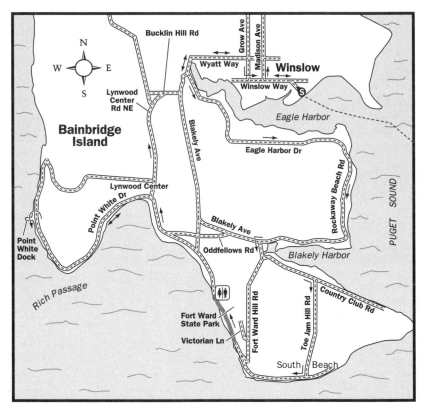

Relaxing on the beach is a Bainbridge Island pleasure.

reverses the full island tour (see Tour 27) by heading south along Eagle Harbor Drive and the island's eastern edge. Here, stylish houses crowd the bluffs above the bay, offering only glimpses of their million-dollar views of Seattle. Prepare for an abrupt and steep hill climb, which comes quickly as Rockaway Beach Drive turns west and becomes Halls Hill Road.

Although you don't see it, you're cycling around the inlet of Blakely Harbor before heading toward South Beach, first by climbing Country Club Road, then by screaming down Toe Jam Hill Road. Prepare for some hard braking toward the bottom, and be glad you're not huffing up this curving, wooded grade.

At the bottom of the hill lies South Beach, and you're rewarded with a waterfront spin at the island's southernmost point. First you're waterside, and the modest homes that brave this briny face are to your right. Then the road jogs up half a block, and the houses sit between you and the water. Soon you arrive at the ramparts of Fort Ward, accessed via a short gravel connector.

Fort Ward displays the remains of Battery Vinton, one of the four gun batteries installed at the fort at the end of the 1800s. The plan was to protect the Bremerton Naval Shipyard from enemy ships with forts that began farther north, at Port Townsend and Whidbey Island. Fort Ward was a second line of defense. The water beyond, which contained an underwater minefield, was the third protection.

From the boat dock and picnic area in Fort Ward State Park, pause to look across the demined passage to the greenery of Manchester State Park and, just south of it, the U.S. Navy's fuel depot at Orchard Point. Picturing the Bremerton ferry that navigates this narrow passage as an enemy frigate, it's easy to see how such a ship would be a sitting duck from gun batteries on each side and mines lurking below.

The guns were never used against an enemy, however, and were removed from Fort Ward in 1920 and sent to France, expected to be needed in World War I. Along with Forts Casey, Flagler, and Worden, Fort Ward sits as a reminder that preparation is the best defense.

A short road, closed to car traffic, cuts through the west edge of Fort Ward, near the shoreline, then exits onto Pleasant Beach Drive as you head north toward Lynwood Center. Another look at waterfront living is afforded with an out-and-back ride to Point White Dock, a public fishing area on the island's southwest edge. The flat road hugs the coastline, providing great views across to Bremerton; stately homes face the road and water. The tour concludes by climbing Bucklin Hill, dropping back to Eagle Harbor, and then rising again into Winslow.

MILEAGE LOG

0.0 Exit ferry; merge to left lane near stoplight.

0.3 Left onto Winslow Wy.

0.6 Right onto Madison Ave.

0.9 Left onto Wyatt Wy., which becomes Eagle Harbor Dr. as it curves left.

1.9 Merge into left lane; turn left at Y to stay on Eagle Harbor Dr. Caution: congested area, busy road with fast downhill traffic.

4.6 Eagle Harbor Dr. becomes Rockaway Beach Dr., which becomes Halls Hill Rd.

7.0 Left onto Country Club Rd.

7.9 Right onto Toe Jam Hill Rd. Caution: steep downhill; use moderate speed.

9.3 Curve right onto South Beach Dr.

10.2 At intersection with Fort Ward Hill Rd., go straight into waterfront housing development.

10.3 At street end, go straight onto brief gravel road into park, then left onto paved park road.

10.6 Arrive at Fort Ward State Park picnic area.

11.0 Exit park onto Pleasant Beach Dr. NE.

11.8 Stay left at Y with W. Blakely Ave. to continue on Pleasant Beach Dr.

12.0 Left onto Lynwood Center Rd. NE at intersection with Oddfellows Rd.

12.7 Left onto Point White Dr. NE.

15.1 Arrive at Point White Dock. Reverse route to return to Lynwood Center.

17.5 Left onto Lynwood Center Rd. NE.

18.7 Merge right onto Bucklin Hill Rd. at stop sign.

18.9 Left at stop sign to continue on Bucklin Hill Rd.

19.2 Merge left onto Eagle Harbor Dr. Caution: busy intersection.

19.3 Curve right, then road becomes Wyatt Wy. NW.

19.9 Right onto Grow Ave.

20.5 Left onto Winslow Wy.

21.4 Right onto Olympic Dr. to ferry.

21.6 Arrive at ferry dock to end tour.

29 Point No Point and Little Boston

DIFFICULTY: moderate
TOTAL TIME: allow 3 hours
TOTAL DISTANCE: 27.9 miles
TOTAL ELEVATION GAIN: 1270 feet

Driving directions: From I-5, take exit 177, Edmonds, and proceed west on SR 104. Continue on SR 104, which becomes Edmonds Wy. Follow signs to parking at Washington State Ferries dock, or choose day parking at fringes of downtown Edmonds and cycle to ferry. Route begins at Kingston end of ferry ride.

This spin out to Point No Point Lighthouse from Kingston provides some moderate challenges and interesting sights in a fairly short ride. It's a good option if your group gets a late start at the ferry or if you want to combine a Kitsap Peninsula ride with a city ride, such as Green Lake to Edmonds (Tour 5).

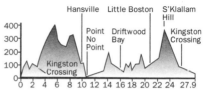

Begin and end in friendly, accessible Kingston, which offers a variety of shops, cafés and pubs, as well as a lively Saturday-morning farmers market in the park adjacent to the ferry dock. If you're aiming for a

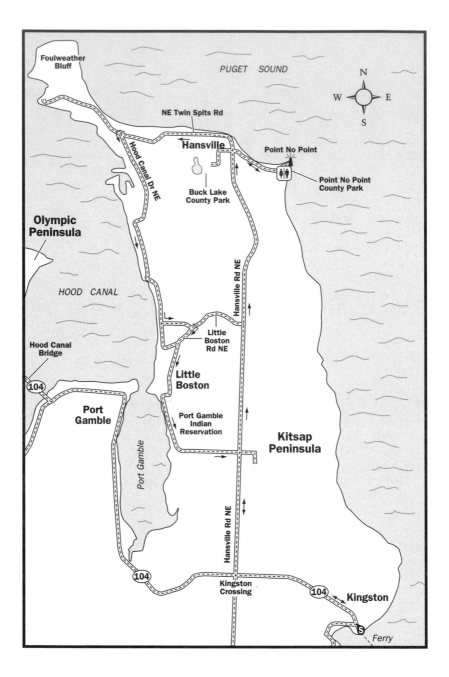

picnic lunch at the beach by the lighthouse, you can carry it from Kingston, stop at the grocery at Kingston Crossing as you turn toward Hansville, or pick up deli sandwiches at the small grocery in Hansville.

The Hansville Road offers rolling hills and pleasant scenery of farms, forests, and a couple small lakes, but the country idyll is marred by lack of shoulder on its northern half and a fairly steady stream of vehicles, including the occasional gravel truck or semi. You pass Point No Point Casino, operated by the S'Klallam Tribe, whose community center you'll ride through on the return trip. Other roadside attractions include Buck Lake County Park and the young vineyards of the Hansville Winery.

As you reach Hansville, a right turn takes you 1 mile down a dead-end road to the lighthouse and beach. Continue a few hundred yards past the turn to shop at the modest grocery.

The small, well-maintained lighthouse, white with red trim and roofs, looks over a curving point on Puget Sound that is a popular fishing destination, both for casting from the beach and from boats moored offshore. Trails take you through the scrubby beach vegetation to explore the county park. Whidbey Island is visible across Admiralty Inlet.

Continuing around this northern tip of the Kitsap Peninsula, churn through the roller-coaster hills west of Hansville. A short detour up NE Twin Spits Road takes you to the Nature Conservancy property near Foulweather Bluff, where a half-mile trail hike on left in ¼ mile

The lighthouse at Point No Point

leads to a stunning beach. Then head south, through the "covenanted" community of Driftwood Bay and the houses overlooking Hood Canal Bridge at Cliffside before coming to Little Boston.

Plan some time for a visit with the S'Kallams, who have an extensive community center complex here at Port Gamble Indian Reservation. A recently completed longhouse boasts four carved totem poles depicting traditional tribal activities, as well as massive 12-foot-tall doors carved with tribal history that slide to open the cavernous space for gatherings and events. A popular time to ride this tour is the weekend in mid-September when the tribe hosts S'Klallam Days, which has traditional dancing, crafts, and food.

Does it seem strange that the center of a Washington Indian reservation is named Little Boston? Early settlers found that the adjacent waterway reminded them so much of Boston Harbor, they named it such, and it stuck. Here, you're more likely to be served wild rice than baked beans with your smoked salmon, however.

This short but interesting loop holds one challenge on the return to Kingston: S'klallam Hill. A long, steady grade keeps you churning as you head back toward Hansville Road. Topping the hill, you retrace the remaining route to downtown Kingston.

MILEAGE LOG

0.0 Depart ferry dock onto Kingston Rd.

0.5 Stay right to continue out of Kingston west on SR 104.

2.7 Right onto Hansville Rd. NE at Kingston Crossing.

9.7 Arrive at Hansville.

10.5 Right onto NE Point No Point Rd.

11.5 Arrive at Point No Point County Park and lighthouse. Retrace route to main road.

12.7 Right to continue north on Hansville Rd. NE, which curves west and becomes NE Twin Spits Rd.

15.0 Left onto Hood Canal Dr. NE. (Continue straight ahead for side trip to Foulweather Bluff.)

15.7 Arrive at Driftwood Bay.

16.8 Left at stop sign to stay on Hood Canal Dr. NE.

17.8 Caution: road drops and curves, then heads sharply uphill.

18.9 Left onto NE Cliffside Rd. Caution: steep climb.

19.5 Right onto Little Boston Rd. NE.

21.0 Arrive at S'Kallam Tribe's community center and longhouse.

22.3 Road curves, then begins long climb east.

23.2 Right onto Hansville Rd. NE.

25.4 Left onto SR 104.

27.9 Arrive at ferry dock to end tour.

30   Port Gamble and Poulsbo

DIFFICULTY: moderate
TOTAL TIME: allow 3.5 hours
TOTAL DISTANCE: 33.4 miles
TOTAL ELEVATION GAIN: 1225 feet

> **Driving directions:** From I-5, take exit 177, Edmonds, and proceed
> west on SR 104. Continue on SR 104, which becomes Edmonds Wy.
> Follow signs to parking at Washington State Ferries dock, or choose
> day parking at fringes of downtown Edmonds and cycle to ferry.
> Route begins at Kingston end of ferry ride.

Gain a great historic perspective on early settlement of the area in this
33-mile ride that loops west and south from Kingston, a short ferry
ride across Puget Sound from Edmonds. Travel through rolling hills to
small but significant port towns, including an early logging town and
a Scandinavian invasion, and the last resting place of a great Native
American chief.

Begin the tour on the broad shoulder of State Route 104 heading
west toward the Hood Canal Bridge. First stop is Port Gamble, just
before the bridge. Cycle past well-kept Victorian-type homes as you
enter town, and continue straight into its small town center as the
road curves left. Nearly all the shops are visible from the turn, as the
town extends less than two blocks to the hills overlooking the bay.
Within those few blocks, however, sits a miniature history of area
settlement.

Port Gamble is and always has been a mill town. Like many small
towns along Hood Canal, it served the lumber barons who served an
insatiable appetite for wood by settlers flocking to western cities.
Pioneer lumbermen Andrew Pope and William Talbot came up from
San Francisco looking for logging opportunities and created a company
town at this strategic point. The timber mill, which began operating in
the mid-1800s, was shut down in 1995. What remains today is a town
still wholly owned by Pope and Talbot, housing perhaps 100 residents.

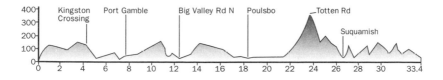

Economic efforts have turned to tourism, and the well-preserved town now has a row of antique shops to accompany its unique general store and an excellent historical museum. Upstairs in the store is a free Of Sea and Shore Museum, which displays crabs, fish, shark teeth, and what claims to be the world's largest collection of seashells. The lower level of the store houses the historical museum, well worth its modest fee.

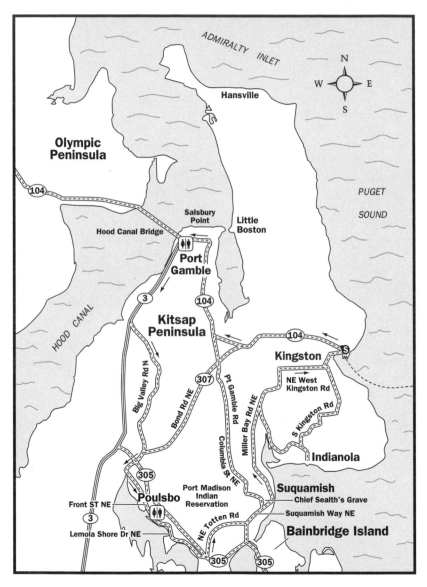

Riders in a cycling event descend briefly on Port Gamble.

Adjacent to Port Gamble is Salsbury Point Park, which offers a great view of the essential Hood Canal Bridge. But don't cross it to the Olympic Peninsula; stay on the Kitsap side.

Head south to Poulsbo via Big Valley Road North, a quiet country highway with small horse farms, a few hay and cattle operations, and much less traffic than the main highway. Located at about halfway through the tour, Poulsbo is a great place for lunch and an extended break.

Poulsbo bills itself as "Washington's little Norway," a statement reinforced by a glance down its main street. The Poulsbohemian Coffee Shop reflects the droll wordplay for which Norwegians are famous. It shares the street with an imposing Sons of Norway lodge. Scandinavian flags vie with overflowing hanging baskets of flowers, and the storefronts are topped with wooden ship's peaks or the floral painted designs known as rosemaling. A Scandinavian bakery, grocery, gift shops, and cafés front a still and scenic harbor on Liberty Bay. This is the Poulsbo never viewed by travelers heading to Olympic National Park or other points west, because the highway skirts the edge of town.

From Poulsbo, drop down along the bay before heading east, crossing busy State Route 305 just west of the Agate Pass Bridge that connects to Bainbridge Island. Follow the coastal road to Old Man House Park and the grave of Chief Sealth, the wise and welcoming Suquamish chief for whom Seattle is named. From behind the painted longboats that are hoisted on pillars around his grave, you can see across the bay to his namesake city.

Climb inland from Suquamish and head north back to Kingston along Miller Bay Road NE, a busy thoroughfare with a comfortable cycling shoulder. (For more of a challenge, ride to Indianola, Tour 31.) Riding the comfortable bike lane on the last leg into Kingston, pass two schools serving the expanding town.

MILEAGE LOG

0.0 Depart ferry dock onto Kingston Rd.

0.5 Stay right to continue out of Kingston west on SR 104.

4.2 Stay right on SR 104 to continue to Port Gamble.

7.9 Arrive at Port Gamble.

8.2 Highway curves, but continue straight for 1 block to town center.

8.7 Return to SR 104 to continue.

9.5 Arrive at intersection where SR 104 continues over Hood Canal Bridge; stay straight on SR 3. Caution: traffic at highway speeds, but good shoulder.

12.6 Left onto Big Valley Rd. N. Caution: busy crossing.

17.7 Right onto Bond Rd. NE.

17.9 Cross SR 305 at stoplight. Caution: busy crossing.

18.4 Left onto Front St. NE at Y with NW Lindvig Wy.

19.2 Right at intersection with Jensen Wy. NE to continue on Front St., which becomes Anderson Pkwy.

19.4 Right onto Fjord Dr. NE, which becomes Lemola Shore Dr. NE and, briefly, Peterson Wy. NE.

22.7 Cross SR 305, after which your road becomes NE Totten Rd. Caution: busy crossing.

25.0 Left onto Suquamish Wy. NE at Y where Totten ends.

25.8 Left onto Division Ave. NE.

25.9 Right onto Totem Ln., 1 block to cemetery containing Chief Sealth's grave. Depart cemetery by turning left back onto Totem.

26.1 Left onto Suquamish Wy. in 1 block.

26.2 Suquamish curves left at town center and becomes Augusta Ave. NE. which becomes Miller Bay Rd. NE.

31.1 Right onto NE West Kingston Rd.

32.7 Left at Y to continue on NE West Kingston into town.

33.3 Right onto Central Ave.

33.4 Left at parking by ferry to end tour.

31 Indianola and Chief Sealth's Grave

DIFFICULTY: moderate
TOTAL TIME: allow 2.5 hours
TOTAL DISTANCE: 18.8 miles
TOTAL ELEVATION GAIN: 1080 feet

> **Driving directions:** From I-5, take exit 177, Edmonds, and proceed west on SR 104. Continue on SR 104, which becomes Edmonds Wy. Follow signs to parking at Washington State Ferries dock, or choose day parking at fringes of downtown Edmonds and cycle to ferry. Route begins at Kingston end of ferry ride.

This short tour from the Kingston ferry dock loops through the rolling hills just south of town and offers stops at the old port landing of Indianola, a salmon hatchery,

and the grave of Chief Sealth, after whom Seattle is named. Try this tour if you don't have a lot of time, or add it on to the Point No Point ride (Tour 29) or Poulsbo ride (Tour 30) if you're filling an afternoon.

As you depart Kingston, pass Arness Roadside Park, a small bayside park with views of the ferry arrivals and departures across the shallows of Appletree Cove. Next to it on private land sits a restored Burlington Northern caboose. The road turns inland and takes you along a forested suburban road, growing busier with a spate of development.

At 5 miles you arrive at Indianola, a small community with one retail business: the inevitable friendly grocery and deli. One block from the store is a private beach and public dock with a storied history. The dock was first constructed in 1916 to deliver ferry service to the area, which lasted until 1951. More recently, the dock was replaced as a pedestrian and fishing pier. From the end of its long walkway is a great view of the container ships, ferries, and cruise ships plying Puget Sound.

Depart Indianola by climbing a short series of hills through this quiet, well-kept residential area. Just before turning onto Miller Bay Road NE, make a stop at the Grover Street Salmon Hatchery, operated by the Suquamish Tribe. Visitors are welcome to walk the grounds and watch the big fish aim for the stream of water coming from a pipe in the small pond. The low-technology operation is worth a look.

The next stop provides another look at the area's heritage. Cycle down into the burg of Suquamish and climb the short hill to visit the burial site of Chief Sealth. His ornate white tombstone is marked by two painted longboats raised on pillars and facing Port Madison Bay. Behind the site sits a magnificent, spreading oak to shade his grave.

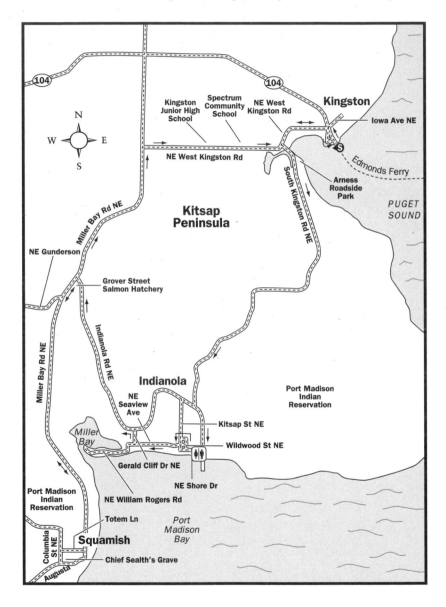

Chief Sealth's grave

Views of Puget Sound and Seattle can be seen beyond the well-kept white church adjacent to the cemetery.

Retrace the route up Miller Bay Road NE, continuing north past Indianola to return to Kingston via a wide bike lane on the road past two of the town's schools. You'll climb a few hills in this short loop, but it is seemly and appropriate to expend some effort to regard the last resting place of a great Native American leader.

MILEAGE LOG

0.0 Depart ferry dock onto Kingston Rd.
0.1 Left onto Iowa Ave. E., which becomes NE West Kingston Rd.
0.6 Left onto South Kingston Rd. NE toward Indianola.
2.9 Left to stay on South Kingston Rd. NE as arterial turns.
4.5 Left onto Indianola Rd. NE.
5.0 Arrive at Indianola town center and dock.
5.1 Right onto NE Shore Dr.

5.2 Right onto Wildwood St. NE, then immediate left onto NE Seaview Ave.

5.8 Right on Gerald Cliff Dr. NE.

6.0 Left onto Indianola Rd NE.

7.7 Arrive at Grover Street Salmon Hatchery.

7.9 Left on Miller Bay Rd. NE, which becomes Augusta Ave. NE as you enter Suquamish.

11.1 Right onto Suquamish Wy. NE at Suquamish town center.

11.2 Right onto Totem Ln., then 1 block to cemetery containing Chief Sealth's grave.

11.4 Depart cemetery by turning left onto Totem Ln. to retrace route.

11.5 Left onto Suquamish Wy. NE.

11.6 Stay on Suquamish as it curves left and becomes Augusta, which becomes Miller Bay Rd. NE.

16.5 Right onto NE West Kingston Rd.

18.1 Left at Y to continue on NE West Kingston into town.

18.7 Right onto Central Ave.

18.8 Left at parking by ferry to end tour.

Opposite: Cyclists exit the ferry onto Shaw Island.

THE ISLANDS

32 South Whidbey Island: Freeland and Langley

DIFFICULTY: strenuous
TOTAL TIME: allow 5 hours
TOTAL DISTANCE: 41.5 miles
TOTAL ELEVATION GAIN: 1910 feet

> **Driving directions:** From I-5 take exit 189, SR 526, and proceed west. Continue on to SR 525, Mukilteo Speedwy., to Mukilteo ferry dock. Paid parking at ferry terminal.

The easiest way to Puget Sound's islands is by bike, as you zip by long lines of car traffic and are ushered first on and off the ferry boats like royalty. At least you might feel royal when you head to such coveted destinations as Whidbey Island atop your shiny two-wheeler. Leave the car behind to sample Whidbey's pleasures on an afternoon ride around the rolling hills of the island's south end. Pop into two small towns, explore a pebbly beach, and find many a quiet side road lined with tall trees or offering views of salt water and mountain peaks.

From the Clinton ferry dock, proceed clockwise around the island's southern bulge, dipping briefly down to the water's edge at Glendale before climbing inland to traverse to the western shore. Ride north along Bayview Road, meeting up with busy State Route 525, which, linked with State Route 20 in the island's north end, comprise the island's arterial highways. Across at this intersection is a business center that includes a bike shop, if needed.

After a brief west stint on the busy road, carefully cross it and head down toward Useless Bay. A side trip would take you to the popular pebbled beach at Double Bluff County Park, where views of Seattle are in the distance and the Kitsap Peninsula's Foulweather Bluff is in the foreground, just across the shipping lanes.

Turn north for a short ride into Freeland, shopping center for the southern island. Skirt the downtown, stopping at the roadside grocery and coffee shop for provisions, then head to the protected town park

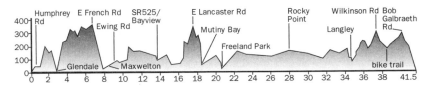

170

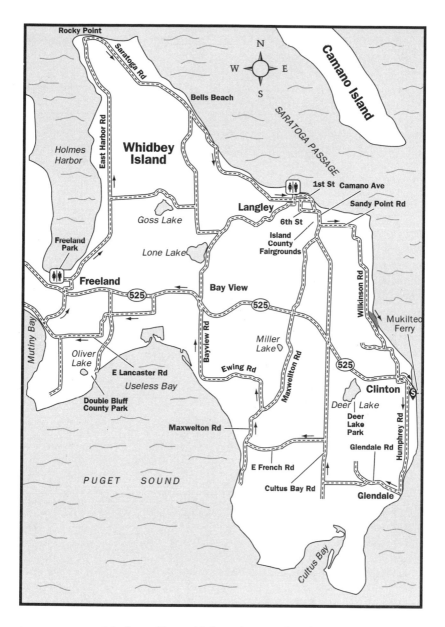

to commune with the gulls amid the salty air of Holmes Harbor. Travel the shady roads north to the round Rocky Point, then gain views of water and Camano Island as you travel south toward Langley.

Word of warning: When you reach Langley, you will probably want to

An amusing entryway sits totem-like in a pasture.

linger. You may check around for a bed for the night (good luck). You'll definitely find plenty to enjoy in this artistic, friendly community. Check out the extensive general store, galleries with local artwork, sidewalk sculptures, and historic eating and drinking establishments. Bear in mind that you still have a few miles to go to finish the tour. If you do plan ahead and stay in Langley for the night at one of the area's many bed-and-breakfasts, you'll find live theater, an old movie house, and many wonderful restaurants at which to cap the day.

The route back to the ferry takes you past an elaborately fenced vineyard before veering off the main road to the old Wilkinson Road, now closed to car traffic. It's a cool, quiet side lane. Upon returning to Clinton, sink your toes into the sandy beach next to the ferry dock while waiting for the boat.

MILEAGE LOG

0.0 Depart ferry onto SR 525.

0.4 Left onto Humphrey Rd.

2.8 Right onto Glendale Rd. as Humphrey Rd. ends.

3.8 Left at Holst Rd. intersection to stay on Glendale Rd.

5.0 Right onto Cultus Bay Rd.

6.1 Left onto E. French Rd.

8.2 Right onto Maxwelton Rd.

9.2 Left onto Ewing Rd., which curves left then right to become Bayview Rd.

13.4 Left onto SR 525. Caution: busy road, but wide shoulder for riding.

14.7 Left onto Useless Bay Ave., which becomes Milliman Rd.

16.2 Milliman becomes Lancaster Rd. as you cross Double Bluff Rd. (Left for side trip to Double Bluff County Park.)

18.2 Lancaster curves and becomes Mutiny Bay Rd.

18.5 Right onto S. Fish Rd.

19.6 Cross SR 525 onto Main St. in Freeland.

19.9 Left onto East Harbor Rd., also signed Stewart Rd.

20.1 Left at Y to stay on Stewart, which becomes Shoreview Dr.

20.4 Arrive at Freeland Park. Restrooms, water, picnic area. Retrace route to East Harbor Rd.

20.8 Left onto East Harbor Rd.

23.3 Pass E. Goss Lake Rd. on the right.

27.5 Arrive at Rocky Point, where the road becomes Saratoga Rd. and curves right.

30.6 Pass Bells Beach on the left.

34.1 Arrive at Langley as Saratoga becomes 2nd St.

34.4 Left onto Park Ave.

34.5 Right onto 1st St. Arrive at viewpoint park, shops, restaurants. Continue east along 1st St. to depart Langley.

34.8 Right onto Cascade Ave. at intersection with 2nd St.

35.0 Left onto Camano Ave. by the unique Langley Motel.

35.5 Left on Sandy Point Rd.

36.3 Right onto Wilkinson Rd.

38.9 Left onto signed bike route, past trail gate.

39.3 Forward onto old Wilkinson Rd. as exiting bike trail.

39.4 Continue through another trail gate onto Zimmerman Rd.

39.8 Left to return to new Wilkinson Rd., which becomes Bob Galbraeth Rd., then S. Hinman Dr.

40.7 Left onto SR 525 into Clinton.

41.5 Arrive at ferry dock to end tour.

33 Central Whidbey Island: Coupeville and Fort Casey

DIFFICULTY: easy
TOTAL TIME: allow 2 hours
TOTAL DISTANCE: 13.6 miles
TOTAL ELEVATION GAIN: 440 feet

Driving directions: To reach Coupeville on Whidbey Island, either take the Mukilteo ferry (see Tour 32), then from Clinton take SR 525 north to SR 20 north, or from I-5 take exit 230, SR 20, and follow SR 20 west to Deception Pass Bridge, then south to Coupeville. Turn north onto NW Broadway Ave., then right onto NW Coveland St. in 0.6 mile. Coupeville Town Park is on the left.

The long crescent of Whidbey Island is most pleasing to cyclists in its center section, from Penn Cove to Admiralty Bay. Here you'll

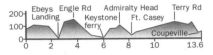

find historic towns, scenic coastline roads, old military installations, and flat, open riding. Nowhere do all these elements come together as nicely as in this Coupeville and Fort Casey loop.

Begin the tour from the Coupeville Town Park. Its free, shady parking is just two blocks from the town's waterfront shops and the island historical museum. Save the town center for last, unless you intend to picnic at Fort Casey State Park, the ride's halfway point. If that's the case, stop at the shops on Front Street or Main before beginning the ride. Snacks also can be purchased at the Keystone ferry landing, which is 0.25 mile from the state park.

Head south out of town on NW Broadway Avenue, taking care when crossing busy State Route 20 to exit town toward Fort Casey. If traffic

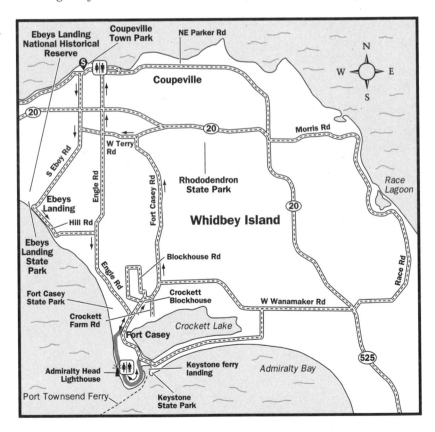

Fort Casey's vast, blooming lawn invites repose.

is especially heavy, detour a couple blocks east to the signal at Main Street. Across the highway, Broadway becomes South Ebey Road, which loops around and drops down briefly along the coast, where you'll find a nice beach and walking trails up to viewpoints at Ebey's Landing National Historical Reserve and State Park. Continue by climbing aptly named Hill Road, then drop down to the entrance to Fort Casey and the Keystone ferry dock beyond.

The old fort offers plentiful scenic areas and picnic spots. The military fortifications—cement bunkers and grassy, covered tunnels—dating from the late nineteenth century—are well worth exploration. Two 10-inch "disappearing" guns are on display atop the battlements, aiming toward the placid shipping lanes of Admiralty Inlet. Nearby, the simple, elegant Admiralty Head Lighthouse provides a high vantage point over the area. The fort's old barracks and administration buildings have been converted into a conference center operated by Seattle Pacific University. Exiting the fort, look for the well-preserved Crockett Blockhouse, a wooden relic by the edge of the road that looks out over the Crockett Farm and Admiralty Bay.

The road back north to Coupeville offers a look at the other side of this flat farm valley, heading back into town via the long Main Street. (Or you can extend the tour by continuing east on West Wanamaker Road and crossing State Route 20 to ride the east edge of the island along Race Road, which leads north, then loop back to Coupeville on

Morris and Parker roads.) On Main, make a stop at the cyclist-friendly Miriam's Coffee Shop before crossing the highway again and heading into the main part of this historic town.

Spend some time exploring Coupeville, Washington's second-oldest town. Its history is clearly on display with the restored homes and buildings that line its few streets. Nautical touches reveal that it was once the home of sea captains. Learn more by picking through the exhibits at the Island County Historical Society Museum, adjacent to which is the Alexander Blockhouse, a protective enclosure dating from the mid-1800s.

End the tour by riding along picturesque Front Street, walking out to the Harbor Store on the Coupeville Wharf, or kicking back at one of the welcoming establishments overlooking famous Penn Cove. For a slight extension, continue west out of Coupeville on NW Madrona Way, a winding waterfront road that overlooks the Penn Cove mussel-farm rafts. The 3.3-mile lane is also a link to Oak Harbor and the Fort Ebey area (see Tour 34).

MILEAGE LOG

0.0 Right onto NW Coveland St. to depart Coupeville Town Park.

0.2 Left onto NW Broadway Ave.

0.7 Cross SR 20. Caution: busy road. Continue south as Broadway becomes S. Ebey Rd.

1.0 As main road curves at Y at W. Terry Rd., right to stay on S. Ebey Rd., which becomes Hill Rd. after curving left at beach.

3.7 Right onto Engle Rd.

5.1 Stay right at intersection with Fort Casey Rd.

5.7 Arrive at entrance to Fort Casey State Park. Continue forward to ferry dock.

6.1 Arrive at Keystone–Port Townsend ferry. Reverse route.

6.6 Left into Fort Casey.

7.0 Arrive at main parking, picnic area. Right to lighthouse.

7.2 Arrive at Admiralty Head lighthouse. Reverse route to exit park.

8.1 Left onto Engle Rd.

8.6 Right at intersection onto S. Fort Casey Rd.

8.9 Pass Crockett Blockhouse.

11.6 Left onto W. Terry Rd.

12.2 Right onto Main St. S.

12.5 Cross SR 20 at signal.

13.2 Left onto Front St. NE.

13.3 Left onto Alexander St. NW as Front St. ends. Museum on the right.

13.4 Right onto NW Coveland St.

13.5 Right at Y to stay on NW Coveland St.

13.6 Arrive at town park to end tour.

34 Central Whidbey Island: Oak Harbor and Fort Ebey

DIFFICULTY: moderate
TOTAL TIME: allow 3 hours
TOTAL DISTANCE: 20.5 miles
TOTAL ELEVATION GAIN: 1220 feet

Driving directions: To reach Oak Harbor on Whidbey Island, either take the Mukilteo ferry (see Tour 32), then from Clinton take SR 525 north to SR 20 north, or from I-5 take exit 230, SR 20, and follow SR 20 west to Deception Pass Bridge, then south to Oak Harbor. Reach intersection of SR 20 and W. Pioneer Wy. From the north, go straight ahead (south) on SW Beeksma Dr.; from the south, turn right on W. Pioneer Wy., then turn right on SW Beeksma Dr. Go 0.2 mile to parking area at city park.

A tour out of bustling Oak Harbor is replete with coastal views. In fact, you get a look at beaches along both sides of Whidbey Island. Although the city of Oak

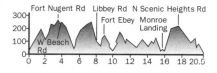

Harbor itself is not included in this tour, the island's largest town deserves some exploring. It's home to a U.S. Navy air base, and you can still see influences of the Dutch people who were the first colonists in the area in the 1850s. A beach walk curves around the harbor from Windjammer Park, adjacent to a developing downtown.

Start at Windjammer Park (formerly City Beach Park) at the south edge of town, easily found just two blocks off SR 20. If you're planning a picnic, stop for provisions at the shopping district along Pioneer Way before leaving town. Except for water and restrooms at Fort Ebey, there are no services on this rural ride.

The tour departs Oak Harbor fairly quickly, climbing along Fort Nugent Road and then cutting across prime farmland. At the intersection with Zylstra Road, the Hummingbird farm and its popular display gardens invite a walk-through. Continue to the island's west coast, where a southbound ride rewards cyclists with stunning views of the Olympics

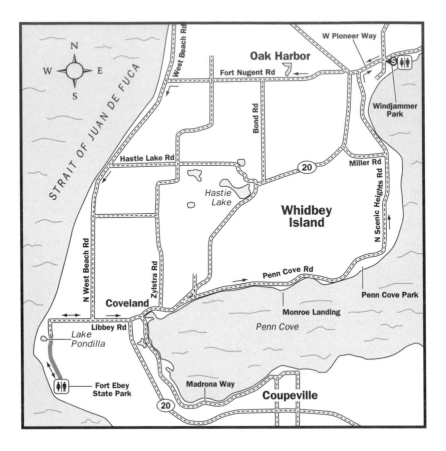

beyond the verdant valleys and glittering Strait of Juan de Fuca.

At nearly 10 miles, arrive at Fort Ebey State Park, the smaller and more recent of the two former military battlements strategically placed on Whidbey to defend the entry to Puget Sound. Fort Casey, a few miles to the south, offers more extensive relics of its defenses—which date to the 1890s—as well as a picturesque lighthouse and extensive open areas for picnicking, kite-flying, and views (see Tour 33).

But Fort Ebey, which was made a military installation during World War II, has its own charms. Hiking and mountain-biking trails snake through the wooded hillsides and to the freshwater Lake Pondilla, and a dirt trail at the end of the road leads to a bicycles-only camping area. Both parks are part of Ebey's Landing National Historical Preserve, managed by the National Park Service.

After a picnic and exploration at the park, return toward Oak Harbor by traveling east to State Route 20. Turn north onto the island's busy "main drag" just south of Madrona Way, the scenic 3.3-mile ride along Penn Cove to Coupeville (see Tour 33). Exit State Route 20 to ride the east edge of the island along much-less-traveled Penn Cove Road, which becomes North Scenic Heights Road, to finish the ride.

This section of the route offers shortcuts available only to those on two wheels. Your first opportunity to join Penn Cove Road comes just as State Route 20 rounds the bay and departs the coastline. There, at the imposing Penn Cove Pottery building, you can slip through a break in the parking lot barriers and drop down to the end of Penn Cove Road, a couple of feet below the parking grade. Then, at the intersection of North Scenic Heights and Miller Roads, a sign warns of a dead end. Don't believe it. The road, which skirts a bluff right by the water, was closed to vehicle traffic, but bikes can again traverse the barriers and continue, rewarded with great views of Oak Harbor and snowy Mount Baker beyond. Such traffic revisions make for quiet, pleasurable riding, enhancing an already excellent central Whidbey excursion.

For more scenic island viewing, you could visit north Whidbey by driving north on State Route 20 to Deception Pass and stop for a hike and tour of its state park and stunning bridge.

A group of Oak Harbor friends cycles around Penn Cove.

MILEAGE LOG

0.0 Exit parking at Windjammer (City Beach) Park onto Beeksma Dr. north toward SR 20.

0.3 Left onto SR 20 at light. Caution: busy intersection.

0.9 Right onto SW Swantown Ave.

1.0 Left onto Fort Nugent Rd.

3.9 Left on N West Beach Rd.

8.0 Right onto Libbey Rd.

8.3 Left onto N. Fort Ebey Rd.

9.0 Right into park.

9.4 Right to beach overlook, trails, restrooms. Gun battery relic on the left.

9.8 Arrive at parking, restrooms. Retrace route to exit park.

10.7 Left to return to Libbey Rd.

10.9 Curve right and stay on main road to retrace route.

11.4 Right onto Libbey Rd.

12.4 Left onto SR 20.

12.6 Cross Madrona Wy.

13.4 Right into parking at Penn Cove Pottery; proceed through barrier to join Penn Cove Rd. Alternate route: Ride to mile **13.5**, turn right onto Holbrook Rd., then left onto Penn Cove Rd. in 1 block.

15.6 Arrive at Monroe Landing, beach and historic marker. Continue forward on Penn Cove Rd.

17.4 Road becomes N Scenic Heights Rd.

18.4 Continue forward at intersection with Miller Rd., ignoring sign saying DEAD END NO OUTLET. Bike access available to continue on N Scenic Heights Rd. into town.

18.7 Traverse street closure barrier.

19.8 Right onto SR 20 into town.

20.2 Right onto SW Beeksma Dr.

20.5 Arrive at parking to end tour.

35 Lopez Island

~~~~~~~~~~~~~~~~~~~~~~~~~~~~~~~~~~~~~~~

DIFFICULTY: moderate
TOTAL TIME: allow 4.5 hours
TOTAL DISTANCE: 37.2 miles
TOTAL ELEVATION GAIN: 1330 feet

Driving directions: Take I-5 north to exit 230; turn left at exit onto SR 20 west to Anacortes. Right onto Commercial Ave., then left onto 12th St., following signs for Washington State Ferries. Paid parking at ferry terminal.

If you're looking for a bike-friendly island ride on quiet roads, Lopez is your mecca. Amiable locals wave from the few cars that pass you along the mostly gentle terrain. This loop explores the island's shoreline parks and mostly avoids the center road, which handles the bulk of car traffic. Although the route loops to and from the ferry, an overnight stay is suggested to really enjoy the island; easy camping locations exist, as well as a number of bed-and-breakfast accommodations.

After the ubiquitous hill climb from the ferry dock, pass the entrance to Odlin County Park. Continue south to Lopez Village, the only town on the island. In a few short blocks, it contains two grocery stores, a bike shop, a bakery, espresso stands, and a few cafés, two of which are open in the evening. Near the village is picturesque Lopez Island Winery, whose wines are available in the shops. Purchase the makings of a picnic lunch here, as additional stops for provisions are few and far between.

Watch for blue herons standing sentinel in the shallows of Fisherman Bay as you exit the village and head south for Shark Reef. Pass the area's second bike shop as you cycle by protected Fisherman Bay. To the right is Otis Perkins County Park, which offers beachcombing and a great view of the village.

Take a lunch break at Shark Reef, which is reached via a 0.25-mile walk through the woods, ducking branches and stepping over tree roots. At the south end of the trail, seals are often visible on the rocky shore. Just across the channel is San Juan Island. You can also save your lunch break for tiny Agate Beach County Park, another stop about halfway through the tour.

Next, venture inland a bit to visit the picturesque Center Church, whose white steeple overlooks the Union Cemetery and an expansive agricultural valley. The church and cemetery date from the 1880s.

At the intersection of Mud Bay Road and MacKaye Harbor Road is Islandale, which has a small grocery and deli, with restrooms. Three miles south is Agate Beach County Park.

After your visit to the island's southern tip, turn north and cycle through the middle of the island, heading for its east shore via quiet Port Stanley Road, where alder trees meet overhead to create a quiet, shady lane.

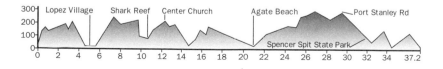

Finally, detour slightly east to Spencer Spit State Park, a popular camp spot for kayakers and bikers. It has restrooms and a historic log cabin. Both Odlin and Spencer Spit are easily attainable destinations for camping, although reservations must be made well ahead. Return to the ferry by looping around Swifts and Shoal Bays, fronted by a small community of shore homes.

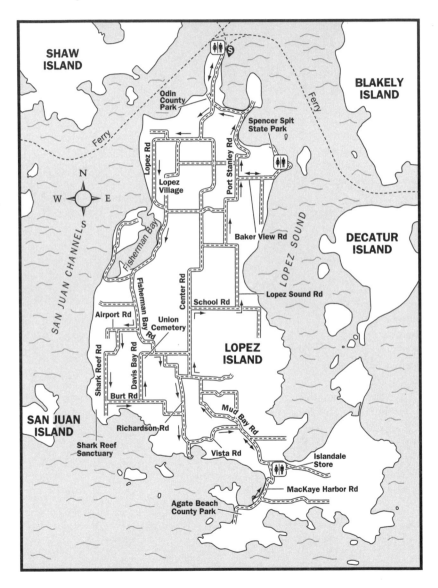

Bicycle recycling, Lopez Island style

MILEAGE LOG

0.0 From ferry dock, head south on Ferry Rd.

1.1 Cross Port Stanley Rd. and pass entrance to Odlin County Park.

2.1 Curve right at intersection with Center Rd. onto Fisherman Bay Rd.

2.6 Right onto Military Rd., which becomes Lopez Rd.

4.6 Arrive at Lopez Village.

4.9 Right onto Fisherman Bay Rd. to depart town center.

5.6 Pass Bayshore Rd. to Otis Perkins County Park.

7.9 Right onto Airport Rd.

8.4 Left onto Shark Reef Rd.

10.3 Arrive at Shark Reef Recreation Site. Depart by returning on Shark Reef Rd. to Burt Rd.

10.6 Right onto Burt Rd.

11.4 Left onto Davis Bay Rd.

12.3 Arrive at Center Church and Lopez Union Cemetery.

12.7 Right onto Fisherman Bay Rd.

13.0 Right onto Kjargaard Rd.

13.8 Right onto Richardson Rd., which becomes Vista Rd. as it curves east.

16.7 Right onto Mud Bay Rd.

17.9 Right onto MacKaye Harbor Rd.

20.8 Arrive at Agate Beach County Park. Depart by returning on MacKaye Harbor Rd. to Mud Bay Rd.

22.2 Left onto Mud Bay Rd., which becomes Center Rd.

26.9 Right onto School Rd., which becomes Lopez Sound Rd.

29.5 Left onto Port Stanley Rd.

31.4 Right onto Baker View Rd.

31.9 Arrive at Spencer Spit State Park. Depart by returning on Baker View Rd. to Port Stanley Rd.

33.4 Right onto Port Stanley Rd.

36.1 Right onto Ferry Rd.

37.2 Arrive at ferry to end tour.

36   Orcas Island

DIFFICULTY: strenuous
TOTAL TIME: allow 3 hours
TOTAL DISTANCE: 22.2 miles
TOTAL ELEVATION GAIN: 1440 feet

> **Driving directions:** Take I-5 north to exit 230; turn left at exit onto SR 20 west to Anacortes. Right onto Commercial Ave., then left onto 12th St., following signs for Washington State Ferries. Paid parking at ferry terminal.

Orcas Island is a conundrum shaped like a horseshoe. On one hand, it provides some of the most beautiful, challenging terrain in the San Juans and some wonderful places to shop, eat, and

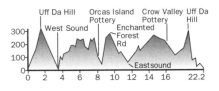

sleep. On the other hand, that tough terrain is made even more so by narrow, winding roads, most of which do not have shoulders, and by drivers who are not as welcoming or tolerant as are those on the other San Juan Islands. It's a combination of factors that, in the end, makes Orcas an island that should be visited only by experienced cyclists who are pretty fit. This tour route provides access to the island's easier half, the west, and leaves you at a jumping-off point if you want to tackle the more challenging east side.

As with all ferry departures, cyclists should pull over as soon as

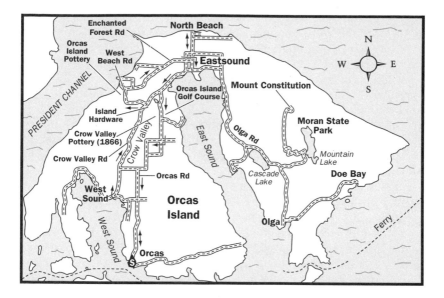

they're clear of the ferry and let the cars depart. It's safer and more efficient, and you breathe a lot less car exhaust. That's especially true on these islands, which invariably have a steep hill to climb as you leave the ferry dock. The small cluster of buildings around the Orcas ferry dock include a hotel, a grocery, and a couple of eateries, the only services available until you reach Eastsound, which is the tour's destination. But it's just 12 miles to Eastsound, and there are great lunch and picnic choices there, so riders should just fill their water bottles in Orcas and climb that first hill. Once the ferry has emptied, the traffic is generally pretty light, although the route makes liberal use of the island's main road.

Depart the main road at the top of the first big hill, fittingly named by some wag as "Uff Da Hill" (note the sign naming the small lane at the top of the hill as Uff Da Hill Road). Loosely translated from the Norwegian, another name for the long climb would be #$*^!$% Hill. You'll see a couple more of these hills, but first you enjoy a quiet road that takes you west through picturesque West Sound and then north to rolling hills and beautiful scenery on the west side of Crow Valley. The valley holds working farms flanked by forests and two pottery studios. On the way north, visit Orcas Island Pottery in its stunning setting at the end of a wooded lane above West Beach. The outbound route continues north to meet the cunningly named Enchanted Forest Road (with a 16 percent grade, another "uff da" experience you may find yourself walking up).

If you're staying the night, book a place in or near Eastsound, which is at the top of the horseshoe, and make the island's main town your home base for other rides. Its dozen blocks contain a great variety of eateries, a well-stocked market, and shops representing the plentiful local artisans.

A delightful jaunt out of Eastsound takes you 1 mile north to touch the waters on the north side of the island. Ride up North Beach Road to its end, where sits a small beachfront park. Across the pebbled beach and blue water can be seen Patos, Sucia, and Matia Islands. Another great picnic spot, adjacent to downtown Eastsound, is the Madrona Point Preserve, just east around the bay from Main Street.

The adventurous could depart Eastsound up another Viking-vexing hill east toward Moran State Park on the far side of the island (not charted in this tour, but obvious on a map). The 4 miles to the park's entrance, just beyond Rosario Road, are pretty much one big climb, but if the spirit is willing, the shoulder is generous. The biggest climb, of course, comes within the park, if you ascend nearly 2000 vertical feet to the top of Mount Constitution in 5.5 miles. You can visit Cascade Lake and Mountain Lake along the way, or make one of those bracing, beautiful spots your destination. Hardy souls wanting to complete the island can ride 2 more hilly miles from the park to the burg of Olga, and 3 similar miles farther to Doe Bay Resort, which has much-anticipated hot tubs and accommodations ranging from camping to hostel beds to yurts.

Grandmother Janice and grandson John, with guide, prepare to ride Orcas.

Return from Eastsound via the main road, which takes you by Crow Valley Pottery, the oldest occupied building on the island, dating from 1866, which is now a potter's studio. The main road, although containing more traffic, has a shoulder suitable for use part of the way, and of course you get to take your revenge on Uff Da Hill in a screaming ride down it back to the ferry dock.

MILEAGE LOG

0.0 Depart ferry dock up Orcas Rd.

2.5 Left onto Pinneo Rd.

3.5 Right onto Crow Valley Rd. just beyond West Sound.

7.3 Left at Island Hardware onto West Beach Rd.

8.0 Pass lane to Orcas Island Pottery, a **0.5**-mile round trip detour.

8.4 Right onto Enchanted Forest Rd.

10.6 Enter Eastsound, crossing Lover's Ln. at a stop sign.

11.2 Left at T onto North Beach Rd.

12.2 Arrive at North Beach. Reverse route to return to Eastsound.

13.2 At intersection with Enchanted Forest Rd., continue south into town.

13.7 Arrive at Main St. in the center of town. Turn right on Main St. to begin return route.

14.1 Right onto Orcas Rd. to depart Eastsound.

15.0 Bear left at clearly marked Y to stay on Orcas Rd.

16.1 Arrive at Crow Valley Pottery on west side of road, just beyond golf course entrance.

16.9 Continue south on Orcas Rd. as it curves right at triangular intersection, then left, then right and left again.

22.2 Arrive at ferry dock to end tour.

37 San Juan Island: Lime Kiln and Roche Harbor

DIFFICULTY: moderate
TOTAL TIME: allow 3 hours
TOTAL DISTANCE: 32.6 miles
TOTAL ELEVATION GAIN: 1860 feet

Driving directions: Take I-5 north to exit 230; turn left at exit onto SR 20 west to Anacortes. Right onto Commercial Ave., then left onto 12th St., following signs for Washington State Ferries. Paid parking at ferry terminal.

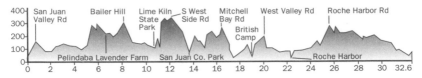

Ah, for a bike and the island life . . . you don't need much more moti-
vation than that for an enjoyable trip to San Juan Island. Although the
riding is more challenging than it is on Lopez, it's less so than on Orcas,
making it the perfect middle ground for a few days of exploration. In
this chapter are two San Juan Island tours—this one encompasses most
of the island and the other (Tour 38) picks up its southeast corner—but
a quick look at the map shows that you can easily depart from either
of these directions to discover your own path. Or combine them for a
complete circuit.

Each tour is a loop from Friday Harbor, the county seat and largest
town in the islands. This loop, the larger of the two, heads west from
town on San Juan Valley Road, with open views of farms and ranches.
Turning south, you encounter Pelindaba Lavender Farm, which fills
one side of a small valley with rows of the fragrant herb. Picturesque
farm buildings and equipment, a gift shop with lavender lemonade
and cookies, and a self-guided walking tour make this a great break.
Restrooms are available here, and you'll probably find your panniers
scented with the purple flowers for the rest of the ride. The farm has a
lavender festival in late July and operates a downtown Friday Harbor
store, if you want to load up on lotions and soaps as gifts but don't want
to lug them up the island's hills.

Speaking of which, the next leg takes you to the most beautiful views
on any of the island tours, as you head for the island's west side. Turning
west, you crest Bailer Hill Road at Edwards Point and burst upon the expanse of Haro Strait far below. West Side Road then snakes its way north,
with continuous views along an open expanse of road until you reach
Lime Kiln State Park, also known as Whale Watch Park. Exploration
here is a must. You may or may not see orca acrobatics in the waters
of Deadman Bay, but you will enjoy a picturesque lighthouse, a rocky
shoreline, and the unique "lime kilns," which were used to cook lime-
stone into lime, a lucrative business when the island was first settled. A
hulking stone kiln still perches on a bluff, and remnants of the operation
can be seen throughout the park. Restrooms and water with a high so-
dium content are available at the parking area of this popular park.

Continuing north, you can drop down to the water at San Juan
County Park or take a short side trip into Snug Harbor on a steep gravel
road before turning east, then north again to head for "British Camp"
and Roche Harbor.

The San Juan Island National Historical Park British Camp is one of two sites on the island that commemorate the "pig war" that began in 1859 when an American settler on the island killed a British settler's pig. Get the full story of the ensuing 12-year standoff between American and British soldiers at this park or the American Camp, which is visited on Tour 38. Today the British Camp flies a mammoth Union Jack above a small formal garden and restored blockhouse, and a walk along the brief trails reveals great views from Mount Young, a cemetery, and other relics.

Roche Harbor offers a delightful final stop on this loop tour. A bustling harbor for big yachts is presided over by the Hotel de Haro, built in 1886 by the founder of the settlement, who also was the owner of the lime mining company. Open-air cafés serve up sandwiches and fish-and-chips in an idyllic waterfront setting. The town has recently been expanding, and new rows of brightly painted townhomes line

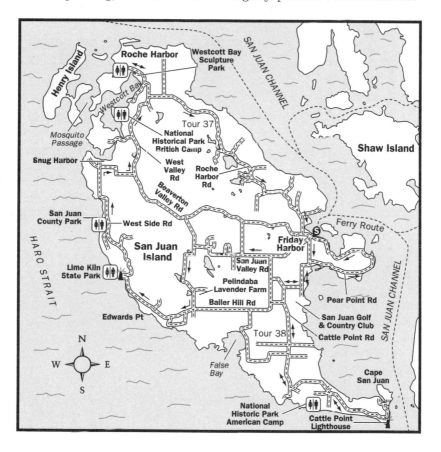

Rolling hills, cattle, and few cars are found on San Juan Island.

the road down to the old hotel. At the town's entrance is the Westcott Bay Reserve and sculpture park, which offers self-guided tours of more than 100 sculptures in natural settings, supported by modest donations requested of visitors.

Ride back southeast to Friday Harbor on Roche Harbor Road. Although it's the island's busiest drive, it offers a good shoulder for safe cycling.

MILEAGE LOG

0.0 Right off ferry dock onto Front St., then left in 1 block onto Spring St., heading west.

0.8 Spring St. becomes San Juan Valley Rd. as you leave town.

4.5 Left onto Wold Rd.

6.5 Arrive at Pelindaba Lavender Farm.

7.2 Right onto Bailer Hill Rd., which becomes S. West Side Rd.

10.4 Left into Lime Kiln State Park.

10.6 Arrive at parking area in park.

10.8 Left onto S. West Side Rd. when leaving park.

13.4 Left into San Juan County Park. Retrace route to depart park.

14.6 Curve right onto Mitchell Bay Rd.

17.0 Left onto West Valley Rd.
18.5 Left into park at British Camp.
18.9 Arrive at British Camp parking lot. Retrace route to depart park.
19.2 Left onto West Valley Rd. when leaving park.
20.6 Left onto Roche Harbor Rd.
22.1 Arrive at town of Roche Harbor.
22.2 Take first right to hotel and harbor. Retrace route to depart town.
22.4 Left onto Roche Harbor Rd.
22.5 Right into parking at Westcott Bay Institute Sculpture Garden. Depart park by making right onto Roche Harbor Rd.
28.6 Pass San Juan Vineyard tasting room in an 1896 schoolhouse.
31.4 At Friday Harbor town limits, road becomes Tucker Ave.
32.2 Left onto Guard St.
32.5 Left onto Spring St.
32.6 Arrive at ferry dock to end tour.

38 San Juan Island: Cattle Point

DIFFICULTY: moderate
TOTAL TIME: allow 3 hours
TOTAL DISTANCE: 27.5 miles
TOTAL ELEVATION GAIN: 1000 feet

> **Driving directions:** Take I-5 north to exit 230; turn left at exit onto SR 20 west to Anacortes. Right onto Commercial Ave., then left onto 12th St., following signs for Washington State Ferries. Paid parking at ferry terminal.

This shorter, less hilly tour of southeast San Juan Island offers a mellower form of entertainment. Although fewer points of interest are found along its 25-mile route

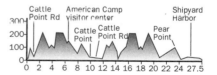

and there is no glittering marina socked away at the end, there are similarities. You'll find plentiful water views, a historic park, and a lighthouse. On clear days, you'll also be treated to views of stunning snow-capped peaks. This tour provides a wonderful opportunity to while away an afternoon, perhaps with a snack stop or relaxation at one of the beaches in American Camp. Restrooms and water are available at the park's visitor center, but no other services are to be found along the route. Depart Friday Harbor through its southern neighborhood and enjoy the well-kept, Victorian-style homes on Argyle Road. Skirt the fairgrounds, airport, and golf course as you pedal south. A detour west to False Bay, via Little Road, Bailer Hill Road, and False Bay Drive (partly unpaved), gains views south toward the Olympic Peninsula.

At 6 miles from town you arrive at San Juan Island National Historic Park American Camp. The visitor center provides details of the American-British boundary dispute that led to this military camp being occupied between 1859 and 1872. A packed-gravel road through the windswept grasses of the park provides wonderful views of the Strait of Juan de Fuca. A lower foot trail goes to the beach. There are also two beaches on the northern side of this narrow spit occupied by the park, and they provide worthwhile short hikes or picnic spots.

One interesting site high on this overlook is Robert's Redoubt. This "redoubt" was an earthen fortification dug to contain the large cannons the Americans planned to use to blast British ships out of the bay below. Although a naval standoff took place during the "pig war," only once was a gun fired from this redoubt, and that was to salute the camp's commander. The redoubt is named for Second Lieutenant Henry M. Robert, who supervised its construction and went on to later, greater fame as the author of *Robert's Rules of Order*. Clearly a good person to have in charge of a standoff.

After exploring the park, venture farther south to the end of Cattle Point Road. You'll enjoy a long, gradual hill that provides stunning

Cattle Point Lighthouse

views of the Cattle Point Lighthouse and land masses beyond; Lopez Island is just to the east. A clear day will treat you to more wondrous mountain views, as Mount Rainier looms above the verdant lands to the south and Mount Baker is visible above the islands to the east.

This lighthouse, as with the one at Lime Kiln State Park on the other San Juan tour (see Tour 37), must be visited on foot. Until 2004 a horn sounded every 30 seconds from this lighthouse to aid navigation through the San Juan Channel. Just up the road is a rocky overlook with an interpretive area that includes a small building where a military radioman was stationed to listen for the navigational call "QTE," which in the language of the mariner means "where am I?" You won't need directional aids on your ride, however, because the road dead-ends at a private marina, forcing you to loop back and return to the park and, ultimately, to Friday Harbor, via Cattle Point Road.

As you near town, detour east onto Pear Point Road, which skirts North Bay past a gravel pit (where the road is smooth but unpaved for 0.3 mile) and through pastoral scenes before curving back around, above a shipyard and through a dense section of town overlooking Brown Island. The route drops you into downtown just two blocks from the ferry.

MILEAGE LOG

0.0 Right off ferry dock onto Front St., then left in 1 block onto Spring St., heading west.

0.2 Left onto Argyle Rd.

1.3 Left onto Cattle Point Rd.

6.2 Right into American Camp at driveway beyond sign.

6.5 Arrive at American Camp visitor center. Ride through American Camp on gravel road at east end of parking lot.

7.7 Right onto Cattle Point Rd. at end of park road.

9.9 Arrive at path to lighthouse (no bikes allowed on path).

10.1 Arrive at Cattle Point Interpretive Area.

10.8 Reach end of road at Cape San Juan private dock. Retrace route to return to Cattle Point Rd.

15.5 Pass entrance to American Camp visitor center. At all intersections, stay on Cattle Point Rd.

22.1 Right onto Pear Point Rd.

22.6 Pass gravel pit, where road is unpaved for 0.3 mile.

24.8 Road becomes Turn Point Rd.

26.3 Pass Shipyard Harbor.

26.9 Right at Y onto Warbass Wy.

27.4 Right onto Harrison St.

27.5 Right onto East St. to return to ferry in 1 short block.

39 Shaw Island

DIFFICULTY: easy
TOTAL TIME: allow 2 hours
TOTAL DISTANCE: 14.9 miles
TOTAL ELEVATION GAIN: 840 feet

> **Driving directions:** Take I-5 north to exit 230; turn left at exit onto SR 20 west to Anacortes. Right onto Commercial Ave., then left onto 12th St., following signs for Washington State Ferries. Paid parking at ferry terminal.

A leisurely spin around the smallest of the four San Juan islands served by the state ferries holds some quiet revelations. Walk the grounds of the school if it's closed;

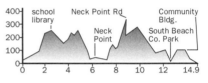

you may see the alphabet spelled out in pieces of driftwood, mounted in rows on an exterior wall. Riding the main road, where a car goes by

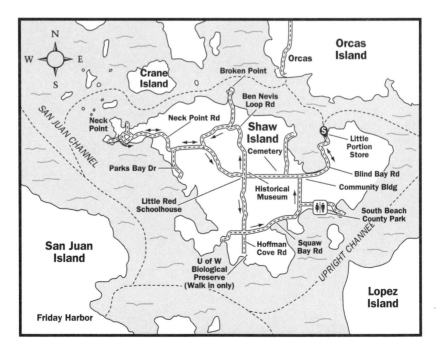

The well-kept Little Red Schoolhouse

every fifteen minutes or so, you may startle a deer bounding off into the opposite ditch, hind hooves kicking soil onto the road in its haste.

Those delightful moments are a fitting way to end a visit to the San Juan islands, and this tour can be easily managed in the middle of a day returning to Anacortes, or plan for it to be an easy day trip out and back from a multiple-day stay on another island. Shaw is 7.7 square miles of mostly wooded land snuggled between Lopez, Orcas, and San Juan Islands. Its ferry dock is visible from the Orcas dock, and the other islands seem so close you feel you can almost touch them. Take a boat from San Juan or Orcas first thing to be on Shaw's quiet roads by midmorning, and you can easily complete the island ride and be somewhere else by lunch. Or take the day, pack a picnic, and spend the afternoon on the beach at Shaw's one public resting spot: South Beach County Park.

The only road from the ferry, Blind Bay Road, leads south then west past the cemetery and to an intersection with the island's main side roads. Here you'll find the small public library and even smaller museum. Across the road sits the well-kept school, its meticulous red-and-white paint job masking its age; it is the oldest continually operating school in the state. A comfortable playground and newer classrooms centered around a courtyard behind the classic old "little red schoolhouse" complete a picture of an educational haven. No wonder it's on the National Register of Historic Places.

Head north from the main road onto Ben Nevis Loop, which comes out near the west edge of the island. Complete the cross-island ride by taking the road all the way to the end, even though the views are mostly of trees and a few houses on the road end's cul-de-sac. Head back to the school intersection, this time heading south on the other side road, Hoffman Cove Road. This takes you past the University of Washington Biological Preserve, where walk-in viewing is allowed. Continue along Squaw Bay Road east past South Beach to the county park, which has pit toilets, water, and a curving stretch of sandy beach. Lopez can be seen across Upright Channel, in which sailboats often ply the waters.

From the county park it's a quick 3 miles back north to the ferry. At the dock, visit the General Store, open on Sundays during the summer.

MILEAGE LOG

0.0 Depart ferry onto Blind Bay Rd.

1.5 Pass community center at intersection with Squaw Bay Rd.

2.5 Arrive at four-way intersection; school and library. Turn right onto Ben Nevis Loop.

4.5 Right onto Neck Point Rd.

5.0 Stay right at Y with Parks Bay Dr.

6.2 Stay left at Y at Harbor Wy.

6.3 Stay right at Y at Sylvan Circle.

6.5 Stay left at Y with Cameron Rd. to stay on Sylvan Circle.

6.8 Right onto Neck Point Rd.; retrace route.

9.6 Right onto Hoffman Cove Rd. at four-way intersection with schoolhouse.

10.7 Left onto Squaw Bay Rd.

12.0 Right onto unpaved road signed for camping.

12.4 Arrive at South Beach County Park. Retrace route to depart park.

12.8 Right onto Squaw Bay Rd.

13.4 Right on Blind Bay Rd.

14.9 Arrive at ferry to end tour.

Opposite: Tulips bloom at Roozengaarde display garden.

SKAGIT COUNTY

40 Skagit Flats and Tulip Fields

DIFFICULTY: moderate
TOUR TIME: allow 4 hours
TOTAL DISTANCE: 38.9 miles
TOTAL ELEVATION GAIN: 50 feet

Driving directions: Take I-5 to Mount Vernon; depart at exit 226, Kincaid St./SR 536. Left at stoplight onto Kincaid. Cross railroad tracks, then right onto S. 3rd St. Road curves left and turns into Division St. Continue 2 blocks, cross bridge, then first left onto N. Front St. into Edgewater Park.

Here's a tour for those longing for the open road—the flat, open road. It's 35 miles of farm roads, punctuated by a visit to the small tourist town of La Conner. Former Midwestern farm kids will feel at home, and city dwellers will definitely know they're not in urbanity any more.

Park at convenient Edgewater Park, just across the river from downtown Mount Vernon. It's free, easy to find, and very accessible to Interstate 5. Bike across the rusty bridge and cycle through the town's homey business district, then in a few minutes you're south of town, riding along a dike that protects the residences from the annual rising of the Skagit River.

As you ride south, the Cascades loom to the east. A quick right over the bridge at Conway puts you on Fir Island, actually a riverine delta where the fertile sponginess of the soil is evident in the abundant rows of crops. Ride north along the other side of the dike on Skagit City Road to circumnavigate the northern edges of the island. This is the most secluded, verdant segment of the ride. Look for many varieties of birds, keeping an eye open for hawks and eagles that are known to soar the thermals and perch in the trees along the river.

Exit the island via a busy bridge with no shoulder on Best Road. Coast down off the short bridge into the waiting arms of the Rexville Grocery, with its jaunty promise of "Foods Galore." Adjacent to this well-stocked grocery-deli is the Rexville Farmers Market, bursting every Saturday in the summer with local vegetables, baked goods, smoked fish, and other delicacies.

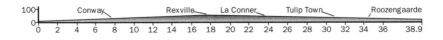

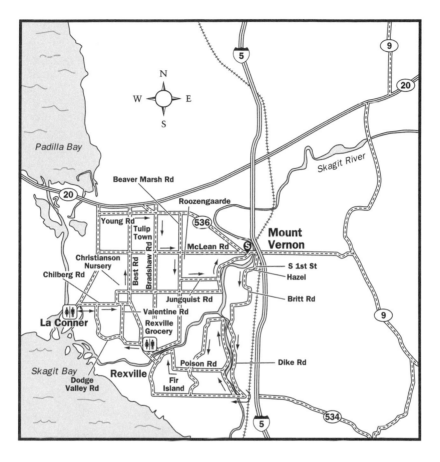

Next stop is La Conner, a sophisticated small town. Head west into town on Chilberg Road, idling alongside the inevitable tourist traffic past the town's many curio shops and antique stores. Highlights include the glass and sculpture of the Museum of Northwest Art on South First Street. There are plenty of places for a coffee or snack stop.

Refreshed and feeling fully like a tourist, head toward the tulip fields. Take care to note intersection signs that warn "crossing traffic does not stop." Nor does it slow down. But most of the busy roads in this area have wide, clean shoulders, so ride north with confidence. Along the way you'll pass Christianson Nursery and, in season, plenty of colorful tulip fields. But the real tulip show is yet to come, at Tulip Town, one of the area's two major show gardens. As you wheel by the long lines of cars inching toward the paid parking, you'll feel quite superior and free.

After a visit, shake off the tulip-color dizziness and get back on the road heading south. For comparison, stop at Roozengaarde, the other tulip haven. This one boasts a larger windmill and outdoor show gardens with swaths of tulips in every color, stripe, and crinkle style. (Note: Both tulip farms charge a small entrance fee.) Wheel out of there, again heading south, making the first left to head back to Mount Vernon. At the edge of the valley, ride north along the dike once again to head back to Edgewater Park.

If you'd like a quicker tour of the tulips, skip the Fir Island portion of the ride and head straight west on McLean Road from the start. You can easily navigate the grid of roads and follow your own path through this wide-open country, simply meeting up with a familiar road should you stray.

Skagit Flats has much to offer beyond tulips. Although the spring flowers are the most colorful example of Northwest farming, they're only a part of Skagit Valley agriculture. Farmers post signs along the

Cyclists enjoy the tulip fields.

roads listing their crops, from wheat to berries to seed crop for spinach, beets, and cabbage. Riding along the fields provides a connection with those farms and our amazing abundance of healthy food. That's why on this tour, perhaps more than any other, slow your pedaling a bit when you see a farmer out working in the fields and raise a hand in appreciation. You most certainly will get a friendly wave in return.

MILEAGE LOG

0.0   Right out of parking lot onto N. Front St.

0.1   Right onto sidewalk on Division St. to cross bridge into downtown Mount Vernon.

0.3   Right onto S. 1st St., which becomes Cleveland St.

1.0   Right onto Hazel.

1.4   Hazel curves left and becomes Britt Rd.

3.7   Left onto Dike Rd. as Britt Rd. ends.

7.7   Right onto Fir Island Rd.; cross over bridge onto Fir Island.

8.0   Right onto Skagit City Rd. immediately after bridge. It turns west, then south to become Dry Slough Rd.

13.2   At stop sign, cross Moore Rd. to continue south on Dry Slough Rd.

14.5   Right onto Polson Rd.

16.1   Left onto Moore Rd.

17.0   Right onto Best Rd.; cross over bridge to leave Fir Island. Caution: no bike lane or shoulder on bridge.

17.6   Arrive at Rexville Grocery.

18.0   Left onto Dodge Valley Rd. Caution: busy stretch of road; traffic can be fast.

18.9   Left at Y at Valentine Rd.

21.4   Left onto Chilberg Rd. Caution: highway speeds; cross traffic does not stop.

23.1   Continue west through roundabout into La Conner.

23.6   Arrive at La Conner town center. Retrace route to depart La Conner.

24.1   Continue east at roundabout on Chilberg Rd.

26.2   Left onto Best Rd.

30.3   Right onto Young Rd.

31.4   Merge onto SR 536 at stop sign, then turn right onto Bradshaw Rd. Caution: busy highway; traffic can be fast.

31.7   Arrive at Tulip Town display gardens.

32.9   Left onto McLean Rd.

33.9   Right onto Beaver Marsh Rd.

34.5   Arrive at Roozengaarde tulip display gardens.

34.9   Left onto Jungquist Rd.

36.4 Left onto Penn Rd.
37.8 Right onto McLean Rd.
38.7 Left onto Wall St.
38.8 Right onto Division St. at light.
38.9 Right onto N. Front St. to return to parking and end tour.

Opposite: A ferry docks next to the waterfront park in Edmonds. Photo by L.J. McAllister.

SNOHOMISH COUNTY

41 Interurban Trail and Mukilteo

DIFFICULTY: strenuous
TOTAL TIME: allow 5 hours
TOTAL DISTANCE: 47.7 miles
TOTAL ELEVATION GAIN: 1380 feet

Driving directions: From I-5, take exit 178, Mountlake Terrace/ 236th St. Turn left onto 236th St., which becomes Lakeview Dr. Turn left into golf course parking at Ballinger Park.

In the somewhat dated newspaper comic staple "Family Circus," little Billy often is shown taking the most circuitous route from one location to another, simply to satisfy curiosity or get a few more precious minutes outside. If that's the mood you're in, try this 50-mile tour along Snohomish County's section of the Interurban Trail. It's a patchwork of streets, trails, overpasses, and parking lots, just barely held together by a series of fading signs.

The former streetcar route also provides a fairly safe and interesting connection to the Mukilteo ferry terminal, for those interested in a Whidbey Island excursion (see Tours 32–34). Along the way, you spin by two malls, travel along both sides of Interstate 5, and explore some nice Everett residential neighborhoods. Trail planners say the kinks will be worked out eventually, providing an off-street trail stretching from downtown Everett to Seattle's Ballard neighborhood. Meanwhile, this meandering route—mazelike though it may be—is the best option for navigating through these cities.

Start at the south end of the trail, which currently is close to the Snohomish County line, or ride up from Green Lake using the Edmonds route (see Tour 5) to connect with the trail. On the first leg, which bisects Lynnwood and Mountlake Terrace, you ride behind office parks and along busy retail corridors.

Cross over Interstate 5 and ride a tree-lined corridor that heads briefly

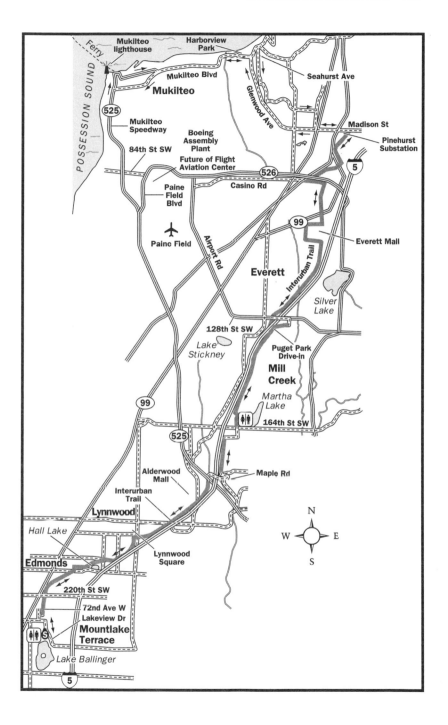

Mukilteo lighthouse and Washington State Ferry

toward Martha Lake and then crosses back to the west side of the inter-state as you enter Everett. A new bike/pedestrian bridge was recently built over Interstate 5 just north of 128th Street, making it a much safer crossing.

Stay with the trail until it turns into street riding in south Everett, then head northwest toward Mukilteo Boulevard, a wide, winding road with excellent bike lanes. Endure the traffic to get to Mukilteo, and you won't be disappointed. The ferry-side burg hosts a small col-lection of shops and cafés, and a picturesque lighthouse sits adjacent to the ferry dock.

If you're feeling adventurous, extend the ride by continuing south out of Mukilteo on the Mukilteo Speedway to a left turn at 84th Street South that will take you to Paine Field Boulevard and the recent at-traction, Boeing's Future of Flight Aviation Center. You're greeted by a shining, luxurious company museum that is the new starting point for tours of the world's largest building by volume, the company's jet assembly plant. If you're taking this detour, which adds a half-dozen miles on a busy road with a bike lane, I recommend retracing your steps to the ferry dock and rejoining the tour route, because the busy highways south of Paine Field carry heavy traffic and do not connect well to the Interurban Trail.

Besides, it's a good challenge to try to hit all your marks when re-turning via the snaky Interurban route. You won't quite need a treasure map to follow this course, but spotting each of the many links can become something of a circus.

MILEAGE LOG

0.0 Left out of parking onto Lakeview Dr.

0.3 Right onto 73rd Pl. W.

0.4 Right onto 226th Pl. SW.

0.5 Left onto Interurban Trail at its start.

1.3 Proceed through underpass at 220th St. SW.

1.8 Left onto 212th St. SW as trail ends, then first right, onto 63rd Ave. W.

1.9 Right onto 211th St. SW.

2.1 Right into South Lynnwood Neighborhood Park between playfield and tennis courts to rejoin trail.

2.6 Jog left as trail ends at 54th Ave. W., then right onto 208th St. SW to continue in bike lane.

2.8 Left onto 50th Ave. W. briefly, then right onto trail.

3.4 Left onto near sidewalk on 44th Ave. W.

3.5 Right at stoplight onto 200th St. SW.

3.9 Right onto trail.

5.4 Stay left at Y to trail end, then ride briefly on mall frontage street to rejoin trail.

5.8 Merge into bike lane along 26th Ave. W.

6.0 Right onto Maple Rd. to go under SR 525, then over I-5.

6.5 Right onto Butternut Rd., then right in ½ block to rejoin trail.

7.8 Left to continue on 13th Ave. W.

8.4 Left onto trail about 1 block north of 164th St. Caution: busy road.

10.7 Left onto 130th St. SE after passing drive-in theater.

10.9 Left onto 3rd Ave. SE.

11.1 Left onto 128th St. SE at light. Merge onto north sidewalk. Caution: heavy traffic.

11.3 Right onto trail just before northbound freeway on-ramp.

11.7 Right onto trail when exiting bike/pedestrian overpass.

13.8 Left off trail at Everett Mall onto sidewalk, then curve left around mall buildings.

13.9 Right onto sidewalk to continue.

14.1 Right along SE Everett Mall Wy. Cross street at light, then turn north to continue in bike lane on West Mall Dr.

14.5 Rejoin trail at end of street.

14.9 Left onto 84th St. as trail ends; follow SR 526.

15.3 Right onto 7th Ave. SE, follow trail signs; curve right again at E. Casino Rd., stay on near sidewalk.

15.4 Right onto trail again after passing under SR 526.

15.7 Continue forward onto Kossuth Ave. as trail ends.

16.3 Cross Beverly Blvd. onto sidewalk, then turn left next to Beverly Park Substation to rejoin trail.

16.8 Left onto Wetmore Ave. as trail ends at Pinehurst Substation.

16.9 Left onto Madison St., which curves north and becomes Glenwood Ave.

20.0 Left onto Mukilteo Blvd., which becomes 5th St.

23.2 Right onto Mukilteo Speedwy. to waterfront.

23.5 Left onto Front St. to lighthouse. Return from lighthouse, cross Mukilteo Speedwy., and continue east on Front St.

23.7 Right onto 1st St.; cross railroad tracks.

24.0 Left onto Mukilteo Ln.

24.4 Left onto Mukilteo Blvd. to depart town.

27.2 Right onto Seahurst Ave. Caution: steep climb first block.

28.1 Seahurst becomes 52nd St. SW, then 51st Pl. SW, then back to Seahurst.

28.5 Left onto Brookridge Blvd., which becomes Pecks Dr. at Beverly Ln.

29.7 Right onto Fleming St.

30.1 Left onto Madison St. Caution: busy street.

30.7 Right onto Wetmore to rejoin trail.

30.9 Right onto trail at Pinehurst Substation.

31.5 Cross street to right at Beverly Park Substation to rejoin trail.

32.3 Right off trail back onto E. Casino Rd.

32.4 Stay on near sidewalk under SR 526, then left onto 7th Ave. for 1 block, then left into bike lane on 84th.

32.8 Right onto trail as road ends at SE Everett Mall Wy.

33.0 Exit trail onto West Mall Dr.

33.6 Cross SE Everett Mall Wy., then right onto south sidewalk.

33.9 Left onto West Mall Dr., then rejoin trail on the left as road curves right.

36.2 Exit trail at 128th; stay on near sidewalk to cross I-5.

36.4 Cross 128th at light after east on-ramp, then turn left on south sidewalk to continue east.

36.6 Right onto 3rd Ave. S., which curves right to become 130th St. SE.

37.0 Right at Puget Park Drive-in to rejoin trail.

39.3 Right onto Meadow Rd. as trail ends. Meadow becomes 13th Ave. W.

39.9 Right onto trail.

41.1 Left onto Butternut Rd. as trail ends.

41.2 Left onto Maple Rd. Cross over I-5, then under SR 525.

41.9 Merge into left lane for left onto 26th Ave. W. Caution: busy intersection.

42.0 Rejoin trail as road curves right.

42.2 Trail ends, rejoins street briefly, then resumes.

43.8 Exit trail onto near sidewalk on Alderwood Mall Blvd.

44.0 Cross 44th Ave. W. at stoplight, then left onto sidewalk.

44.2 Right onto trail just before freeway on-ramp.

44.9 Left onto 50th Ave., then right onto trail.

45.1 Exit trail into bike lane on 208th St. SW, then left at 54th Ave. W. to rejoin trail.

45.6 Left out of South Lynnwood Neighborhood Park onto 61st, which curves right to become 211th St. SW.

45.8 Left onto 63rd Ave. W.

46.0 Right onto 212th St. SW, then cross street to rejoin trail.

46.4 Cross 220th, then right on sidewalk briefly, then left on trail.

47.1 Right onto 226th Pl. SW.

47.2 Left onto 73rd Pl. W.

47.3 Left onto Lakeview Dr.

47.7 Return to parking to end tour.

42 Centennial Trail

DIFFICULTY: moderate
TOTAL TIME: allow 4 hours
TOTAL DISTANCE: 47.5 miles
TOTAL ELEVATION GAIN: 620 feet

> **Driving directions:** From I-5 in Everett, travel east on US 2 toward Wenatchee. Take third exit off US 2 into Snohomish. Turn right onto 92nd St. SE, then right onto Pine Ave. Turn right onto Maple Ave., which becomes S. Machias Rd. Pilchuck trailhead is on the right in approximately 2 miles.

This is a flat, relaxing ride, mostly in the country, on a trail that's been much expanded recently to create a great link between the towns of Snohomish, Lake Stevens, and Arlington. If you start your tour in Snohomish and loop the entire distance, switching to roads for most of the last few miles into Arlington, you'll put in about 50 miles (half a

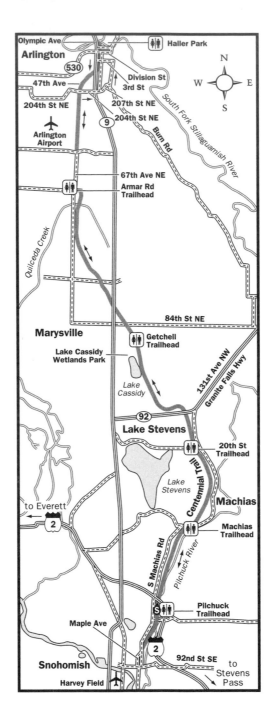

century, in cycle-event lingo). But for better access to parking and services, I suggest starting at the Pilchuck Trailhead, which is just north of Snohomish off US Highway 2.

Head north as the trail runs close to the Pilchuck River. There's only a portable toilet at Pilchuck, but there are seasonal services at Machias Station, which is your first stop, just 3 miles ahead. The converted rail depot now has a snack shop, water, and restrooms, and in the summer of 2005 they began renting bicycles and in-line skates. With picnic tables and a covered shelter, it's a nice place to stop and a great meeting point.

Next you skirt the edge of the town of Lake Stevens (detour at 20th Street for a side trip to its town center) and pick up the new section of the trail, noticeable by the lack of tree roots that can heave the asphalt under your tires (for an example of this, see Burke-Gilman Trail, Tour 1). At about 10 miles you reach Lake Cassidy, on the eastern edge of Marysville, which has trail access to a dock and wetland interpretive area. There are picnic tables here as well. The trail continues north through denser tree cover, and as it nears Arlington, you begin to get views west through the valley.

An equestrian trail parallels the flat, rural Centennial Trail.

You do make a bit of a climb over the entire course of the trail, but it's so gradual you might not notice it until you reach the end, where you cross Quilceda Creek and coast down to the Armar Road Trailhead. If you sought just an easy off-street pedal, reverse course here and return to Pilchuck for a 34-mile ride. The trailhead has a portable toilet but no other services. This tour continues another few miles into Arlington for restrooms and refreshments.

To visit Arlington, turn right onto 67th Avenue NE (also known as Armar Road) and pedal north. You spend 1 mile on this moderately busy, shoulderless road before picking up another section of the trail, a 12-foot-wide sidewalk that takes you into town. This short trail section ends at Cemetery Road. Turn right onto 204th Street NE and ride two blocks to the well-equipped Haagen's Supermarket to sample its deli selections and facilities. Continue 4 miles on city streets into Arlington, using a short bike lane through downtown Arlington that parallels its main street and connects to riverside parks. The county has plans to finish the trail into Arlington, then link these sections and extend the trail north to the Skagit County line.

On the return, after the initial climb from Armar Road you begin to notice the downhill slope, as you find yourself coasting along or really picking up speed. The trail has a posted speed limit of 15 miles per hour, which is mostly a concern on the busy sections or where you reach a crossing with cars, pedestrians, and horses.

A bridle trail parallels the bike and pedestrian trail, mostly set a few feet away on a dirt path in the adjacent ditch. However, equestrians do join the trail at bridges and other crossings, and it's a good idea to leave plenty of space and approach at a moderate speed. At one point, Snohomish County was the dairy capital of the state, but today the closest you'll get to livestock near the trail will be seeing well-groomed, well-behaved horses. As with many communities in the Interstate 5 corridor, the towns along this trail are sprawling into the rural landscape. If that process continues, the Centennial Trail will become another two-wheel commuter link, but for now it's mostly a recreational trail that offers at least the feel of a country ride.

MILEAGE LOG

0.0 Left onto trail from Pilchuck Trailhead.

3.2 Arrive at Machias Trailhead. Restrooms, water available.

9.0 Arrive at town of Lake Stevens.

9.9 Arrive at Lake Cassidy picnic area, dock.

17.0 Arrive at Armar Rd. Trailhead.

17.1 Right onto 67th Ave. NE, also known as Armar Rd.

18.1 Cross 172nd St. onto sidewalk bike path on east side of road.

20.5 Right onto 204th St. NE, which crosses SR 9, then curves left to become 207th St. NE.

21.7 Left onto Stillaguamish Ave.

22.4 Left onto 3rd St.

22.9 Right onto downtown trail just past Olympic Ave.

24.2 Arrive at Haller Park. Restrooms available. Reverse route to return through downtown.

25.5 As trail ends, right onto West Ave.

25.9 Left onto NE 47th Ave.

26.9 Cross 204th St. NE to rejoin trail adjacent to 67th Ave. NE.

30.3 Rejoin Centennial Trail at Armar Rd. Trailhead.

37.4 Pass Lake Cassidy picnic area.

38.3 Pass town of Lake Stevens.

44.3 Pass Machias Trailhead.

47.5 Arrive at Pilchuck Trailhead parking to end tour.

43 Snohomish to Everett

DIFFICULTY: moderate
TOTAL TIME: allow 3 hours
TOTAL DISTANCE: 23.7 miles
TOTAL ELEVATION GAIN: 690 feet

Driving directions: From I-5 in Everett, travel east on US 2 toward Wenatchee. Take third exit off US 2 into Snohomish. Turn right onto 92nd St. SE, then right onto Pine Ave. Turn right onto Maple Ave., which becomes S. Machias Rd. Pilchuck Trailhead is on the right in approximately 2 miles.

Central Snohomish County is a region where the rural areas are giving way to suburbs, although north and east of Bothell, Mill Creek, and Everett, you can still see open land and wildlife. Finding them is

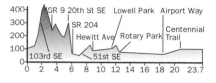

the goal of this tour, which includes rolling hills but also a stretch of moderate rural highway along the verdant Snohomish River valley.

The tour begins north of the Snohomish town center, then skirts Ebey Slough, downtown Everett, and the winding river. Coming back through Snohomish provides a lunch or snack visit to the town's touristy main street, from where you can connect to another tour: to

Monroe (Tour 44) or onto the Centennial Trail (Tour 42) if the spirit moves you. Because of this tour's fairly modest length, plenty of time is left for exploration or relaxation along the way.

Begin at the Pilchuck Trailhead just north of Snohomish. Ride a bit north, then turn west and cross the valley. The route takes you on a climb, then across busy State Route 9, before dropping back down onto the flats of Ebey Slough, at the point where US Highway 2 comes across on a trestle from Everett and splits with State Route 204 to Lake Stevens. This is a tricky interface with a major highway, but cyclists ride under the ramps where the roads diverge. Choosing the road not taken by either highway allows avoidance of most of the commotion.

Ride west along the north edge of the slough, hard up against the highway on one side, viewing a raised set of pipelines on the other. Halfway through the slough, you curve south into Ebey Island a bit, and you can further explore this farm-centric floodplain by making a detour south on Home Acres Road. That route would take you quickly back to Snohomish via Riverview Road, but to see a bit of Everett, this tour follows the signed bike route to the north, up onto the protected pedestrian–bike lane bridge that joins US Highway 2 over the Snohomish

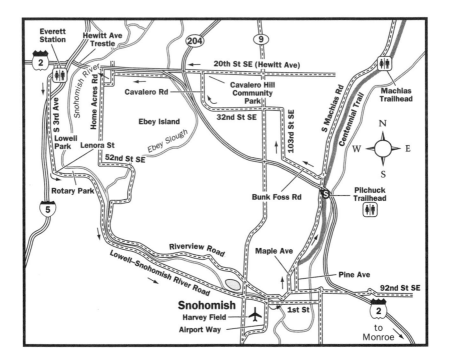

A heron ignores nearby Highway 2 while fishing in Ebey Slough.

River. Drop into downtown Everett, riding past the recently combined train and bus transit center called Everett Station.

A few blocks north and west is the Everett Events Center, with its distinctive masts and wires looking like a frigate without sails. From here you could continue northwest to Everett's waterfront, west to Mukilteo, or north to the bike paths of Smith Island. But this tour continues south and east along the river. A relaxing break can be had at Lowell Riverfront Park as you cross from the city streets to Snohomish River Road. Continue along this relatively quiet road, which has signs cautioning cars about the presence of bicycles, back to Snohomish.

As you cross the bridge into downtown Snohomish, you'll find a visitor information center. On busy First Street, the town's true touristy nature is revealed: six blocks jammed with eateries, tea shops, and antiques, plus a great gourmet coffee shop, just on the left. Visitors line up at the ice cream shop, which also carries a vast array of collectibles, such as all things Coca-Cola or Betty Boop. Another popular stop is the

Pie Company, which sells sandwiches and dessert pies, whole or by the slice. Finish the tour by exiting stage right and heading up Maple to connect with the Centennial Trail.

MILEAGE LOG

0.0 Left onto Centennial Trail and ride north.

0.7 Left off trail onto Ritchey Rd. Cross Old Machias Rd. and proceed west across valley. Climbing out of valley, Ritchey becomes Bunk Foss Rd.

1.8 Right onto 103rd St. S.E.

2.9 Left onto 32nd St. SE.

3.3 Cross SR 9. Caution: busy intersection; highway speeds.

3.7 As 32nd St. SE curves right, it becomes 91st Ave. SE.

3.8 Left onto S. Lake Stevens Rd., which curves north and becomes Cavalero Rd.

5.5 Left onto 20th St. SE, also called E. Hewitt Ave.

5.9 Merge into left lane and stay on 20th when approaching ramps to US 2 north, which exits to right, and US 2 south, which exits to left.

6.0 At stop sign, cross SR 204 onto a marked bike lane on the left side of 20th. Note: At this point, 20th becomes an eastbound one-way, and cyclists ride against traffic in a wide bike lane on this little-used road.

7.2 Left onto 51st Ave. SE toward Home Acres Rd.

7.9 Right onto bike path as road curves left and becomes Home Acres Rd. Follow bike path up and along US 2 over river.

8.8 Left onto Hewitt Ave. at base of trestle.

8.9 Right onto Chestnut St., which becomes Pacific Ave. and goes under I-5, then rises on a bridge over railroad tracks.

9.6 Left on Smith Ave. as you come off west side of bridge. Restrooms at Everett Transit Station immediately on the left.

10.7 Right onto Lowell-Larimer Rd. at stop sign at 38th St. It becomes S. 3rd Ave.

11.5 At Lowell Park, road curves and becomes S. 2nd Ave.

12.2 Left on Lenora St. Road curves right at railroad tracks and becomes Lowell–Snohomish River Rd.

12.3 Pass Rotary Park on your right.

18.6 Left onto Airport Wy.

18.8 Right onto 1st St. into downtown Snohomish. Public restrooms on the right at mile 19.0.

19.5 Left onto Maple Ave. S. after 1st St. curves right.

20.7 Cross Pine Ave. and join Centennial Trail.

23.7 Arrive back at Pilchuck Trailhead.

44 Snohomish to Monroe

DIFFICULTY: moderate
TOTAL TIME: allow 3 hours
TOTAL DISTANCE: 33.5 miles
TOTAL ELEVATION GAIN: 600 feet

> **Driving directions:** From I-5 in Everett, travel east on US 2 toward Wenatchee. Take third exit off US 2 into Snohomish. Turn right onto 92nd St. SE, then right onto Pine Ave. Turn right onto Maple Ave., which becomes S. Machias Rd. Pilchuck Trailhead is on the right in approximately 2 miles.

There are many routes that will take you through the farm communities of Snohomish County, and this one serves as an introduction to the communities and major roads that can lead to much more exploration. Begin this tour on the Centennial Trail, riding south into downtown Snohomish. Here you'll find a visitor information center and a town center tailor-made for tourists.

Head down Maple to First, then east along First until Lincoln, which takes you out of town, past soccer fields and into grazing fields. The route uses Old Snohomish Monroe Road, which has relatively light traffic except at peak hours, due to the presence of US Highway 2 just beyond the valley to the north. But much of this road does not have a shoulder and there are plenty of curves, so caution is warranted. Watch for the curious blue "Fish Crossing" signs, which lead to musing on the presence of evolution continuing in the valley.

About halfway between Snohomish and Monroe is the turnoff to Lord Hill Regional Park, a 2-mile climb south of the road. The heavily wooded park, which borders the Snohomish River, offers hiking, horse, and mountain-biking trails but not much for road cyclists. The valley, however, is a beautiful ride, and you rise up a bit along the edge of the foothills to get a look at Monroe on the approach.

Enter Monroe at a roundabout and cycle down Main Street, a long, wide, quiet lane leading to the town center. Ride past schools and the

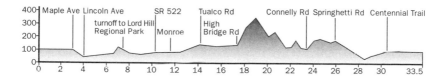

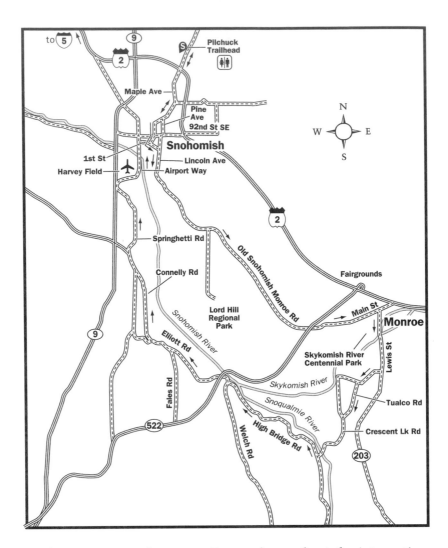

Washington State Reformatory. Just to the north, at the intersection of US Highway 2 and State Route 522, sits the sprawling fairgrounds where the Evergreen State Fair is held every September. There is also much commercial development along US Highway 2.

Downtown Monroe, a four-block radius around the junction of Lewis Street and Main, includes a couple cafés, a bakery, antique shops, and a bike store, which is on the south side of Main one block before Lewis. Exit the homey town center by turning right on Lewis and heading south. Cross the Skykomish River and continue south for a bit on busy State Route 203 to a right turn at Tualco Road. This begins the loop back to Snohomish, through a flat, verdant river valley fed by both the Skykomish and the Snoqualmie. Tualco Road stands up well as an idyllic setting for river valley farming, and you cycle by a great variety of market crops, from corn to raspberries.

Cross the Snoqualmie and climb out of the valley via High Bridge Road, entering a section of rolling hills. The road winds through more picturesque farm- and ranchland before dropping back down to the Snohomish River valley. As you turn north onto Connelly, then Broadway for a quick descent to the valley, be mindful of a right turn onto Springhetti that comes quickly. Development along State Route 9 has stretched north into this bluff above the Snoqualmie River valley, and traffic can be an issue as you skirt the edge of it. The final leg is again a flat, farm-road route back into town.

MILEAGE LOG

0.0 Right onto Centennial Trail to ride south into Snohomish.
3.0 Cross Pine Ave. and ride south on Maple Ave.
3.9 Left onto 1st St.
4.0 Right onto Lincoln Ave.
7.4 Pass entrance to Lord Hill Regional Park on the right.
10.4 Cross under intersection with SR 522; stay in right lane and go halfway around the roundabout to continue onto Main St.

Rolling ribbon of road west of Monroe

11.5 Arrive in downtown Monroe.

12.4 Right onto Lewis St., which is also SR 203.

14.0 Right onto Tualco Rd.

14.9 Curve left and stay on Tualco Rd. at intersection with Tualco Loop Rd.

15.9 Curve left onto Crescent Lake Rd.

17.3 At T after crossing Snoqualmie River, right onto High Bridge Rd. Caution: winding road with no shoulders climbing out of valley.

20.9 At Y with Welch Rd., stay right as High Bridge becomes Elliott Rd., then cross under SR 522.

22.9 Continue on Elliott at intersection with Fales Rd.

23.4 Right onto Connelly Rd.

25.4 Right onto Broadway Ave.

25.9 Right onto Springhetti Rd. Caution: Be prepared for the turn on this steep downhill segment.

27.9 Right onto Airport Wy.

29.0 Cross bridge into downtown Snohomish.

29.2 Right onto 1st St.

29.6 Left onto Maple Ave.

30.5 Cross Pine Ave. and join Centennial Trail.

33.5 Arrive back at Pilchuck Trailhead.

45 Monroe to Sultan

DIFFICULTY: moderate
TOTAL TIME: allow 2.5 hours
TOTAL DISTANCE: 24.7 miles
TOTAL ELEVATION GAIN: 740 feet

Driving directions: From SR 522, travel east toward Monroe and take the W. Main St. exit. Follow sign to City Center/W. Main St. around the roundabout. Turn right onto Lewis St. at 1.7 miles. Turn left into parking just beyond Lewis Street Park entrance at 2.2 miles.

From US Hwy 2, travel east toward Stevens Pass and turn right on Lewis St. in Monroe, proceeding to parking at Lewis Street Park at 0.7 mile.

There is a point where communities along US Highway 2 shake off the atmosphere of suburban Snohomish County and settle down into "mountain time," and you might feel that shift on a quick tour of the foothills between

Monroe and Sultan. Exploring the side roads that roughly parallel the Stevens Pass Highway, you will find an abundance of scenic views: snowcapped mountains, rushing rivers, tree-lined lanes, and pastoral valleys.

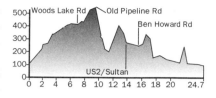

Start the loop in Monroe. Settled in the 1860s because of its rich farmland, the area is best known today for hosting a state reformatory (read: prison) and the Evergreen State Fair; I'm not aware of any connection between the two other than location. Monroe is also the last shopping metropolis for people heading across Stevens Pass, so a crowded strip of businesses line the highway on the edge of town. This tour mostly avoids that mess, crossing the highway at a stoplight when you're heading out of town.

Begin at Lewis Street Park, which sits beside the Skykomish River on the south edge of town. The Skykomish and its sister from the south, the Snoqualmie, join forces and become the Snohomish River southwest of Monroe. The Snohomish empties into Puget Sound at Everett. The park has restrooms, picnic areas, and an interpretive trail through riverside wetlands.

Head northeast out of Monroe into the Woods Creek Valley along Old Owen Road, where bedroom communities are reaching farther into the countryside. A view of the Cascades' jagged peaks makes it easy to see why high parts of the valley would be coveted for homes. For a bit of variety, swing north along Woods Lake Road, then loop back along Reiner Road, which follows the Sultan River down into Sultan. These quiet lanes expose the desirable side of country life being sought a few yards off a main road: the whinny of horses, odors of wood smoke and freshly cut hay, and a casual wave from a neighborly farmer.

After climbing out of the river valley, drop down back onto Old Owen Road and then to US Highway 2 at the edge of Sultan. Take a break and explore this small town: Have coffee at the renowned bakery, check out the barbecue joint or art gallery on Main Street, or kick back at Sportsman Park. Then cross the highway onto Mann Road (311th Avenue SE) and head for Ben Howard Road, which heads west to Monroe. Cross a series of bridges that span the sloughs and tributaries of the Skykomish.

The undulations of Ben Howard Road seem to be beloved by motorcycle riders. Along its 10-mile stretch you're very likely to encounter that other style of biker: the noisy one who makes the scene with gasoline. The road parallels the Skykomish and opens onto ranching valleys

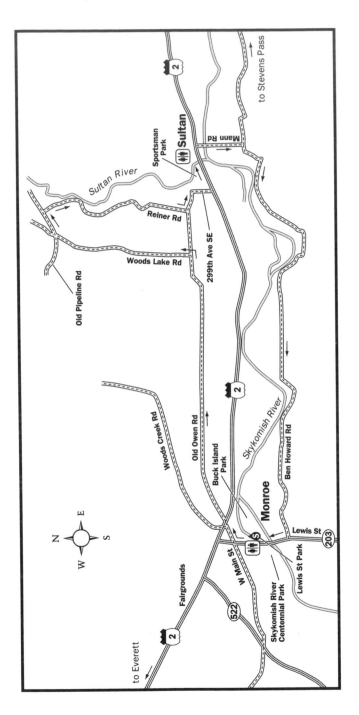

The North Cascades provide a stunning backdrop to rural Snohomish County scenes.

but also offers a couple of hill climbs to bring that crisp mountain air deep into the lungs.

At the end, Ben Howard Road meets up with State Route 203, the Duvall-Monroe Road. Join this busy thoroughfare briefly as you cross the Skykomish and head north back to the park to end the tour. Mind the bridge, as it—like most country bridges of a certain age—makes no allowance for cyclists. Slowing the impatient car traffic by pedaling across a bridge makes one appreciate the niceties of modern design that allow for the comfort and safety of non-motor-vehicle bridge users.

MILEAGE LOG

0.0 Right out of parking onto Lewis St.
0.5 Right onto Main St.
0.9 Cross US Hwy. 2 at stoplight on Main St. On north side of highway, road becomes Old Owen Rd.
1.1 Bear left at Y to stay on Old Owen Rd.

6.6 Left onto Woods Lake Rd. (Note: You could continue straight on Old Owen Rd. to shorten tour by approximately 4 miles and skip one challenging hill climb.)

9.3 Right onto Old Pipeline Rd.

9.7 Right onto Reiner Road at Y. Caution: sharp downhill curve.

13.1 Left onto Old Owen Rd. at stop sign. Road curves to become 299th Ave. SE.

13.7 Left onto US 2 at stoplight; Sportsman Park on your right before signal.

13.8 Arrive at Sultan. Visit bakery or cafés or stop at park for a break.

14.5 Right onto Mann Rd. to begin return.

15.4 Right onto Ben Howard Rd.

24.2 Right onto SR 203 to go into Monroe. Caution: no shoulder or bike lane on bridge.

24.7 Arrive at park to end tour.

Opposite: Mount Rainier looms over the Foothills Trail.

PIERCE COUNTY

46 Downtown Tacoma, Point Defiance, and the Narrows

DIFFICULTY: moderate
TOTAL TIME: allow 4 hours
TOTAL DISTANCE: 27.5 miles
TOTAL ELEVATION GAIN: 1200 feet

Driving directions: From I-5 take exit 133, Tacoma Dome; follow "City Center" off-ramp, then make first right onto E. 26th at light. In 0.1 mile, turn left onto E. D St., then right onto E. 25th St. to arrive at Freighthouse Square. Parking on street and in adjacent park-and-ride lot.

A tour through Tacoma can include many interesting sights and stops, from art to parks to waterfronts to wonderful neighborhoods. Why not combine them all into one ride and make a day of it?

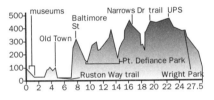

Begin at Freighthouse Square, the old-is-new transit center area tucked near the Tacoma Dome just southeast of downtown. It's got great freeway access and cheap or free parking, and the transit stop makes it ideal for tourists not using a car to visit Tacoma.

The downtown Tacoma area is experiencing a renaissance, visible in the first leg of this tour. Travel carefully through a busy traffic corridor before reaching the renovated Union Station and federal courthouse, new Tacoma Art Museum, and Washington State History Museum. This handsome strip sits just above the waterfront digs of the Museum of Glass, which you reach by looping down onto Dock Street. The modern building, with its glass funnel angling skyward like a postindustrial factory smokestack, provides a welcome connection to the picturesque Thea Foss Waterway and its marina.

Cycle along the promenade, past the Working Waterfront Museum and Thea's Park, then climb up to ride a safe sidewalk along the fast-moving Schuster Parkway to skirt the city along the shore of Commencement Bay. Climb briefly into the Old Town neighborhood before dropping down to the park trail alongside Ruston Way. Here you'll find sculptures, an old fireboat, fishing piers, and the remains of an old mill, along with plenty of people on a nice afternoon. Climb a

challenging hill to enter the Ruston neighborhood, then reward yourself with a treat at the old-fashioned soda fountain in Don's Ruston
Market before heading into Point Defiance Park, just beyond the ferry
terminal to Vashon Island.

Point Defiance makes a great midway stop, with many attractions
along its 5-mile-long road: a Chinese garden and pagoda; sandy Owen
Beach; historic displays at restored Fort Nisqually; a logging museum;
and picnic areas in the towering, moss-covered forest. The big attraction, of course, is the Point Defiance Zoo and Aquarium. The polar
bears are sometimes visible from the road.

Exit the park and head south toward the impressive twin spires
of the recently expanded Tacoma Narrows Bridge. The route takes
you over the broad hill of northwest Tacoma, then drops into the
neighborhood adjacent to the suspension bridge, where you get great
views of the magnificent structure. The new bridge includes a safe,
grade-separated bicycle trail. Across from the trail's entrance is the
relocated War Memorial Park, whose shaded benches provide a nice
break area.

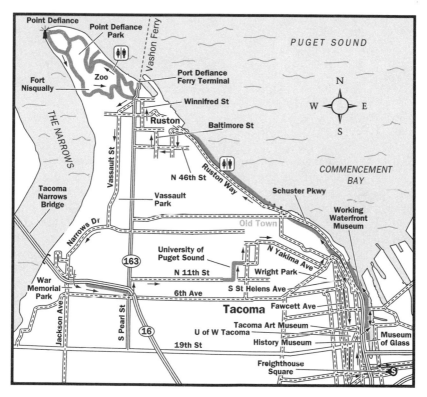

The Museum of Glass is a newer attraction on Tacoma's downtown waterfront.

Head back east through quiet Tacoma neighborhoods to finish the tour. The route travels through the University of Puget Sound campus for a glimpse of college life. Continue on over the car-free Yakima Bridge and through the neighborhood of stately old homes and apartment blocks on Yakima Avenue. Skirt the edge of Wright Park and end the tour by riding along a relatively quiet street above downtown Tacoma. Drop down one of the steep cross streets to get a closer look at the city's commercial center, or stay above the busy downtown streets and enjoy the view.

MILEAGE LOG

0.0 Left onto E. 25th St. to depart Freighthouse Sq.
0.2 Right onto Pacific Ave. Pass Washington History Museum.
1.1 Right onto Hood St. at Tacoma Art Museum.
1.2 Right onto S. 15th St. and curved overpass.

1.4 Left onto Dock St.

1.6 Left at pedestrian entrance to Museum of Glass, then right on promenade to end of walkway at Thea Foss Waterway; reverse route to ride promenade north past Working Waterfront Museum.

2.3 Switch to street as promenade ends.

2.9 At Thea's Park, left to climb overpass and leave waterfront.

3.3 Cross Schuster Pkwy. at light and turn right onto far side sidewalk, which is a pedestrian-bike trail.

4.6 Cross under overpass to turn left onto Schuster as trail ends. Schuster becomes N. 30th St. as you enter Old Town.

4.9 Right onto McCarver St.

5.0 Cross Ruston Wy. and turn left onto waterfront trail.

7.3 Left at end of park, cross Ruston, and go uphill at N. 49th St. Go under railroad tracks and curve right, use protected walkway on right to climb hill; N. 49th becomes Ferdinand St.

7.8 Right onto N. 46th St.

8.0 Right onto Baltimore St.

8.4 Left onto N. 49th St.

8.6 Right onto Winnifred St. (unmarked) in 2 blocks.

8.9 At intersection with N. 51st., go straight across onto divided street.

9.1 Left on N. 54th St. at a Y.

9.3 Right into Point Defiance Park. Caution: busy five-way intersection with ferry traffic.

10.1 Arrive at restrooms, main park picnic area.

10.4 Take middle fork at stop sign with Owen Beach Rd.

13.3 Right into short loop through Fort Nisqually Historic Site.

13.5 Return to Five Mile Drive; take short loop through logging museum displays on the right if desired.

14.5 Soft right onto Park Wy. when exiting Point Defiance Park.

15.0 Park Wy. becomes Vassault St.; continue forward.

16.9 Right onto Narrows Dr.

17.8 Continue forward as Narrows Dr. becomes Jackson Ave.

18.4 Arrive at Tacoma Narrows Bridge. Forward through intersection at off-ramps; to ride the 1-mile bike trail across bridge, turn right on south side of intersection.

18.5 Left at intersection at off-ramps onto east sidewalk to enter War Memorial Park. Proceed forward through park. Caution: busy freeway exit; use pedestrian crossing signal.

18.9 Left to exit park onto Skyline Drive.

19.1 In two blocks, as Skyline ends, cross N. 9th St. onto trail on sidewalk above SR 16.

20.5 Left onto S. Pearl St.

20.7 Right on N. 11th St.

22.5 Left onto path into University of Puget Sound campus to right of sports field. Right at Benefactor Plaza, then left around Wheelock Student Center.

22.9 Right onto 15th St. to exit campus.

23.0 Left onto Cedar St.

23.4 Right onto 22nd St.

23.5 Jog left at street end for ½ block, then right, and cross intersection onto N. Yakima Ave. Continue forward past barriers onto pedestrian- and bike-only Yakima Bridge.

24.8 Left onto Division Ave.; Wright Park to south.

25.0 Right on S. St. Helens Ave.

25.5 Angle right onto Baker St.

25.6 Left onto Fawcett Ave.

27.0 Left onto E. 25th St.

27.5 Arrive at Freighthouse Square to end tour.

47 Foothills Trail

DIFFICULTY: easy
TOTAL TIME: allow 2.5 hours
TOTAL DISTANCE: 29.8 miles
TOTAL ELEVATION GAIN: 380 feet

Driving directions: From I-5, take exit 142 west on SR 18 to SR 161/Enchanted Pkwy. south, which becomes Meridian. Turn east on SR 167/Valley Freeway to SR 410. Take SR 410 to Valley Rd. (SR 162) exit. Turn right on Valley Rd. and travel 0.4 mile south to right turn onto 80th St. E. Trailhead is on the left in 1.3 miles.

Pierce County's recently extended Foothills Trail provides a wonderful leisure ride through small towns, new subdivisions, and wooded countryside that gently rises toward the Lance Armstrong

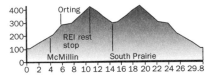

of Washington attractions: Mount Rainier. In fact, the trail is a crucial link in getting cyclists to the challenging roads encircling "the Mountain." The route is a popular destination for Tacoma cyclists looking for a leisurely outing. Developers call it the "Foothills Trail Linear Park," but before its rails-to-trails reincarnation, it was known as the Buckley Line, hosting both Northern Pacific freight and a passenger

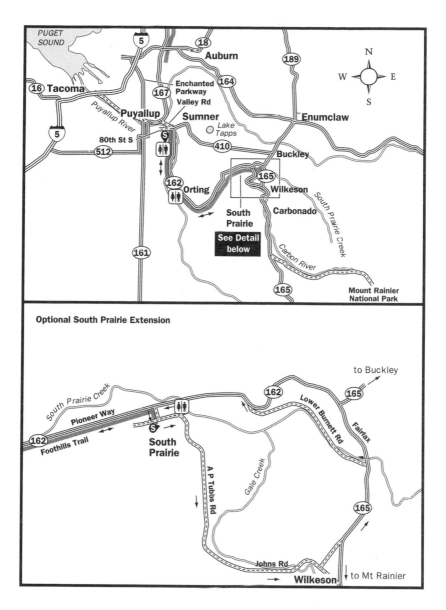

train from Orting to South Prairie, the current southern terminus of the trail.

Begin at the East Puyallup Trailhead, just southeast of the intersection of State Routes 167 and 410. When extensions are created going north, the trail will connect with the in-town trails in Puyallup, and plans call for further connections north to King County's Interurban Trail and south toward Mount Rainier. Going down and back on the current trail, from Sumner to South Prairie, offers an easy, scenic 30-mile spin.

As with the Sammamish River Trail (Tour 15), you will encounter walkers, children, in-line skaters, and dogs. The Puyallup section runs alongside railroad tracks for 4 miles and crosses the tracks four times. You may also see people with fishing poles trying their luck in the glacially colored waters of the Puyallup and Carbon Rivers, which both parallel the trail for long stretches. People used to the busy urban and suburban trails of King County will enjoy the uncrowded feeling here.

Many cyclists stop along the route at the casual Park Bench Café and Eatery, across the street from the trail in Orting's downtown park. South of Orting, the route becomes more rural. Look for a farm with emu and buffalo, and stop at the REI-sponsored wildlife viewing area in a marsh next to the creek. The trail ends at a small park in South Prairie. Nearby are an espresso stand, gas station, and convenience store.

Rural scenes include great views of Mount Rainier.

The tour can be extended via road to points north and south. An additional 7-mile loop onto local roads south of town would offer some variety on a jaunt through the wooded countryside. Take SE Third Street on a precipitous climb out of town, where it becomes A. P. Tubbs Road, then Johns Road; make a left on Carbonado–South Prairie Road, then another left onto State Route 165; turn left onto Lower Burnett Road and State Route 162 to return to the park in South Prairie. Or at Carbonado–South Prairie Road, continue straight on Johns Road, then turn south on State Route 165 through Wilkeson to the Carbon River Entrance to Mount Rainier National Park, where you could get closer to our glacier-covered peak. A third option is to continue on State Route 165 north toward Buckley, cross the White River, enter King County, and continue north through Enumclaw.

Whether you use the Foothills Trail as an out-and-back ride on its own or as a link in a larger loop, riding south on the trail on a clear day may be enough of a treat for many cyclists, as the mountain's snowy slopes quietly fill the skyline above the trees lining the trail. That view might be the most rewarding bit of tourism possible on two wheels.

MILEAGE LOG

0.0 Begin at East Puyallup Trailhead. Caution: railroad tracks; cross at right angles.

4.0 Pass McMillin Trailhead.

5.8 Enter Orting.

6.5 Trail jogs right briefly as it enters Orting Memorial Park.

7.3 Ride by skate park and dirt-bike trail.

11.7 Arrive at REI rest stop at marsh.

14.9 Arrive at South Prairie Trailhead. Retrace route or take sidetrip onto local roads (see above).

18.1 Pass REI rest stop.

23.3 Pass through Orting.

25.8 Pass McMillin Trailhead.

29.8 Arrive at parking at East Puyallup Trailhead.

Opposite: A whimsical bicycling sculpture at the Monarch Sculpture Park

48 State Capitol and Central Olympia

DIFFICULTY: moderate
TOTAL TIME: allow 3 hours
TOTAL DISTANCE: 18.7 miles
TOTAL ELEVATION GAIN: 340 feet

> **Driving directions:** Take I-5 to exit 103, 2nd Ave., and go through first light. Turn left onto Custer Wy. S.W. and cross over bridge. Take first right onto side road that takes you onto a lower bridge. Cross that and turn left onto Deschutes Pkwy. Entrance to Tumwater Falls Park is on left.

Here's a short tour with plenty of stops that will give a visitor a great look at our state's capitol city and seat of government. The ride loops from Tumwater Falls Park, famous as the home of the

Olympia Brewery. It's one of a series of parks around Capitol Lake that celebrate the area's history and connection to commerce.

The falls is the culmination of the Deschutes River. A plaque in the adjacent Tumwater Historical Park notes that this was also the finish line for an overland trading route from Fort Vancouver to Puget Sound. It also marks the end of the settlement route known as the Oregon Trail. If you're there in September, look for salmon in the fish ladders at the adjacent hatchery.

Climb up onto the city streets above the park, and quickly cross over from Tumwater east and north into Olympia. As you cross under Interstate 5 and make your way north into the city center, look for the many murals painted on the sides of downtown buildings.

Cross busy shopping and dining streets as you pedal west on Legion, then turn north toward the city's waterfront on Budd Inlet. Pass Percival Landing Park and arrive at your first stop, the welcoming Farmers Market. With farm stands under arched barn roofs, playful iron vegetable sculptures, and an array of crafts and food for sale, this is a spot to stroll and browse.

Continue exploring the shorelines of the inlet by riding out Marine Drive to North Point, which has been undergoing renovation and is now home to an expansive marina, restaurants, and harborside trails.

Before exploring the capitol campus, head north out of downtown to Priest Point Park. Loop through the park, with its moss-encrusted trees, then stop at the quiet, enclosed rose garden before heading back.

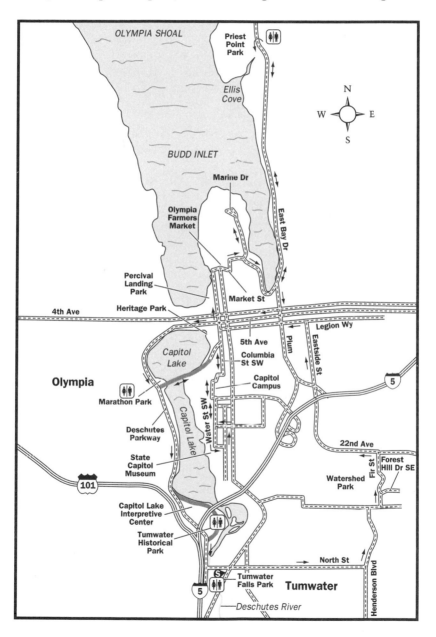

The State Capitol across Budd Inlet

The ride south offers a great view of the serene waters of Ellis Cove and the pleasure-boat haven at the south end of the inlet.

Cross back through downtown to circle around Capitol Lake. A division in the lake's two sections holds a path for hikers and bikers through Marathon Park. The park honors America's first women Olympic marathon runners; Olympia hosted the trials before the 1984 Los Angeles games.

Exit into Heritage Park, which skirts the northeast edge of Capitol Lake. From there it's a short climb south to the state government buildings. Tour the grounds to view war memorials, sculptures, and gardens. Poke your head into the legislative building, whose grand dome was restored after the 2001 earthquake. Completed in 1928, it was America's last great domed state capitol to be built.

Ride south a few blocks to the State Capitol Museum, in the historic South Capitol neighborhood. Return through the capitol grounds and back between the lake segments, then complete the ride along the west side of Capitol Lake to return to the series of parks at the end of the tour.

MILEAGE LOG

0.0 Right out of parking onto Deschutes Pkwy.
0.1 Right to go over falls onto low bridge.
0.2 Right onto Custer Wy SW. Caution: busy street.
0.5 Merge into center lane to go straight across Cleveland Ave. Road becomes North St.
1.5 Left onto Henderson Blvd.
2.0 Right onto Eskridge Ave. SE.
2.2 Left onto Forest Hill Dr. SE.
2.3 At a Y, left onto Fir St.

2.7 Left onto 22nd Ave. Road curves under I-5 and becomes Eastside St.

4.2 Left onto Legion Wy.

4.9 Right onto Columbia St. NW.

5.3 Arrive at Percival Landing Park.

5.5 Right onto Market St. In 1 block, arrive at Farmers Market. Continue east on Market St.

5.8 Left on Marine Dr.

6.4 Arrive at North Point, end of Marine Dr. Return south along Marine Dr.

7.1 At intersection with Market St., left to stay on Marine Dr.

7.6 Left onto East Bay Dr.

9.1 Left into Priest Point Park.

9.6 Follow "South Exit" signs next to restrooms and rose garden, then merge onto East Bay Dr. to return south to city center, where East Bay becomes Plum St.

11.7 Right onto 5th Ave.

12.3 Arrive at Heritage Park by Capitol Lake.

12.5 Merge into left-turn lane, then turn left onto Deschutes Pkwy.

13.2 Left into Marathon Park, in middle of Capitol Lake. Ride or walk packed-gravel path that bisects two parts of lake.

13.5 Stay right to join paved trail on far side of lake.

14.0 Right onto Columbia St. SW. Caution: railroad tracks with bad angle.

14.2 Right onto access road in front of General Administration Building across from capitol grounds. It curves left, then runs in front of capitol building.

14.5 Arrive at state capitol.

14.6 After road curves left beyond capitol, right onto Water St. SW. Turn between Newhouse and Cherberg office buildings. Water St. SW becomes 21st Ave. SW.

14.9 Arrive at State Capitol Museum.

15.0 Left (north) onto Columbia St. SW.

15.1 Left onto 19th Ave. SW, then right onto Water St. SW.

15.4 Return through capitol grounds.

15.7 Left onto Columbia St. SW to exit capitol campus.

16.0 Left onto trail to return across lake.

16.7 Left onto Deschutes Pkwy.

17.6 Left into Capitol Lake Interpretive Center. Follow waterfront trail under freeway to Tumwater Historical Park. Exit park by taking left branch of Y.

18.4 Left onto Deschutes Pkwy.

18.7 Left into Tumwater Falls Park to end tour.

49 Chehalis Western and Woodard Bay Trails

SOUTH SECTION
DIFFICULTY: easy
TOTAL TIME: allow 3 hours
TOTAL DISTANCE: 29.8 miles
TOTAL ELEVATION GAIN: 200 feet

NORTH SECTION
DIFFICULTY: easy
TOTAL TIME: allow 1.5 hours
TOTAL DISTANCE: 14.7 miles
TOTAL ELEVATION GAIN: 120 feet

Driving directions: Take I-5 to exit 108, Sleater Kinney Rd. Drive 0.8 mile south, turn right onto 14th St., then turn left after trestle in 0.3 mile into Chehalis Western Trailhead parking at Chambers Lake.

The Olympia area has much to offer touring cyclists. The small city and navigable suburbs are surrounded by tremendous natural beauty, from the Capitol Forest to the inlets of south Puget Sound to the foothills of Mount Rainier. If such a description makes you want to relocate there, use your bike to scout the area for suitable homes. You'll find quiet roads to meander, plenty of rest stops, and striped-and-signed bike lanes on the busier roads, which greatly aid the bike commuter.

Most helpful is a major bike route that bisects Thurston County north to south. The Chehalis Western Trail began—as did so many of our bike trails—as a rail line. Owned by Weyerhaeuser, the line was put into operation in 1926 to bring logs to the sound. Taken out of operation in the 1980s, the right-of-way was purchased by the state from the Weyerhaeuser Foundation in 1988. By the mid-2000s, development as a multi-use recreational trail was nearly complete. The 5.8-mile north

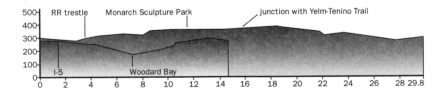

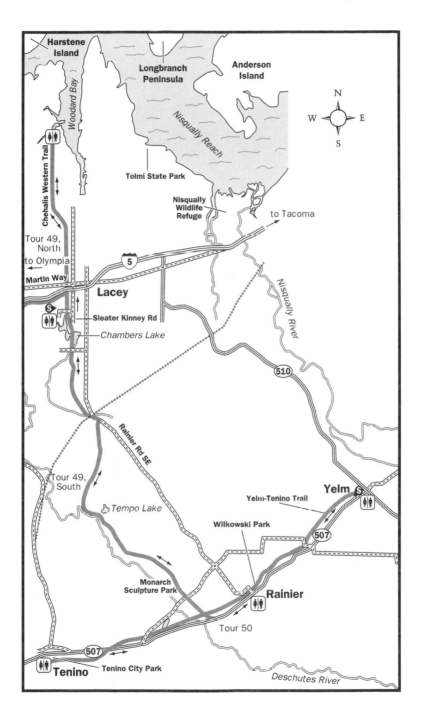

Trail barriers help avoid accidents where the trail crosses a street.

section, from Woodard Bay to Interstate 5, is maintained by the state Department of Natural Resources. The longer south section, whose 14.5 miles run from south of Interstate 5 to an intersection with the Yelm-Tenino Trail (Tour 50), is operated by Thurston County. The two were due to be linked with new bridges over busy arterials and the freeway in 2006.

While the northern section is largely a shaded, woodland run, the southern portion offers a variety of environments, from suburbs to farmland to river frontage. Because of easy freeway access, this tour starts at the Chambers Lake Trailhead, the northern terminus of the southern section. Cyclists can go down and back on this trail, then add on a trip up to Woodard Bay if more riding is desired. Connections to the Interstate 5 commuter trail, which reaches nearly to downtown Olympia, and to the aforementioned Yelm-Tenino route, offer variety for those wanting to design their own tours. Linking the southern trail, the commuter trail, and the downtown–state capitol loop (see Tour 48), for example, offers the widest range of Olympia attractions.

Departing from Chambers Lake, the C-W's south section bisects residential areas of Olympia and Lacey. By the time you cross 37th Street, homes and golf courses give way to woodland. At the 69th Street Trailhead, the scenery begins to open up into farms and pastureland, with views of Mount Rainier. Just south of that junction, riders must endure a brief (0.2 mile) section of gravel before popping out onto a road to cross under a railroad trestle and climb a short hill to rejoin the trail. The only other obstacles on the line are barriers at road intersections that one must slow to a near stop to navigate.

An interesting sidelight awaits toward the south end of the trail. The Monarch Sculpture Park sits trailside at mile 11, beckoning visitors with free admission to the grounds. It also hosts an outdoor café in summer. Art in the park includes a whimsical permanent sculpture of a woman and two children wildly balancing atop a small bike. This clearly marked attraction is a good turnaround point or a welcome rest stop if you're going on to the Yelm-Tenino Trail (Tour 50).

Those heading up the northern section encounter the sights and smells of farms and ranches, as well as a well-used equestrian trail that meanders next to the paved route. Small wildlife is in abundance, and a hike out to the muddy flats of Woodard Bay and Henderson Inlet is worth the time at the end of the line. The return can be made more challenging by navigating the hilly local roads, but a map is required for this endeavor.

MILEAGE LOG—SOUTH SECTION

0.0 Right out of parking onto trail.

3.2 Trail curves left and becomes gravel for 0.2 mile.

3.4 Right onto near-side sidewalk at Rainier Rd. SE to travel under a trestle. Caution: road narrows at trestle.

3.6 Right onto trail just beyond first intersection.

11.3 Pass Monarch Sculpture Park on the left.

14.4 Arrive at intersection with Yelm-Tenino Trail. (Town of Rainier is 2 miles east; left onto Yelm-Tenino Trail.) Reverse route to return.

25.2 Left off trail onto near-side sidewalk at Rainier Rd. SE. Caution: busy road.

25.4 Left onto gravel trail section just beyond trestle.

29.8 Arrive at Chambers Lake Trailhead to end section.

MILEAGE LOG—NORTH SECTION

0.0 Left out of parking onto 14th St.

0.3 Left onto Sleater Kinney Rd.

1.1 Cross I-5.

1.3 Left onto Martin Wy. Caution: busy road; use turning lane.

1.6 Right onto sidewalk to merge onto Woodard Bay Trail.

7.4 Arrive at Woodard Bay Trailhead. Reverse route to return.

13.2 Left onto near sidewalk at Martin Wy. Stay on sidewalk to Sleater Kinney Rd.

13.5 Right onto Sleater Kinney Rd. Cross I-5; continue to 14th St.

14.5 Right onto 14th St.

14.7 Left into Chambers Lake Trailhead parking to end section.

50   Yelm–Tenino Trail

DIFFICULTY: moderate
TOTAL TIME: allow 3.5 hours
TOTAL DISTANCE: 27.2 miles
TOTAL ELEVATION GAIN: 320 feet

> **Driving directions:** From I-5 take exit 111, SR 510, and follow SR 510 southeast approximately 13 miles into downtown Yelm. Just prior to first stoplight in Yelm, turn right onto Railroad St. SW in front of Yelm City Hall. Trailhead parking area is ½ block on the left.

Just a few years ago, Olympia-area cyclists were offered the choice of roads or more roads for their touring pleasure. Not that there's anything wrong with that—the country lanes around our capitol city are as inviting and uncrowded as you're likely to find within an hour or so of Seattle.

But then the upside-down T was created. The bottom half of the grand off-road route through Thurston County is the Yelm-Tenino Trail, which traverses the eastern half of the county and runs through three small towns: Yelm, Rainier, and Tenino. It's an eminently useful and very pleasant amenity.

Begin in Yelm, the most developed of the three modest towns along the route. Situated 13 miles south of Interstate 5 along the Nisqually River, Yelm is a cross between bedroom community and farm town. Park at the trailhead behind the town hall (where restrooms and water are accessible if you visit on a weekday) and quickly depart town as the trail winds through newly constructed neighborhoods.

The east-west trail, acquired by the county from Burlington Northern Railroad in 1993, is 14.5 miles long and quite flat. The first leg out of Yelm runs right alongside State Route 507, which makes for a noisy experience, but it is a great reminder of the benefits of not having to use the highway.

The trail gets away from the road for a quick few miles to the tiny town of Rainier. Ride by modest Wilkowski Park and then through the town center, which has a gas station and market if amenities are desired.

Two miles west of Rainier, the trail intersects with the Chehalis Western Trail (Tour 49), the longer, more scenic north-south route that goes into Olympia. An interesting side trip, taken on either direction of this ride, is to detour north onto the C-W for a 6-mile round-trip visit to the Monarch Sculpture Park, whose free grounds, found trailside just north of the

Military Road crossing, provide an enjoyable break. The bike-friendly facility has dozens of permanent sculptures scattered along winding paths, and in the summer it sports an outdoor café. The ride up and back takes you through the Deschutes River valley, containing ranches and equestrian facilities.

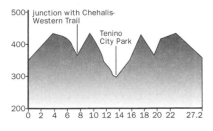

Back on the Yelm-Tenino Trail, cross the Deschutes, then ride along

Thurston County's shadiest, quietest trail

the southern edge of McIntosh Lake before arriving at the end of the line in Tenino City Park. The park provides restrooms and water, and just beyond the trail's end is the Tenino Depot Museum and Quarry House. The museum houses all manner of old rail memorabilia, while across the parking lot the old house features walls of locally quarried stone. The quarry is now a public swimming pool, bustling on a hot summer day.

Ride into town for a look at the businesses along Sussex Avenue, the main street. Provisions for a park picnic can be found here, or just view the historic Landmark Tavern building at the corner of Howard Street, which dates from 1906.

The return can be made simply by retracing the trail route, making the trip just over 27 miles without the sculpture park detour. For an additional challenge—in length, if not in difficulty—you could head south from Tenino on Crowder Road SE, North Craft Road, Skookumchuck Road SE, and Johnson Creek Road SE to loop around through the Skookumchuck River and Johnson Creek valleys back to the trail near Rainier. It's 14-plus miles of rolling hills on country roads, replacing 5 miles on the trail, which would make the trip about 36 miles total. On the return, look for Mount Rainier's glacial cap peeking over the trees beyond your right handlebar grip.

MILEAGE LOG

0.0 Depart Yelm onto trail from terminus at parking.
5.7 Arrive at town of Rainier.
7.7 Left at Y with Chehalis Western Trail to stay on Yelm-Tenino Trail.
9.9 Ride along McIntosh Lake.
12.0 Cross SR 507 and rejoin trail. Caution: busy road.
13.4 Arrive at Tenino City Park.
13.6 Arrive at Depot Museum and Quarry House, just beyond trail's end. Retrace route or take side trip on local roads (see above).
19.5 Pass junction with Chehalis Western Trail.
21.5 Arrive at town of Rainier.
27.2 Arrive at parking in Yelm to end tour.

RECOMMENDED RESOURCES

Start your research at this book's accompanying website, *www.bikingpuget sound.com*, which contains many links to the resources listed below.

CYCLING CLUBS

Bicycling membership organizations typically offer group rides, socializing, and community events. Some hold classes, maintain trails, negotiate discounts with bike shops, or serve as advocates to governmental entities.

Backcountry Bicycle Trails Club, Seattle; *www.bbtc.org*. Statewide advocacy of backcountry trails.

Boeing Employees' Bicycle Club, Seattle; *www.bebc-seattle.org*. You need to be associated with Boeing to be a member but not to participate in their rides.

Capital Bicycle Club, Olympia; *www.capitalbicycleclub.org*.

Cascade Bicycle Club, Seattle; *www.cascade.org*. The area's largest club; sponsor of the Chilly Hilly, Seattle to Portland (STP), annual Bike Expo, and many other events.

Different Spokes, Seattle; *www.differentspokes.org*. A cycling club for the gay, lesbian, bisexual, and transgender communities.

Evergreen Tandem Club, Seattle; *www.evergreentandemclub.org*. Promotes the joy of riding tandem in the Puget Sound area.

Marymoor Velodrome Association, Bellevue; *www.marymoor .velodrome.org*. Promotes track and cyclocross racing and events at the Velodrome.

Mountaineers; *www.mountaineers.org*. Some local chapters have cycling outings.

Redmond Cycling Club, Redmond; *www.redmondcyclingclub.org*. Sponsor of Ride Around Mount Rainier in One Day (RAMROD); club slogan: "Where hill is not a four letter word."

Seattle Bicycle Club, Seattle; *www.seattlebicycle.org*. Sponsors social rides and a series of short tours around Washington State each summer.

Seattle International Randonneurs; *www.seattlerandonneur.org*. A club focused on randonneuring—long-distance, unsupported, noncompetitive cycling.

Skagit Bicycle Club, Mount Vernon; *www.skagitbicycleclub.org*.

Snohomish County B.I.K.E.S. Club; *www.bikesclub.org*. Sponsor of the McClinchy Mile ride.

squeaky wheels, Bainbridge Island; *www.squeakywheels.org*. A "bicycling support group" that promotes safe biking on Bainbridge Island.

Tacoma Wheelmen's Bicycle Club, Tacoma; *www.twbc.org*. Sponsors the Daffodil Classic ride.

West Sound Cycling Club, Silverdale; *www.westsoundcycling.com*. Sponsors the Tour de Kitsap ride.

ADVOCACY ORGANIZATIONS
You can support safety, education, and expansion of bicycle routes or transit amenities for cyclists by joining a group that advocates for the cause.

Bicycle Alliance of Washington, Seattle; *www.bicyclealliance.org*. Among its many safety-related activities, BAW operates the Safe Routes to School program; offices co-located with Bikestation Seattle in Pioneer Square.

Bike Works, Seattle; *www.bikeworks.org*. A Rainier Valley bike shop that recycles bikes for youth in its Earn-a-Bike program.

Foothills Rails-to-Trails Coalition; *www.piercecountytrails.org*. Assists in the creation and maintenance of a connected system of nonmotorized trails from Mount Rainier to Puget Sound.

Friends of the Burke-Gilman Trail, Seattle; *www.burkegilmantrail.org*. Supports the completion and maintenance of the granddaddy of Seattle's rail-trails.

BIKE MAPS
Look for links to these maps, text updates, and many more bicycle-related links on this book's accompanying website: *www.bikingpugetsound.com*.

County:

King: *www.metrokc.gov/kcdot/roads/bike/map.cfm*

Kitsap: *www.visitkitsap.com*

Pierce: *www.co.pierce.wa.us/pc/services/recreate/bike.htm*

Skagit: *www.beactiveskagit.org/maps.cfm*

Snohomish: *www.commtrans.org*, click on "Bikes" in the Riding the Bus menu

Thurston: *http://www.olympiawa.gov/community/transportation/biking/*

City:

Bellevue: *http://www.bellevuewa.gov/walking_biking.htm*

Kent: *http://www.ci.kent.wa.us/parksplanningdevelopment/parksguide.asp*

Redmond: *www.redmond.gov/cityservices/citymaps.asp*

Seattle: *www.seattle.gov/transportation/bikemaps.htm*

State:

A Washington bicycle map showing the average daily traffic of major roads and highways across the state—and highways where bicycles are prohibited—can be ordered through the state Department of Transportation: *www.wsdot.wa.gov/bike/Planning_Maps.htm.*

SUGGESTED READING

Bell, Trudy. *Bicycling with Children.* Seattle: Mountaineers Books, 1999.

Spring, Vicky, and Tom Kirkendall. *Bicycling the Pacific Coast.* Seattle: Mountaineers Books, 2005. How about a two-wheeled adventure from Vancouver to San Diego? This book tells you how.

Toyoshima, Tim. *Mountain Bike Emergency Repairs.* Seattle: Mountaineers Books, 1999. This slim little book is big on practical advice. It identifies hundreds of bike parts and problems and offers a diagnosis, emergency repair, and permanent repair for most gear maladies.

Wert, Fred. *Washington's Rail-Trails.* Seattle: Mountaineers Books, 2004. A guide to forty-eight of the former railroads that can now be enjoyed on foot, by bike, or on horseback.

Woods, Erin, and Bill Woods. *Bicycling the Backroads of Southwest Washington.* Seattle: Mountaineers Books, 2002. Forty-six scenic tours from Bremerton to Portland. There's great riding in Grays Harbor and Lewis Counties and other points south.

INDEX

ABOUT THE AUTHOR

Bill Thorness is a freelance writer and editor based in Seattle. His articles on business and lifestyle topics have appeared in many regional publications, including the *Seattle Times* and *Seattle Business Monthly*, and online. He has been a recreational cyclist since the mid-1980s and was a bike commuter into downtown Seattle in the 1990s, where he found that the challenge of traffic can be every bit as sweat-inducing as climbing one of the city's numerous hills. When he's not ditching the computer screen by researching another bike route, he enjoys gardening, hiking, and skiing. Bill is a member of Cascade Bicycle Club and The Mountaineers. Professional affiliations include Northwest Independent Editors Guild and Society of Professional Journalists. See more of Bill's work at *www.billthorness.com*.

Continue to explore new routes and receive updates to this book by logging on to *www.bikingpugetsound.com*, the book's website. The author provides an e-newsletter with ongoing articles, tips, and route updates, as well as cycling links and event listings.

Bill Thorness and Susie Thorness (photo by L.J. McAllister)

THE MOUNTAINEERS, founded in 1906, is a nonprofit outdoor activity and conservation club, whose mission is "to explore, study, preserve, and enjoy the natural beauty of the outdoors. . . . " Based in Seattle, Washington, the club is now one of the largest such organizations in the United States, with seven branches throughout Washington State.

The Mountaineers sponsors both classes and year-round outdoor activities in the Pacific Northwest, which include hiking, mountain climbing, ski-touring, snowshoeing, bicycling, camping, kayaking, nature study, sailing, and adventure travel. The club's conservation division supports environmental causes through educational activities, sponsoring legislation, and presenting informational programs.

All club activities are led by skilled, experienced instructors, who are dedicated to promoting safe and responsible enjoyment and preservation of the outdoors.

If you would like to participate in these organized outdoor activities or the club's programs, consider a membership in The Mountaineers. For information and an application, write or call The Mountaineers, Club Headquarters, 7700 Sand Point Way NE, Seattle, WA 98115; 206-521-6001. You can also visit the club's website at www.mountaineers.org or contact The Mountaineers via email at clubmail@mountaineers.org.

The Mountaineers Books, an active, nonprofit publishing program of the club, produces guidebooks, instructional texts, historical works, natural history guides, and works on environmental conservation. All books produced by The Mountaineers Books fulfill the club's mission.

Send or call for our catalog of more than 500 outdoor titles:

The Mountaineers Books
1001 SW Klickitat Way, Suite 201
Seattle, WA 98134
800-553-4453
mbooks@mountaineersbooks.org
www.mountaineersbooks.org

The Mountaineers Books is proud to be a corporate sponsor of The Leave No Trace Center for Outdoor Ethics, whose mission is to promote and inspire responsible outdoor recreation through education, research, and partnerships. The Leave No Trace program is focused specifically on human-powered (nonmotorized) recreation.

Leave No Trace strives to educate visitors about the nature of their recreational impacts, as well as offer techniques to prevent and minimize such impacts. Leave No Trace is best understood as an educational and ethical program, not as a set of rules and regulations.

For more information, visit *www.LNT.org*, or call 800-332-4100.

OTHER TITLES YOU MIGHT ENJOY FROM
THE MOUNTAINEERS BOOKS

BICYCLING THE PACIFIC COAST
A Complete Route Guide, Canada to Mexico, 4th Ed.
Tom Kirkendall and Vicky Spring
The most comprehensive guide available for touring the
Pacific Coast

PADDLING WASHINGTON:
Flatwater and Whitewater Routes in
Washington State and the Inland Northwest
Rich Landers, Dan Hansen, Verne Huser, &
Douglass A. Norton
The only all-in-one guide to the best of Northwest
flatwater and whitewater paddling routes.

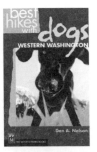

BEST HIKES WITH DOGS
Western Washington
Dan Nelson
Where to hike with your four-legged partner; all trails
recommended as dog-legal, dog-friendly, and dog-fun!

CONDITIONING FOR OUTDOOR FITNESS:
A Comprehensive Training Guide, 2nd Ed.
David Musnick, M.D. and Mark Pierce, A.T.C.
Training and fitness for all outdoor activities

WATERFALL LOVER'S GUIDE TO THE PACIFIC
NORTHWEST
Where to Find Hundreds of Spectacular
Waterfalls in Washington, Oregon, and
Idaho, 4th Ed.
Greg Plumb
Drive-ups, hike-tos, and paddle-fors—634 waterfalls waiting for you
to explore

KAYAKING PUGET SOUND,
THE SAN JUANS, AND GULF ISLANDS:
50 Trips on the Northwest's Inland Waters, 2nd Ed.
Randall Washburne
Take advantage of a world-class kayaking destination with a
guide to all the best trips.

The Mountaineers Books has more than
500 outdoor recreation titles in print.
Receive a free catalog at
www.mountaineersbooks.org.